HUNGARY BETWEEN WILSON AND LENIN: THE HUNGARIAN REVOLUTION OF 1918-1919 AND THE BIG THREE

PETER PASTOR

EAST EUROPEAN QUARTERLY, BOULDER
DISTRIBUTED BY COLUMBIA UNIVERSITY PRESS
NEW YORK

1976

EAST EUROPEAN MONOGRAPHS, XX

Peter Pastor is Associate Professor
of History at Montclair State College

To my parents and to my twin brother

PREFACE

This monograph is the outgrowth of my doctoral dissertation, which I completed at New York University in the Spring of 1969. My inspiration for the examination of the relations between Hungary and the Big Three was the 1967 publication of Arno J. Mayer's *Politics and Diplomacy of Peacemaking*. In this work Professor Mayer examined the impact of revolutionary Hungary on the peacemakers. In the preface, however, he recognized that his treatment of the Hungarian question had some flaws as he had had "difficulty to strike a satisfactory balance between internal and external aspects." My aim was to fill the gap which was probably caused by Professor Mayer's lack of Magyar and by the inavailability of archival documents, still closed at the time of the publication of his award winning book.

I am grateful to my dissertation advisor, Professor Hans A. Schmitt, who guided me through the intricacies of researching and writing a book length monograph. I also owe thanks to my admired friend, Professor Béla K. Király who read the dissertation and encouraged me to do further research at foreign archives which recently opened documents relevant to my inquiry.

I must also thank my colleagues, here and abroad, with whom I corresponded or conversed on topics related to my manuscript. Their advice and direction during its shaping was most valuable. In the United States the list includes Dr. Richard Allen and Dr. Joseph Stasko, Professors István Deák, Nándor Dreisziger, Thomas Karfunkel, Iván Kovács, Arno Mayer, Iván Völgyes and Gábor Vermes. In Great Britain they are Professors Norman Stone and A.J.P. Taylor and in France, Dr. Károly Kecskeméti and Professor Georges Haupt. Lastly, in Hungary, my thanks are due to Drs. Tibor Hajdu, Elek Karsai, Zsuzsa L. Nagy, György Litván and György Ránki.

I am especially indebted to Vice-principal Eva Linder in Hungary, who during the last decade has tirelessly supplied me with recent publications on the topic, and to my uncle Gyorgy Pasztor in Budapest and my cousin Denise Dale in Paris, who during my visits were tireless companions on the endless hunts for out-of-print books at used book stores.

Appreciation is due to Mr. Peter Beales for editorial help on portions of the text and to my typist, who prefers to remain anonymous, for his very careful work. Equally appreciative am I to the staff and directors of archives and libraries for the assistance I received from them. To the witnesses of the events of 1918-1919 who provided me with personal recollections, including Countess Catherine Károlyi, widow of the President, I owe my thanks.

The grants-in-aid covering travel expenses, which I received from Monmouth College, New Jersey during my tenure at that institution, were invaluable. The College Development Fund grant and the release time from my present employer, Montclair State College, greatly helped me to prepare the manuscript for publication.

When faults are found in the monograph, responsibility, as always, will rest with the author.

TABLE OF CONTENTS

INTRODUCTION

The Hungarian communist revolution of 1919 has been long considered by the students of history as an important episode in the genesis of national communism. The birth of the Béla Kun regime on March 21, 1919 and its 133 day existence jolted the world into realizing that communism was not just a passing fad in Russia, thus making the peacemakers in Paris fear the spread of communism to the west. Yet, in spite of the spectacular rise of communism in Hungary, the communist revolution was an alternative revolution. Communism had few, if any, roots in Hungary. As contemporary observers have noted and historians concluded, Hungarians chose communism out of desperation and fear that Hungary, like 18th century Poland, would be partitioned among her neighbors. Communism was chosen not because the Hungarians believed in the superiority of a dictatorship of the proletariat but because the ideology seemed to be forging an international alliance. This alliance held the promise of destruction of the seemingly insatiable appetite of the successor states of the Austro-Hungarian Monarchy.

While Béla Kun and the communist interlude in Hungary have even been subjects of European history surveys, little or no attention has been paid to the Frostflower Revolution, led by Mihály Károlyi. The revolution, which became victorious on October 30, 1918, had its roots deeply set in the Hungarian past. World War I was seen by the rulers of the antiquated Habsburg Monarchy as a barricade against the revolutionary ideology that demanded changing Hungary from a semi-feudal state to a parliamentary democracy of the western type. Contrary to the expectations of the Hungarian leaders, the war accelerated the revolutionary process. The military defeat of the Austro-Hungarian Monarchy in October 1918 lead to the virtual collapse of the state, a development which provided the revolutionary forces in Hungary with power and authority.

Hungarians have experienced western type democracy twice in the course of the twentieth century. Both democracies were established after a war. Their life was brief. Failure of these democracies came about in both instances as a consequence of the international situation and not by internal design. No case can be made in argument of the thesis that the Hungarians had a "course of history" that inevitably led them to accept authoritarian systems.

The survival of Károlyi's People's Republic depended on the support of the victorious powers whose political ideology was now shared by Hungary. The leaders of France, Great Britain and the United States failed to buttress the young Hungarian republic. Their responsibility was not to prop up the revolution against its internal enemies. A "positive revolution" enjoys popular support and the Károlyi government, with its social and political program, enjoyed veritable consensus. Neither the monarchists nor the "bourgeois opposition" was able to muster enough popular support to threaten the life of the republic. The great powers were needed to support Hungary against its hostile neighbors whose territorial demands were exaggerated. In this respect Hungary remained unprotected.

The United States and Great Britain decided to remain neutral in the affairs of the successor states of the Austro-Hungarian Empire. This area became a French sphere of interest by default. France showed marked hostility toward the Hungarians. This policy was not shaped by "revanchisme," but instead was the by-product of French military intervention in Russia, supported by two of Hungary's neighbors—Czechoslovakia and Rumania. French military representatives in Hungary, led by Colonel Vix, were sympathetic toward the Hungarians. Their superiors in the Balkans—General Henrys, General de Lobit, and the Commander-in-Chief of the Allied Armies of the Orient, General Franchet d'Esperey—were equally even-handed in Hungarian affairs. Hostility toward Hungary was shared by those Frenchmen to whom Hungary was merely a part of an Eastern Europe which also included Russia. These men favored the appeasement of Hungary's neighbors as long as they supported French intervention in Russia. General Henri Berthelot, the commander of the French forces in Rumania and in southern Russia, supported Rumanian intransigence against Hungary in return for Rumanian help in Russia. He played a major role in the demise of the Károlyi republic as constant Rumanian-Hungarian flare-ups provoked by Bucharest led to border changes that were unacceptable to the republic. French leaders of greater authority also subscribed to anti-Hungarian policies shaped by their preoccupation with Russia. Foreign Minister Pichon supported all Czechoslovak demands against Hungary largely because of the activities of the Czechoslovak Army in Russia. Marshal Foch, the generalissimo of all Allied forces, was also an exponent of war against Russia. His plans included the retailoring of the frontiers of Hungary in such a manner as could best provide victory for his forces. Prime Minister Clemenceau, as the leader of France, could be equally faulted for not seeing the potential danger of French policies toward Hungary. It was he who ordered the transmission of the famous Vix ultimatum of March 20, 1919, in which Rumania was given the green light to occupy more Hungarian territory. He expected that, in return, the Rumanian military could salvage the French-led Allied intervention in southern Russia. Clemenceau's hopes were soon shattered while the Vix ultimatum caused the collapse of the Károlyi régime and ended the liberal democratic revolution in Hungary.

A policy of Anglo-American neutrality with a "wait and see" attitude could hardly countervail French hostility. Even though members of visiting American and British missions favored active support for the Károlyi régime, the important decision makers in the U.S. government favored no new course towards Hungary. Neutrality at times when action is needed can be considered a bad policy. The Anglo-American leaders—President Wilson, Secretary of State Lansing, Prime Minister Lloyd George and Foreign Secretary Balfour—could be faulted for their lack of commitment in East Central Europe and, specifically, toward Hungary.

While these men could be criticized for their policy of neutrality, they should be lauded for not shaping an anti-Hungarian policy in the emotion-charged atmosphere of that period. Though the Anglo-American leaders feared Bolshevism, they were not convinced by the anti-revolutionary propaganda of the right and of Hungary's neighbors claiming that Károlyi was leading Hungary to Bolshevism. Rising anti-Semitism, a companion of the Red Scare, had created hostility toward the republic by some. Many of the leaders of the government were Jewish. Yet there is no indication that this influenced the Anglo-American leadership in any way. The only exception to this observation could be made in the case of Róza Bédy-Schwimmer. Hostility towards her was, however, more on the grounds that she was a woman than that she was a Jewess. As the first woman ambassador in modern history she was pioneering equal opportunities for women. Her appointment by Károlyi should be praised on philosophical grounds, but in 1918 it created a diplomatic fury.

The above exposé indicates that, in the opinion of the author, the role of personalities and their perception of Bolshevism, could be considered decisive for the fate of Károlyi's republic. Moreover, it is also evident that in spite of the polarization of French and Anglo-American activities *vis á vis* Hungary, there is a common underlying theme in the relations of the Allied powers with Hungary. It could be defined as a policy of "no policy." Thus, it is impossible to substantiate the claims of the Hungarian revolutionary leaders' memoirs that the Allied leaders consciously aimed to bring down the Károlyi government. Nor is it possible to subscribe to Marxist historiography which claims that the "bourgeois-democratic" republic was the victim of the institutional conspiracies of interest groups within and outside of Hungary.

Hungarian policies toward the "Big Three" were well defined. Károlyi's policy emphasized seeking United States' support. He firmly embraced Wilsonian idealism and hoped that his government's policy would gain American backing. The novelty of Wilsonism in Europe was also welcome to Károlyi because a democratic Hungary was equally new to the Europeans. While this period of Hungarian history had been seen mostly in the light of territorial squabbles, it is important to consider Károlyi as a revolutionary leader. Under his guidance social and political reforms brought Hungary into the twentieth century. It was the collapse of this revolution that subsequently led to the return of a whig autocracy in Hungary. Károlyi was also a visionary comparable to Wilson. His failure, however, was less spectacular than that of the American President's. At the time of the revolution only Wilson's close friend, George Creel, was able to note the stature of the Hungarian President.

The British were considered to be junior partners of the Americans. Though the Hungarians hoped to establish friendly relations with the government, there was no special emphasis put on British support. It was the counter-revolutionary elements in Hungary who hoped to find an affinity between the British and Hungarian aristocracy and thus hoped to muster support for the counter-revolutionary cause. The Hungarians had little success with their efforts. The attitude of Lewis Namier, the Austro-Hungarian specialist of the Foreign Office, prevailed. Namier supported the social revolution that was taking place in Hungary. Balfour and Lloyd George were of the same opinions.

Hungarian foreign policy toward France was markedly different from the pro-Anglo-American policy. France was considered as an unfriendly state and Hungarian leaders gave up on ameliorating relations soon after the arrival of the Vix mission to Hungary. The Vix mission was to supervise the armistice agreement but was also in charge of transmitting French demands to the Hungarians. Since these demands required territorial concessions, Vix and his superiors came to be considered as instigators and executors of the harsh demands of the French government. The bitterness of the Hungarians toward Vix, however, was not wholly justifiable. Vix and his immediate superiors were sympathetic to the Hungarian cause. The Hungarians were not aware that in the French military command there was a conflict of authority over Hungary. Even though General Franchet d'Esperey was theoretically in charge, General Berthelot constantly interfered in Hungarian affairs. Berthelot's designs often prevailed because he was in charge of the southern theater in Russia. Emphasis was put on the success of France's Russian policy.

In the long run, Budapest's pro-Entente policy was considered a failure Anglo-American neutrality had allowed Hungary's neighbors to blockade her with impunity. Czechoslovakia prevented the flow of coal—the life-blood of the nation. The Yugoslavs slowed the emergency food shipment destined for Hungary. Such hostile activities created economic hardships. The Vix Ultimatum of March 20 demanded Hungary's yielding of Transylvania and a considerable part of the lowlands to Rumania. The terms, had they been submitted to at the time, would have led to the immediate and total collapse of the economy. The Allied threat of force was met with defiant rejection. Károlyi and his Cabinet resigned and this brought about the collapse of the Hungarian People's Republic and the rise of Béla Kun's communist régime.

Béla Kun promised to reply to Allied force in kind by using Bolshevik aid. Thus, Allied bayonets did not bring democracy to Hungary in 1918-1919. The threat of bayonets led to the collapse of the five month democratic experiment. Hungary had tried democracy and had failed in spite of herself.

Since the life of the Károlyi government depended on the disposition of the great powers, the relations of Hungary and the Big Three warrants the detailed study of this monograph.

CHAPTER I
THE ROAD TO REVOLUTION

For the Hungarian part of the Austro-Hungarian Empire the First World War was a last-ditch effort to forestall conflicts arising out of the social and nationality problems of the multi-national state. The national awakening of the various nationalities and their struggle for independence had been evident for a century. The revolutions of 1848 in Central Europe were nationalistic, while the 1867 Compromise between Austria and Hungary was an attempt to strengthen the Austrian and Hungarian ruling classes so as to combat more successfully the nationalism of the ethnic groups living in Austria and Hungary.[1] Both the Magyar and non-Magyar masses were exploited in Hungary. Whereas the latter could find consolation for their inferior status by blaming the Magyars for their misfortunes and thus find escape in their nationalism in this fashion, the former could not.

The compromise aggravated, rather than alleviated the nationalities problem. The Czech intelligentsia wanted equal partnership with the Austrian Germans; the Croat intelligentsia demanded equality with the Hungarian Magyars. South of the border, with Russian encouragement, Serbia was waging a propaganda war against the Dual Monarchy and was aiming for the alienation of the southern Slav minorities of Hungary from the Crown of Saint Stephen.

The appeal of nationalism was not restricted solely to the non-Magyar nationalities. The Magyars themselves were carried away by its attraction. The conservative Hungarian ruling classes of wealthy landowners and less numerous capitalists used the appeal of nationalism to perpetuate their political hegemony over the Magyar and non-Magyar masses alike. The Magyar nationalist aim was to establish a personal union with Austria through a common monarch. This meant that even the existing common ministries of Foreign Affairs, Finance, and Defense would have to be separated. This policy appealed to Magyars of all classes. Most could neither forget nor forgive the defeat of their newly independent country in 1849 by the Austrians who had been aided by Russian military forces.

In 1904 the nationalists in the Budapest Parliament aimed at sabotaging the efficacy of the assembly through the barrage of endless filibusters.

Reaction presented itself in the person of Prime Minister István Tisza who on November 18, 1904, through a well-executed parliamentary maneuver, changed the rules of the house and put a limit on such obstructionist tactics. The reaction of the parliamentary opposition was swift: in a beerhall-like atmosphere, they went on a rampage, destroying the furniture of the Chamber of Deputies. The uproar caused the dissolution of the Chamber and forced new elections. The January 1905 campaign brought an end to Tisza's reign, and to the domination of the Free Thought Party, a faithful supporter of Dualism. The victory of the opposition parties through a coalition was disregarded by the Emperor Francis Joseph who, instead of choosing his next Prime Minister from among the victorious party leaders, appointed Géza Fejérváry, a trusted royalist. Ferenc Kossuth, the leader of the most powerful party of the coalition, the Independence Party, declared that such an arbitrary act could not be accepted and called for a nation-wide passive resistance movement. However, Francis Joseph intimidated the coalition by threatening to introduce universal suffrage in Hungary. This measure, promising a strong political voice to the non-privileged classes and, most importantly, to the ethnic minorities, forced the coalition to abandon the pursuit of nationalistic aims in return for the Court's retraction of its threat. In April 1906, the leading politicians of the Hungarian independence movement thus reaffirmed the principles of the Compromise of 1867, which assured continued aristocratic dominance while betraying the "national cause."

Thus it was evident that, for both the leaders of the oppressed Hungarian nationalities and the Magyars, nationalism was a means of serving different ends. The leaders of the oppressed nationalities believed that independence meant freedom to reform, to educate, to build—to modernize. For the Magyar nationalists in power, nationalism's functional purpose was to preserve a semi-feudal social and political system. In the course of the years following the 1906 compromise, the Hungarian Government continued its harsh policies against the awakening nationalities of the realm. On October 27, 1907, at the Slovak village of Černova a group of Slovak peasants, congregating for the consecration of their church, was fired upon by the Hungarian gendarmerie when they demanded the presence of Father Andrus Hlinka, their imprisoned national leader. The fusillade resulted in fifteen deaths and some sixty wounded.[2]

Such governmental reaction forced the Slovaks to choose between complete passivity or mass emigration, especially to the United states.[3] In the meanwhile, the seven Slovak representatives in the Budapest parliament organized themselves into a nationalities bloc. The group was under the leadership of the journalist Milan Hodža. Its aim was to propagate the ideas of the heir-apparent Francis Ferdinand, calling for concessions to the national minorities. Soon the fifteen Rumanian as well as the four Serb representatives joined Hodža's group. The forty member Croatian delegation did not follow until 1908 after the central government's confrontation with Croatia.[4]

That year, in "autonomous" Croatia, the Hungarian government's requirement that the state railway employees know the Magyar tongue, brought about the victory of a Croat-Serb political coalition at election time. The Hungarian government, disregarding these results, introduced a virtual dictatorship, while Croat leaders were arrested, accused of *lèse majesté* and sentenced to prison terms of from five to twelve years.[5]

As a result of the elections of 1910, the emasculated coalition gave way to the party of Tisza, rechristened the National Party of Work. It aimed to preserve Magyar dominance within the framework of the Compromise. In November of that year Tisza clearly expressed this goal:

The nationalities question is one of the basic questions of our national policy. The Hungarian Nation can fulfill its *raison d'être* and establish its future on solid foundations if it resolves this great problem. With severity if necessary, with understanding and level-headedness wherever possible, we must insure that every citizen of the country will bow before the Hungarian constitutional ideals, which are based on the political unity of the Hungarian state.[6]

If Tisza's party stressed Magyar national preponderance, it certainly did not stress the interest of the worker but rather that of the worker's masters. Hungarian labor was represented by the Hungarian Social Democratic Party, which, as a result of the restrictive suffrage laws, was not able to send representatives to parliament. Under the existing system the demands of the Social Democratic Party for universal suffrage were utopian, and on one occasion, on May 23, 1912, a demonstration organized for that very reason was met with violence. Workers demonstrated in front of the Parliament building and in other parts of the city. The explosive situation had a number of victims: seven died, four were critically wounded, while another two hundred and sixty persons required medical attention.[7] The near-revolutionary situation of this date lives on as Bloody Thursday and its seriousness can be measured by the fact that Tisza demanded the imprisonment of the socialist leadership, though this suggestion was voted down by the Council of Ministers.[8]

In the Chamber of Deputies, the newly elected Speaker of the Chamber, István Tisza, disregarded certain parliamentary rules, which caused one irate opposition member to lose his temper and fire at him. The deputy's assassination-suicide attempt failed, but the critically wounded perpetrator was hailed by public opinion as a hero and martyr. On the following day, June 8, a young Croat student attempted to assassinate the Croatian governor in Zagreb. When he was captured he confessed that his crime was motivated by events taking place in Budapest.[9]

The Social Democratic Party journal *Népszava* lauded the crime of the deputy who was seen as a victim of the "decadence of the Party of Work and of the mad villain who occupies the Speaker's chair." The only complaint of the writer of the article was that "the poor man's aim was bad." The bourgeois daily, *Polgár*, sized up the situation in its true significance when it claimed that the general feeling in the city and the countryside was like dry peat-moss which could be set afire by a solitary spark engulfing the whole country in flames.[10]

Thus, it is evident that the Hungarian state faced social revolutionary as well as ethnic revolutionary opposition. The traumatic experience of the assassination of Archduke Francis Ferdinand and his wife at Sarajevo by the Bosnian fanatic Gavrilo Princip added a new twist to the Hungarian situation. The assassinated Archduke, the heir to the Austrian and Hungarian thrones, had plans favoring the trialistic reorganization of the Dual Monarchy and opposed Magyar domination over the Hungarian nationalities.[11] It was, therefore, widely held in 1914 that the crime was perpetrated with clandestine Magyar support to prevent the resulting redistribution of political power in favor of the non-German non-Magyar nationalities. It soon became evident, however, that strong groups whose influence was felt in Serbian circles were partly responsible for the act. Serbia was a long-time external nucleus of South Slav nationalism and wanted to frustrate all attempts of reconciling the Slav nationalities to the Empire. If their discontent died, Belgrade's dream of a greater Serbia, including Croatia, Bosnia and Herzegovina, would die with it.[12]

The death of the Archduke was nevertheless no cause for tears among Hungarian nationalists, whom the deceased regarded as "rabble Huns," and who viewed his ideas as a threat to their political hegemony. Furthermore, his assassination was an indication of the intricacy of the nationalities problem which had to be dealt with. It became evident that Serbia had to be crushed for Budapest's sake as well as for Vienna's.

For this reason, the son and namesake of the late Gyula Andrássy, the chief architect of the Dual Alliance, assailed the act in no uncertain terms. Andrássy, who was a member of the presidium of the opposition Independence Party eulogized the dead heir-apparent as one "who was filled with noble ambitions and a will to greatness, wishing to help the nationalities of the Monarchy. . . . For this reason he was killed because he represented a position which was in the vital interest of Hungary."[13]

Even if most of the politicians were in favor of forceful action against Serbia, the Hungarian Prime Minister, Count István Tisza, was opposed to it, knowing that Russia would intervene on behalf of the Serbs. The consequences of such action would be disastrous to the Dual Monarchy.[14] Tisza was aware of the ineptitude of the Austro-Hungarian army in a possible confrontation with the "Russian steam-roller." As soon as he was assured of German military assistance, however, Tisza abandoned his opposition. For the Hungarian leaders, the war had to be waged for no other reason than the preservation of the status quo of "Thousand Year Old Hungary."[15]

Tisza saw the war not only as an opportunity to find a cure for the nationalities problem, but thought that it would still all important political opposition in parliament. The reinvigorated Independence Party under the leadership of Mihály Károlyi would have been a prime target in this drive.

Mihály Károlyi was one of the richest magnates in Hungary, with over 60,000 acres of land in his possession. His wealth was valued at twenty-five million Pounds. He first became active in politics in 1901, when at the age of twenty-six he made an ill-fated attempt to get into parliament on the Independence Party platform. His second attempt in 1905 brought success which led him to party leadership by 1913.[16] Under his leadership, the Independence Party revived its drive for a personal union.

Tisza expected that the war would disarm opposition coming from the Independence Party, which could be reminded of the will of its dead apostle, Lajos Kossuth. Kossuth, at the time of the outbreak of the Russo-Turkish crisis in 1877, called on the Hungarians to support Austria in case of an Austro-Russian conflict. The self-exiled opponent of the Compromise had seen in a possible Russian victory the end of Hungary:

> In case of such defeat, Hungary would be the stake at which the Austrian Eagle would be burned.[17]

Time especially seemed opportune, as Mihály Károlyi, at the invitation of the wealthy New York banker, the Hungarian-American Alexander Konta, was on a speaking tour in the United States. Károlyi's aim was to gather funds for his political platform, which aimed to reorient the Austro-Hungarian foreign policy from a pro-German to a pro-Entente position.[18] In Károlyi's absence, the pro-German faction seemed to carry the Independence Party and welcomed the war with relief. As a member of the party's presidium, the former minister of education, Count Albert Apponyi endorsed with enthusiasm the declaration of war against Serbia with a resounding "at last," which seemed to indicate the birth of a Hungarian *union sacrée*.

Tisza also expected to eliminate the crisis in Hungarian society by the new war. In a declaration, made to an editor who impressed upon him the extreme importance of the suffrage question, Tisza emphasized that after the war a new *Biedermeier* epoch (an allusion to the relatively peaceful, conservative 1830's) would characterize the world and soldiers would be happy if, after their terrible sufferings, they could return to their work and their families.[19] Thus, for Tisza the war became a cure for all the ills of Hungary.

If the war at its outbreak was considered as a vehicle for the salvation of the Dual Monarchy and, in its narrower context, for the survival of traditional Hungary, its course indicated that not one of Tisza's expectations bore the expected fruit. Instead, it sharpened existing internal conflicts. In respect to political unity, Hungary remained the only country among the belligerents where a party truce never materialized and a truly national government never took shape.[20]

In the month of August, while all the parliamentary parties of the countries involved in the conflict surged to support their government, Hungary's two major parties were contesting for the glory of being solely responsible for the war. The opposition Independence Party claimed that it had pressured the indecisive Tisza to accept war. The Party of Work's case rested on its traditional support of military preparedness, while the opposition continually sabotaged the army bills of the Monarchy. If Tisza had not used force to break the obstructionist tactic of the opposition, a poorly furnished army would have faced the Russians and the Serbs. Opposition members grudgingly agreed with Tisza that, for the time being at least, they had history on their side.[21]

Tisza's expectation of an end to the social crisis, however, remained a dream. The Social Democratic Party was in a good position to further dissatisfaction among the urban proletariat, as the Hungarian labor union movement was closely connected with the party. The Party, having no representatives in Parliament, unlike its sister parties in the Entente and Central camps, took no part in the decision to go to war. The party journal *Nepszava*, however, reflected mixed feeling at the very beginning. It was printing anti-war articles alongside those which supported the cause of the Central Powers in the "defense of culture against tsarist barbarism."[22] As early as July 1915, the party's leadership called on the International Socialist Bureau to meet in order to restore peace among the national socialist parties. While the Hungarian Socialists did not participate at Zimmerwald, they approved its anti-war program.[23] The September 25 lead article of *Nepszava* appraised the importance of the meeting in a positive fashion, though it criticized the way the meeting was called together. The party's new platform, which was adopted at the time of the Zimmerwald meeting, declared that it was the duty of the Socialists to start a strong peace movement. The call was justified by the exhaustion of the population.

In January 1916, two members of the party's presidium, Ernö Garami and Manó Buchinger, left for Germany and for Holland in order to mediate differences between the socialist parties of the Entente and the Central camps. The Hungarian socialists drafted a program of conciliation which included the re-establishment of Belgian independence, the creation of an independent Russian Poland, a plebiscite in Alsace-Lorraine, the re-establishment of independent Serbia and the rejection of its "economic annexation."[24]

As early as 1915 major strikes for higher pay and suffrage took place at the Budapest munition factories. As the continuing war meant more and more deprivation and sacrifice, the situation became more explosive. The year 1917 witnessed a new high in work stoppages and general strikes. The miners walked out on most of the mines during the spring, followed by the railway workers. As a result of general labor unrest, the government was forced to permit the celebration of May Day, banned since the outbreak of the war. Over 100,000 workers participated in the Budapest demonstration. On May 2, a one-hour general work stoppage in the entire munitions industry took place. The strikers demanded higher pay and suffrage reforms.

On November 25, the victory of the Bolshevik revolution in Russia was celebrated at a Socialist-sponsored rally of 100,000 workers. One of the party leaders, Dezső Bokányi, called on the workers to follow the Russian example and establish workers' and soldiers' councils. The success of limited socialist activism in general is best reflected in the rapid growth of labor union membership, which increased from 43,381 in 1915 to 215,222 by 1917.[25]

The nationalities problem was not solved by the war either. Instead, it gave new impetus to ethnic leaders to press for hard bargains or to look for support for their policies from the Entente powers. The first major demand for change on behalf of the nationalities came from the enemy. Serbia defeated the Austro-Hungarian forces in the initial phase of the war. A greater Serbia which would include Croatia, the Bánát, and Bácska seemed within reach.[26] The Croatian Sobor, whose majority did not aspire to Serbian citizenship, produced a different utopia following the German-Austro-Hungarian victory over Serbia during the Spring of 1916. It favored a greater Croatia including Bosnia and Herzegovina. This demand, which might have placated Croat nationalistic aspirations, was refused by Budapest. The Budapest government wanted nothing less than the outright annexation of Bosnia and Herzegovina by the Hungarian Crown.[27]

In Bohemia, outstanding political leaders, such as Eduard Beneš and Thomas Masaryk, chose exile in Entente countries and decided to give up the seemingly futile idea of rearranging the Monarchy into a partnership of the nationalities, thus becoming the champions of the creation of a new state of Austrian Czechs and Hungarian Slovaks.

The great number of Rumanians in Transylvania were also beginning to stir and look toward the Rumanian Kingdom, which, until 1916, was undecided as to what course to follow. It was likely, however, that Rumania, like Italy in 1915, would side with the highest bidder. The Hungarian Prime Minister, Count Tisza, was adamant in his refusal to concede territory to these fence-sitters and was afraid that even concessions of non-Hungarian lands to Italy would lead to Rumanian claims in Transylvania.[28] Even following the entry of Italy on the side of the Allies, Tisza refused to grant some limited territorial concessions to Rumania as a price for her continuing neutrality. When in June 1915, there was some German pressure to appease Rumania, Tisza refused and lashed out at the Germans as he wrote to the Austro-Hungarian Foreign Minister Baron István Burián:

> It is appalling that the tragic role that was played by the poor Francis Ferdinand in playing the fool's game with the Rumanians is now taken over by the Germans.[29]

France and England entered the war against Austria-Hungary without aiming to destroy the Habsburg Monarchy and public opinion expected quick victories for Entente arms. It soon became evident, however, that in spite of the expansion of the war and in spite of the immense sacrifices of the soldiers at the front, the Central Powers were holding the initiative. Thus it became necessary for the embattled Entente to embrace high ideals justifying further bloodshed and sacrifices. Therefore, nothing was easier than to find sympathy for the nationalities of Eastern Europe who "struggled" for national self-determination at the very moment when the Entente powers were facing the possibility of losing their own as a result of their declining military fortunes. The immense cruelties of the war, the thousands of crippled and mutilated soldiers who returned from the fronts, and the hundreds of thousands who were never to return made war appear to be a struggle for national existence. By early 1916 it was evident that quick victory was but a chimera: the public became disposed to clamor for the destruction of the enemy who seemingly intended to do the same.

British government officials were first to entertain plans for the make-up of post-war Eastern and Central Europe. For this purpose they began to consider a major policy change. The old Palmerstonian concept of the desirability of a Habsburg-ruled Central Europe gave way to a policy which was to support the centrifugal forces of the Dual Monarchy. Thus, in the autumn of 1916, the Foreign Office began to reshape British foreign policy and to recommend new guidelines for the future. The new project was drawn up in a confidential memorandum that began with the premise that England should "ensure that all the states of Europe, great or small, shall in the future be in the position to achieve their national freedom and security."[30]

Similar changes were evident in France which, like England, entered the war without thinking of destroying the Dual Monarchy. France could hardly be imagined as a sincere champion for the non-Magyar nationalities when French revanchism was clamoring for the return of territories, by far more German than French in culture. The course of war, however, had its result. The government of Aristide Briand accepted the reorganization of Eastern Europe as early as February, 1916.[31] The active participation of Czech volunteers on the side of France furthered the cause of those Bohemian exiles who championed the destruction of the Austro-Hungarian Monarchy. By early 1916, plans of the French military included the utilization of Czech legions organized in Serbia. Later on, in 1918, these troops took part in the fighting at Amiens and were instrumental in preventing the collapse of that front.[32]

The 1916 Treaty of Bucharest represented the convergence of Allied aims in respect to post-war Hungary. It promised Rumania not only Transylvania, Bukovina, and the Bánát, but also a wide band of the Hungarian lowlands almost up to Debrecen. In the hope of such extensive concessions, Rumania declared war on Austria-Hungary to assure the realization of her "national ideal."[33] The January 1917 Inter-Allied Conference at Rome furthered the intention of the Allies to destroy the Dual Monarchy when it adopted a resolution calling for the "liberation of Italians, of Slavs, of Roumanians and of Czechoslovaks from foreign domination."[34]

Only the Russian Monarchy championed the destruction of the Dual Empire and the "liberation" of its nationalities from the very beginning. After initial victories of the Russian armies in Galicia in August 1914, Grand Duke Nicholas issued his manifesto to all "nations of Austria-Hungary," which appeared in nine languages and promised them "liberty and realization of national desires."[35] On November 21, 1914, Tsar Nicholas outlined his view to the French ambassador, Maurice Paléologue, explaining that the defeat of Austria-Hungary would mean the collapse of the Empire as the nationalities would want to reassess their relation with a defeated power. Nicholas's vision in this respect was prophetic. What Nicholas failed to foresee was the collapse of Tsarism in Russia in March 1917, followed by the Bolshevik Revolution in November. The Bolshevik government under the leadership of Vladimir Ilyich Lenin withdrew from the hostilities and was demanding an end to the war with no indemnities and annexations.

The loss of Russia as an ally was compensated by the entrance of the United States into the conflict on the side of the Allies. The exchange of a Russia in turmoil for a country with seemingly inexhaustible resources was a great gain, and for the first time there was definite hope that the military impasse would eventually be overcome by the reinvigorated Allies. For the first time, their military leaders were able to predict total victory by 1919. Yet the threat of Bolshevism at home and general war weariness forced these very same leaders to be on the military defensive and to look for a non-dictated peace that would end the war as soon as possible. The *Fourteen Points* of President Wilson, announced in January 1918, suggested the same intentions. Article Ten of this document did not speak of the dissolution of the Dual Monarchy as a war aim. It merely demanded that "the peoples of Austria-Hungary, whose place among the nations we wish to see safeguarded and assured, should be accorded the freest opportunity of autonomous development." This declaration of war aims toward the Empire came hardly a month after the American break with the Austro-Hungarian Monarchy. President Wilson in his speech to Congress recommending a declaration of war claimed that such an act was necessary as the government of the Dual Monarchy had become separated from the people and had become the tool of Germany. From the speech it seemed to be evident that the aim of the United States was to force on Austria and Hungary a government which was responsive to the people:

> We owe it, however to ourselves to say that we do not wish in any way to impair or to re-arrange the Austro-Hungarian Empire. It is no affair of ours what they do with their own

life, either industrially or politically. We do not propose or
desire to dictate to them in any way. We only desire to see
that their affairs are left in their own hands, in all matters
great or small.[36]

It is clear, therefore, that the cessation of hostilities depended on a twofold Austro-Hungarian response: first of all, the creation of governments
in Austria and in Hungary that responded to the popular will; secondly,
governments which were able to steer clear of German influence. Wilson,
like Lenin, formulated his view toward government in a Rousseauesque
fashion and made it clear that there was a distinction between government
and governed. He hinted that the guilt of war would be borne by those
in government who instigated it, and not by the people.

The other major Western Allies were quick to respond to Wilson's war
aims and their intentions toward the Austro-Hungarian government
became milder. The wild claims of early 1917 gave way to Wilsonian
ideals. Lloyd George, the Prime Minister of Great Britain, declared on
January 5, 1918:

> Similarly, though we agree with President Wilson that
> the break-up of Austria-Hungary is no part of our war aims,
> we feel that unless genuine self-government on true demo-
> cratic principles is granted to those Austro-Hungarian
> nationalities who have long desired it, it is impossible to
> hope for a removal of those causes of unrest in that part of
> Europe which have so long threatened the general peace.[37]

Stephen Pichon, French Minister of Foreign Affairs, accepted Lloyd
George's program and the *Fourteen Points* which were promulgated on
January 8. In a speech which was coupled with a seething attack on the
"usurping" Bolsheviks in Petrograd, he expressed his government's
position in no uncertain terms:

> Coming after those made by Mr. David Lloyd George
> these declarations give world wide character to our claims.[38]

The demand for self-expression of the popular will was not limited
to the Allies. In Hungary, the opposition in parliament continued to

press for universal suffrage. In April 1917, outbursts in the Chamber of Deputies regained their violent character. Shouts of "long live universal, equal and secret voting—nothing shall be discussed here but the franchise" greeted the appearance of Tisza, forcing the Speaker to suspend the session.[39]

May Day was observed with a demonstration for suffrage and peace. On the fifth anniversary of Bloody Thursday, the Károlyi Party, with the co-operation of the Radicals, the Social Democrats and two other smaller parties, established a united front to achieve universal suffrage.[40] The war, which Tisza and his supporters conducted in the hope of preserving the *ancien régime*, did not seem to achieve its aim. The swelling tide of opposition forced King Charles to call on Tisza to introduce a suffrage reform bill. On May 23, rather than accept even the slightest extension of the vote, Tisza resigned as Prime Minister of Hungary.

The Bolshevik revolution in Russia reverberated in Hungary, and in January 1918 workers' strikes became widespread. In some factories workers' councils were formed in the fashion of the Soviets. The mere demand of political revolution through universal suffrage was not satisfactory to many by the time of the Lloyd George and Wilson manifestoes. With the rise of Bolshevism in Russia the workers began to pay more attention to socialism which seemed to promise political revolution with its thoroughgoing social changes.

Fear of revolutionary agitation forced Sándor Wekerle's Minister of Justice, Vilmos Vázsonyi, to introduce strict censorship over strike-reports in the journals. The papers were ordered to refrain from reporting strikes, riots or "similar movements either at home, or abroad, even in the enemy camp."[41] Similarly, he threatened the use of force against Bolshevik movements:

> . . .we shall prevent the seeds of Bolshevism from ever being
> sown in Hungary. This faith I do not tolerate; I will trample
> it under foot.[42]

The fear of Bolshevism induced this influential statesman to oppose even the Brest-Litovsk negotiations which took place at the time, as he rejected any idea of negotiation with the Bolsheviks.

To ameliorate the internal situation, Vázsonyi was empowered to work out the details for a suffrage bill which passed the Budapest Parliament on

June 18, 1918. The new law granted suffrage to male citizens over twenty-four who had proof of literacy and fulfilled a one year residency require-ment. The right to vote was also limited by property or income qualifications. These prerequisites were waived for non-commissioned and commissioned officers and for soldiers decorated for valor. The new law increased the size of the electorate from 1,162,000 (6.9% of popu-lation) to 2,714,000.[43] The Károlyi group derided the bill which fell far short of universal suffrage.

The nationalities problem did not fare better as a result of the war. The Congress of Oppressed Austro-Hungarian Nationalities met in Rome in April, 1918. There, representatives of several national committees in exile proclaimed the right of self-determination and denounced Austria and Hungary. It promised to mount a concerted attack aimed at the destruction of the Dual Monarchy. The emasculated version of the franchise reform could hardly enthuse the nationalities who were looking in the direction of those who promised them self-determination and sovereignty.

It thus seems that the two original war aims of the Hungarian leaders, the solution to the social problem and to the nationalities question had met with hopeless failure by April 1918. In terms of Magyar objectives the war was lost in the spring of 1918, even before the royal armies had laid down their weapons. It was an ironic twist that nothing could now be salvaged of the status quo without accepting the *Fourteen Points* in the international sphere, and without entrusting authority to the enemies of war at home. The latter choice clearly pointed to the selection of Count Mihály Károlyi.

CHAPTER II
THE OUTBREAK OF THE FROSTFLOWER REVOLUTION

A change in attitudes toward the pacifists was accented even more by the fact that by April hopes of arriving at a negotiated peace through existing governmental channels came to naught. In April, secret negotiations between France and Austria broke down. The result of the impasse was the publication of Emperor Charles' letter to Clamenceau in which he promised to support the "just claims of France to Alsace-Lorraine" in Berlin. The German Government was infuriated by these secret dealings, and the embarrassed Charles was forced to apologize. On May 12, he journeyed to Spa to put his signature to agreements for closer military and political alliances between Germany and Austria-Hungary. With this act, Austria-Hungary became a satellite of Germany.[1]

It was clear now that the Wilsonian call for an Austria-Hungary independent of German influence had met with failure. The Allies needed new tactics to weaken the Austro-Hungarian Empire. This meant the return to the old strategy of the Entente—dissolution. At the same time unrest among the nationalities increased. On May 15, representatives of Czechs, Slovaks, Yugoslavs, Poles, Italians and Rumanians gathered in Prague under the pretext of celebrating the golden anniversary of the founding of the Czech National Theater. The meeting turned out to be a replica of the Rome Congress. It was a loud demonstration against the Empire where the names of Masaryk and Wilson were often repeated and hailed. On May 17, a committee, formed by the participating leaders of the nationalities of the Empire, drafted a resolution which promised to do everything in their power "in order that their nations may gain their freedom from this terrible war and on the basis of self-determination rise to a new free life in their independent states."[2]

The initiative to return to the policy of dissolution was initiated by the Americans. On May 29, Secretary of State Lansing drafted a "Memorandum on the Policy of the United States in Relation to the Nationalities included within the Austro-Hungarian Empire." Its purpose was to secure the President's approval of the new policy of the State Department. Lansing thought that a change of policy in the light of the "unwise publication of the Prince Sixtus Letter" and of the situation within the Empire was appropriate:

> It would seem to me not only politic at this time of political unrest and social unrest in Austria-Hungary and of the failure of the offensive in Italy, but just to the nationalities concerned to declare without reservation for an independent Poland, an independent Bohemia and an independent Southern Slav State, and a return of the Rumanians and Italians to their natural allegiance.
>
> This would mean in effect the dismemberment of the present Austro-Hungarian Empire into its original elements, leaving these independent nationalities to form separate states as they might themselves decide to form, especially if the severance of Austria and Hungary resulted. . . [3]

President Wilson approved Lansing's memorandum and on June 26 he wrote his version of a death sentence to the Habsburg Empire:

> I agree with you that we can no longer respect or regard the integrity of the artificial Austrian Empire. I doubt that even Hungary is any more an integral part of it than Bohemia. I have made this judgment in part upon a very interesting and illuminating conversation I had a month or two ago with a group of Magyar Americans who spoke plainly to the point.[4]

The opinion of President Wilson that the separation of Austria and Hungary could be achieved was motivated by the leaders of the Hungarian-American Loyalty League, formed in January 1918. This group was the most vocal of the Austro-Hungarian ethnic organizations in the United States. The organization was under the leadership of Alexander Konta, who in 1917 was appointed to head the government-run Hungarian Bureau of the Committee of Public Information. With the blessing of the C.P.I. Foreign Section Director, George Creel, the Hungarian-American Loyalty League accepted a platform supporting independent Hungary. This policy was later cabled to C.P.I. agents in Russia by Creel for the purpose of its clandestine introduction into Hungary.[5]

The introduction of revolutionary ideas through Russia was made possible by the Brest-Litovsk Armistice and soon after by the Brest-Litovsk Treaty which permitted the return of the Austro-Hungarian prisoners of war in Russia to the Empire. With the aid of his agents, Creel expected to distribute C.P.I. propaganda publications among those Magyar prisoners of war who were still in Russian camps, but were to be repatriated in the near future.[6] It seems, however, that the revolutionary ideology of Bolshevism, rather than U.S. sponsored separatism among the returning prisoners of war, gave the real headache to Hungarian authorities. Reports to the Austro-Hungarian Chief of Staff included strong warnings of the danger of Bolshevism among the prisoners of war[7] and, as a result of the threat, returning soldiers were quarantined and investigated before they returned to duty.[8] One of these camps was at Kenyérmező, where the returning prisoners of war were questioned about the Hungarian revolutionary organization at Omsk, Siberia. The interviewers were especially interested in the activities of the leaders, such as József Rabinovics and Béla Kun. These interrogators insisted that the repatriates "must know these men whose aim was to make revolutions at home also."[9] Some of the insurrectionary activities were also led by returning soldiers. The Chief Prosecutor of the mining city of Pécs, for instance, reported that the instigators of a local rebellion were soldiers back from Russian prisoner of war camps. These men, according to the minutes of military court martials, were "saturated with Bolshevism."[10]

The fear of Bolshevism was serious enough to prompt the German Embassy in Moscow to protest against the communist efforts to subvert the prisoners' of war allegiance to their own governments.[11] During the same month of April, Allied observers were also sent to investigate the activities of the "Red" Hungarian prisoners of war in Russia. This was necessitated by official Allied reports that the activities of the Hungarians were instigated by the Central Powers and were dangerous to the Allied cause. The two investigators, the American Red Cross Attache, Captain William B. Webster, and Captain W.I. Hicks of the British Mission in Moscow, were sent to Omsk, Siberia to survey the activities of the Magyars. In their summary report they dismissed the charge that the prisoners of war attempted to seize "the Trans-Siberian Railway in the interest of the German cause." They could only report a total of nine-hundred and thirty-one Hungarian Red Guards armed for Bolshevik military purposes.

They reported the threat of the Central All-Siberia Soviet, which promised to arm more Hungarians in case of an Allied "uninvited intervention." The Allied investigators thought that the report of German foul play concerning prisoners of war was spread by anti-Bolshevik Allied observers, and that in reality the Red Guards represented a threat to the Central Powers rather than to the Allies:

> We can add after seeing the armed prisoners and the type of men which they are that we feel there is no danger to the allied cause through them. On the contrary, we feel that there would seem to be a large social danger to the course of the Central Empires, as the Socialist activity among the prisoners of war is very far reaching.[12]

The Allies were not able to profit from the disruptive force of Bolshevism which was threatening the Dual Empire. This ideology became a taboo among the Allied leaders as well. They were afraid that its energy could not be harnessed and that it could backfire much as it did in the case of the Germans who were responsible for the return of Lenin to Russia. President Wilson thus felt that, unlike the Central Powers whose policy had been "to foment revolution in the countries with which they were at war," the United States could not do anything "that would directly or indirectly bring revolution even in an enemy country."[13] Secretary of State Lansing had similar views about Bolshevik revolutions:

> The question is as to what will be the result if the proletariat should overthrow orderly governments in Central Europe. A Bolshevik Germany or Austria is too horrible to contemplate. It is worse, far worse, than a Prussianized Germany and would mean an even greater menace to human liberty.[14]

Because of the fear of Bolshevism, the Allies had no other tactic to disrupt the war effort of the Dual Monarchy than the support of the disgruntled Austro-Hungarian nationalities. The allies of the United States were quick to accept the *volte face* that was initiated by Lansing. On June 28, the day the Secretary of State declared that "all branches of the Slav race should be completely freed of Austrian rule,"[15] the

French government recognized the Czecho-Slovak National Council as the "supreme organ of the nation and the first basis of a future Czecho-Slovak government within the historic limits of your provinces."[16] The British government moved in a similar direction. On June 14, Foreign Secretary Arthur James Balfour approved a Foreign Office directive that suspended liasons with the Hungarian opposition led by Károlyi. The policy makers of the Foreign Office claimed that contacts with the Hungarians "would alienate the Slavs of the Empire and like in 1848, would create a pro-Hapsburg feeling."[17] This policy was followed up on August 9 when the British government recognized the Czecho-Slovak National Council as a *de facto* co-belligerent government. The United States followed suit in September.

The recognition of the Czecho-Slovak National Council as a kind of government in exile had far-reaching implications. It meant the nullification of Point Ten of Wilson's *Fourteen Points* by the Allies. This was a concrete fact overshadowing the vague promises made in the past which could be respected or disregarded at will. The existence of the Czecho-Slovak National Council in Paris as a co-belligerent suggested the creation of a new state which had never existed in modern European history. With this act the nationalities question became an international question as far as Hungary was concerned.

The putting of the National Council on such solid grounds was also necessitated by the "uninvited intervention" of the Czecho-Slovak Legion in Russia in May 1918. The Siberian Soviet kept its word and decided to arm the Hungarian prisoners of war. The call was nationalistic in tone and described the murder of several Hungarian Red Guards at Chelyabinsk. Because of the anti-Magyar feelings among the Czechs, the appeal reasoned, Hungarians had to fight for their existence:

> Before us stands open the question: to be or not to be. The Soviet has placed at the disposition of the central organization a thousand rifles. These thousand rifles we must use if we wish to guard ourselves and the Russian revolution which is our ally and the basis for our future revolution.[18]

The chief spokesman for the Czechoslovak cause, Eduard Beneš, was eager to express willingness of the Czechoslovaks to fight in Siberia in return for Allied recognition of Czechoslovak aspirations.[19] Czech anti-Communism was emphasized following the Czech intervention by the fact that of all the Czechoslovak prisoners of war in Russia, only 1,300 threw in their lot with the Bolsheviks. Beneš went on to compare this number with the large number of Magyars in the Bolshevik fold. The Czech statesman claimed that the Magyars were so much influenced by communism that they refused to be repatriated and became serious adversaries of the Czechoslovaks.[20] Reports from the Czecho-Slovak Legion also indicated that captured Magyar Red Guards were summarily executed, while their Russian camarades were merely made prisoners.[21] Thus, the anti-Bolshevik intervention of the Czechoslovaks lead to a civil war between the nationalities of the Austro-Hungarian Empire in distant Siberia. The violent hostility of the neighboring nationalities, however, came to be identified as a struggle of conflicting ideologies. The Czechoslovaks were recognized as warriors in defense of democracy while the Magyars were labeled as supporters of the Bolshevik menace.

If the Czecho-Slovak National Council was recognized because of its anti-Bolshevik position, and if the birth of the Czechoslovak state can be attributed to it,[22] then it can also be said that the death of the historic Hungarian state that included Slovakia was significantly affected by events in Siberia.

In light of the changes taking place in Allied circles, the suggestion of Alexander Konta, dated July 31, 1918, that the Hungarian-American Loyalty League ought to contact the Károlyi party and work together for the dismemberment of the Dual Monarchy became anachronistic. If there were a dismemberment of the Empire, the dismemberment of Hungary was its corollary. For this reason, while Count Károlyi was gaining popular acclaim at home, the time for the application of his policies passed.

At the outbreak of the Sarajevo Crisis Károlyi took an anti-war position which he continued to uphold throughout the conflict. The news of the Austro-Hungarian ultimatum caught him in Cleveland, Ohio,[24] a city with a large Hungarian minority. Seeing that a clash between the two states would destroy the possibility of a future rapprochement between the Magyars and Serbs he took a position against the ultimatum. The August 30 issue of the influential *Pester Lloyd*, representing official opinion and the general war fever, attacked this speech with special vehemence. The paper called Károlyi's views bankrupt and questioned the advisability of Károlyi's return to Hungary. In spite of the fact that he was a "traitor" in the eyes of the Hawks, a *persona non-grata,* the Count returned and, except for a short interval, proceeded to take up a courageous fight for pacifism in Parliament where, in the spring of 1915, he stood almost alone.

In his memoirs, Károlyi later blamed himself for not remaining abroad and for not taking up a struggle "in the style of Masaryk."[25] This belief that his postwar government would have been better treated had he stayed in exile is unconvincing in light of the preceding pages.

Unlike other aristocrats of similar wealth, Károlyi's political platform included demands for land reform and universal suffrage. Like the right-wing members of the Independence Party, he also advocated the nationalistic idea of "personal union" between Austria and Hungary. Unlike the right wing, however, he had a very anti-German outlook. As a patriot, Károlyi saw in the possibility of German victory a change from Austrian to German economic hegemony in Hungary. Károlyi's fears were buttressed by the appearance of Frederich Naumann's *Mitteleuropa.* In this book the author expressed what was soon accepted in German official circles as the war aims of Germany. Naumann saw the necessity of a Berlin-Baghdad axis through the Balkans. Because of its geographic location, Hungary would have been included in Germany's economic orbit.

By July 1916 Károlyi saw that he was unable to force the acceptance of his political platform upon the party over which he presided. He decided to leave the organization, taking some twenty other prominent members with him. The new Károlyi-Independence Party proclaimed a policy pressing for peace without annexations, based on international law, land reforms and universal suffrage.[26]

At the Pacifist Congress which took place in Berne in November 1917, Károlyi had occasion to meet Allied officials in the persons of the French public information officer, Emile Haguenin, and the American Ambassador to Switzerland, Hugh R. Wilson. At these meetings Károlyi attempted to convince the Allied officials that a call for an international conference which, he assumed, the German government would refuse to attend would be the best way to get Austria-Hungary out of the war. In that case, he reasoned, Emperor Charles would have been served a pretext to sever all commitments to Germany.[27] The British Ambassador, Sir Horace Rumbold, also attempted to contact Károlyi and learn the views of the Hungarian opposition leader.[28] Though there is no indication that such a meeting did take place, the Foreign Office was informed of Károlyi's plan for a post-war east-central Europe that would have federated Poland, Austria, Hungary and Yugoslavia under Habsburg presidency. Károlyi claimed that such federation would serve as an effective barrier against German expansion.[29] Even if Károlyi's projects did not materialize, the Berne meeting furthered his reputation as a friend of the Allies.

In January 1918, Mihály Károlyi welcomed Wilson's *Fourteen Points* and became their supporter. During the course of the year, his popularity among the Hungarian masses was greater than that of any one of the socialist leaders. The Austro-Hungarian government, however, did little to accept peace according to the Wilsonian points until the military collapse of Bulgaria. The defeat of the Balkan ally on September 26 shook the whole Central camp and on the 29th, Germany, Austria-Hungary and Turkey agreed to appeal to President Wilson to initiate peace negotiations on the basis of the *Fourteen Points*. Austria-Hungary's appeal arrived in Washington on October 7.[30]

The social and nationality crisis was now coupled with a military crisis. It became evident that if Hungary was hoping for a mild treatment at the hands of the Allies she had to find a man who was always on the side of the Entente. Gyula Andrássy summed up best the feeling of the war party. Referring to his son-in-law, Mihály Károlyi, he said:

> Now it's Mihály's turn. He put his bet on the winner. Now
> he must show what he knows![31]

Károlyi himself expected to be appointed Prime Minister to replace Sándor Wekerle, who would have been happy to resign on the call of the Emperor-King. However, King Charles, ill-advised, refused to appoint Károlyi to the post. He decided to implement the defunct demand of Wilson's Point Ten. His Imperial Manifesto of October 16 proclaimed the federalization of the Austrian realm, stressing that the change did "not touch the integrity of the lands of the sacred Hungarian crown."[32] The exclusion of Hungary was necessitated because Wekerle threatened to cut off Hungary's wheat supply to Austria if the King acted against the Hungarian Constitution.[33] In the same manifesto Charles called on the Reichrat representatives to form national councils that "will represent the

interest of the peoples toward one another as well as toward my government." This call was an attempt to sanction those national councils which
were already forming in ever-growing numbers and at the same time to
keep them within the Imperial confines. The appeal of the Emperor
was unsuccessful.

President Wilson's answer the following day confirmed the failure of
the Imperial Manifesto. Secretary Lansing, conveying Wilson's message,
declared that, due to America's recognition of the Czecho-Slovak National
Council, Point Ten was no longer applicable:

> The President is, therefore, no longer at liberty to accept
> the mere "autonomy" of these peoples as basis for peace,
> but is obliged to insist that they, and not he, shall be the
> judges of what action on the part of the Austro-Hungarian
> Government will satisfy their aspirations and their conception
> of their rights and destiny as members of the family of
> nations.[34]

This new Wilson doctrine supported the notion of national self-
determination as a requisite for peace with Austria-Hungary. For the
nationalities the choice was simple: independence.   Even those who
would have otherwise favored the existence of the Empire would have
had to vote for the dissolution if they followed the rules of logic.
Remaining within the Empire would have meant suffering the consequences of a lost war, while Wilson's offer was an invitation to side
with the winners.

On October 16, the Budapest Parliament met to discuss the meaning
of the Imperial Manifesto for Hungary. Prime Minister Wekerle saw it
as a document proclaiming a personal union between Austria and Hungary.
Károlyi accepted this view but declared that the new situation demanded
the introduction of a new political program: "We lost the war, now it
is important that we ought not lose the peace."

During the parliamentary discussion, a Károlyi partisan lost his temper
and engaged in a shouting duel with members of the Party of Work. He
reminded them that the death of one million Magyar soldiers would
forever be on their conscience. A Work Party member in turn accused the
Károlyi supporter of using treasonous "Entente talk." Tempers flared and,

amidst shouts of "traitors," the Speaker suspended the session. Later the Károlyi partisan was reprimanded for his behavior.[35]

In front of the Parliament building violence also flared. As István Tisza was leaving the building, a young writer made an unsuccessful attempt to assassinate the political leader. The attacker was a member of a self-styled social revolutionary group which had loose connections with the Social Democratic Party. The group thought that the violent death of Tisza would serve as the last act signaling the outbreak of a revolution. A revolution did not break out on that day. Nevertheless, the conspirators justly appraised the situation as nearly revolutionary.

The following day, István Tisza answered Károlyi's charges:

> I recognize what representative Mihály Károlyi said yesterday, that we lost this war. . .[36]

Encouraged by Tisza's admission of defeat, Károlyi pressed on to demand the reigns of the government, but without success. Károlyi saw the desirability of his leadership not only because it might improve Hungary's position *vis á vis* the Allies, but thought that, if no significant social reforms were introduced by the government, a Bolshevik type of revolution would take place in Hungary. On October 22 he declared in Parliament:

> If we do not want here the extreme outbreak of sans-culottism and of Bolshevism, we must act today. If not, then I will hold you, Mr. Prime Minister, responsible for that situation that will come to pass unless you step down immediately.
> . . . And if the government will not act, then I declare and please note, that I will![37]

On the following day Prime Minister Wekerle resigned, but there was no indication that the King would replace him with Károlyi. This negative response forced Károlyi to execute his revolutionary threat. On October 25, he became the president of a newly formed counter-government—the Hungarian National Council. The National Council was a coalition supported by three parties: the Social Democratic Party, the Károlyi

Party, and the Radical Party of Oszkár Jászi. The same day a proclamation was issued by the Council which, like the March 1848 Proclamation of the Hungarian Revolution, had twelve points. It was written by Oszkár Jászi and was printed in several daily newspapers published on that day. The proclamation included a demand for the change of the "corrupt parliamentary and governmental systems in which the country sees its enemies and not its representatives." This program of the National Council included the creation of an independent Hungary, immediate conclusion of a "hopeless war," the repudiation of the "German Alliance," and universal and secret suffrage. It promised civil liberties and amnesty for all political prisoners. Projected social reforms included the redistribution of land and the nationalization of large scale industries. The last three points dealt with the foreign policy program of the National Council.

Point ten called for the recognition of the "newly created Ukrainian, Polish, Czech, South-Slav and Austrian states" and for close economic and political cooperation with them. Next, the program outlined the establishment of embassies abroad led by reputable Hungarian democrats. Their major role was "to stress the ties between the Magyar and sister nationalities out of considerations for their common interests." Point twelve spoke of the need to send to the Peace Conference representatives who favored general disarmament and supported the establishment of strong international organizations. The dictated peace treaties of Bucharest and Brest-Litovsk were renounced with the demand that the "questions of war and peace must be decided by the representatives of all the peoples of the globe."

It is significant that point ten spoke only of the recognition of the Czech and not of a Czecho-Slovak state. Also, point eleven implied the willingness of the nationalities to remain within the Hungarian state. The National Council, which was willing to recognize the secession of the Croats, was unwilling to admit that the other nationalities would do the same. This meant that the boundaries of the historic kingdom of St. Stephen were to be defended by the new government as well. The belief that the nationalities would remain within Hungary was not based on the concept of force but on democratic principles. Jászi, a nationalities specialist of world-wide reputation, was especially sure of his thesis, the theme of point five. He expected that, according to the concept of self-determination, the nationalities would vote to remain within a democratic Hungarian republic:

In a new Hungary the distinction between the nation and the nationalities would lose its malignant significance. The country would change into a brotherly alliance of equal peoples who would support territorial integrity based on common economic and geographic interests and not on national jealousies.

The proclamation of the National Council concluded by asking foreign governments to recognize the Council as the sole legitimate government of Hungary:

> Only the Hungarian National Council can speak or is authorized to deal in the name of the Hungarian nation on whose blood and labor Hungary depends.[38]

In order to build a reputation as a popular institution, the National Council decided to sponsor a peaceful march to the Royal Palace. On the twenty-fifth of October, the demonstrators aimed to express their wish that the King accept the program of the National Council. The march had a mere symbolic purpose as the King was not in Budapest. The demonstrators left a national banner, donated by Károlyi, flying over the Royal Palace. As the orderly manifestation was ready to leave the palace square, they were dispersed by mounted police. In the clash, forty demonstrators were seriously wounded while some two hundred received lighter injuries.[39]

Rejected in his bid to power, Károlyi had one last opportunity to acquire power by legal means. He could persuade the Emperor-King personally to appoint him as Prime Minister of Hungary. King Charles, however, refused and instead sent Archduke Joseph to Budapest to rule as *homo regius* until an acceptable man was found for the post. On October 27, upon his return from Vienna to the Hungarian capital, thousands of people welcomed Károlyi and cheered him as the leader of the now unavoidable revolution. The crowd welcomed him by singing neither the anthem of the Monarchy nor the National Anthem, but the anthem of the revolution: *La Marseillaise.*[40] The man who less than two weeks ago warned Parliament of the danger of sans-culottism accepted the support of the masses who favored orderly change. However spurred on by his deep feeling of patriotism, he now saw that only through the recourse of force could he save Hungary from the threatening abyss.

Károlyi and the other members of the National Council proceeded to organize a forceful takeover. An uprising to install the National Council in power was planned for the first of November.

On the morning of October 29, leaders of the Social Democratic Party decided to send agitators to the military barracks of Budapest in order to win the soldiers over to the cause of the National Council. The National Council attempted to do the same. The following morning posters of the Council appeared on the walls of buildings. The content was a proclamation, addressed to the Hungarian soldiers. It claimed that many of the troops had been brought to Budapest for the sole purpose of crushing a "popular movement which demands an immediate cease fire, universal civil rights, bread and freedom." The manifesto called on the soldiers to organize councils and to establish contact with the National Council. The proclamation ended with the following words:

> . . . Do not shed the blood of your fellow citizen! Do not use
> your arms if they will send you to quell in blood your brothers
> and mothers who are fighting for an independent Hungary, for
> popular rule, for an immediate cease fire! Your place is not on
> the side of the antiquated system but on ours! Be the soldiers
> of the National Council.[41]

The authorities reacted swiftly. On the morning of the appearance of the Manifesto, they ordered the evacuation of the 32nd Infantry Brigade, since it became evident that revolutionary agitation was most fruitful among its soldiers.[42] On the same afternoon government troops raided the headquarters of the Soldiers' Council. This revolutionary organization had been set up on October 25 by twelve young Hungarian officers of various military units, with the ultimate aim of pressuring the authorities to accept an immediate cease fire. In the next few days, its swelling membership and its support for the National Council came to be recognized as a threat to the morale of the army. But the raid did not accomplish its purpose of arresting the leaders of the Soldiers' Council, for they had been warned in advance by a telephone operator who tapped the conversations of the military authorities.[43]

On the evening of the thirtieth, the Soldiers' Council reassembled at another location and discussed the events of the day. In the barracks of the 32nd Brigade, the soldiers refused to obey orders which were to send them to the front. For this seditious act the men were promptly disarmed and arrested. This event produced mixed reactions among the Council members. Some officers and sailors favored an immediate call for revolution, arguing that in the event of delay all Magyar troops with revolutionary sympathies would be pulled out of Budapest and would be replaced with reputedly reliable Bosnian troops. Other members of the Council who represented the minority called on the assembly not to act sooner than planned. While the members were debating what should be done, a demonstration took place in front of their assembly building. The demonstrators came to express their solidarity with the harassed leaders. In this stormy situation the crowds and the Council learned that two companies of the 32nd Brigade were being forcibly sent to the front. The Soldiers' Council decided to act. Some of its members led the demonstrators, approximately ten thousand strong, to the Southern Railway Station to free the captive soldiers from the box cars awaiting departure.[44]

When the demonstrators arrived at the station the guards received orders to disperse them at once. These soldiers refused to obey commands and, instead, some of them handed over their arms and joined the demonstrators. Following the liberation of the two companies, the soldiers led by the officers of the Soldiers' Council and trailed by civilian sympathizers, proceeded to the headquarters of the City Commander. The officers and the soldiers of the crowd tore the Imperial ensigns from their uniforms and replaced them with white frostflowers. This change of symbols baptized the revolution.

At the headquarters, the guards refused to obey the Council officers' plea to open the gates of the fortified building to the rebels who were demanding the arrest of the commander, General Várkonyi. Only after some warning shots from the rebels did they yield. General Várkonyi was arrested and was taken to the Hotel Astoria, the headquarters of the National Council.

Meanwhile, other officers of the Soldiers' Council entered the barracks of the First Infantry Brigade and called upon the officers and enlisted men to join the revolution. Following the successful occupation of the City Command building, the Soldiers' Council ordered the occupation of all important public buildings in the city. These orders were swiftly carried out. The Soldiers' Council took command of the police also.[45]

Other insurgent military groups forced their way into the Army Prison building and freed the imprisoned members of the Soldiers' Council as well as other prisoners.[46]

This unexpected and unprepared revolution caught the members of the National Council off-guard. The sounds of the revolution filled them with apprehension, as they expected loyal troops of the Austro-Hungarian Army to quell the uprising. Their fear was not without foundation as General Lukachich, commander of these forces, had taken preparatory steps to crush any disturbance. The National Council feared that lack of coordination would cause the defeat of this revolution. Although the Council was aware of the success of revolutionary agitation among the troops and of the general deterioration of discipline, what percentage of the troops would side with the revolution was not clear. Council members were also afraid of the Bosnian troops stationed in Hungary, who would be indifferent to "shedding Magyar blood."

The National Council's headquarters at the Hotel Astoria stood virtually without defense. For this reason Mihály Károlyi and the others were expected to be put under arrest by Lukachich. Their new prisoner, General Várkonyi, intensified their anxiety even more by claiming that he would be liberated at any moment.[47] The General was believed to be better informed than he in fact was regarding the military situation. Thus, members of the National Council feared to be arrested for a revolution in which they had no part. Professor Jászi, a member of the National Council, expressed this belief to his companion, the Socialist Kunfi: "We shall probably all hang at dawn! to which a gloomy 'yes' was the answer."[48] Nevertheless, the expected attack on the Astoria by Lukachich's troops never came. A few minutes after three a.m. Lukachich telephoned Vienna and informed the King of the initial success of the rebels and asked for orders. In the course of the conversation he explained the hopelessness of the situation. He also reported that his further orders had little chance of being obeyed and asked the King for reinforcements. The King gave no military orders as to how to handle the rebellion.[49] Instead, he asked for information about the safety of his children, who were staying at the town of Gödöllö, not far from Budapest.

The new Prime Minister, Count János Hadik, spoke to the King next. He announced his desire to relinquish his post to which he had been appointed by the King a day earlier. The Count advised Charles to appoint

Károlyi to the position. The King at this time accepted Hadik's advice and telephoned the Buda residence of Archduke Joseph, instructing him to initiate negotiations with Károlyi. The archduke in turn called Károlyi, who now knew that he had the upper hand and demanded the immediate withdrawal of loyal troops from the streets to their barracks as a price for negotiations. The *homo regius* of Charles accepted the terms.

Following a short preliminary parley at the archduke's residence, Károlyi returned to the Astoria with newly gained confidence. He soon departed again to the bureau of the Prime Minister to reopen negotiations with Archduke Joseph and Count Hadik. Károlyi insisted upon being treated not as a member of Parliament ready to form a cabinet, but as the President of the National Council. This meant that the representatives of the King recognized the revolutionary organization as a legal institution of Hungary. While Károlyi was negotiating, the Social Democratic members of the Council decided to call a general strike in order to strengthen Károlyi's position at the parley. The following proclamation was issued by the Social Democratic Party:

> Workers, Camaraaes! The revolution is on!
> The selfish class rule forced the country into an unavoidable revolution. In the course of Wednesday night military groups, who decided to join the national council, have occupied without bloodshed the important public buildings of the capital. They took the City Command, the Central Post Office and the Telephone building. These soldiers swore loyalty to the National Council.
>
> Workers!
> Now it is your turn!
> No doubt the counter-revolution will attempt to regain power. You must show your solidarity with your soldier brothers. To the streets! Stop work!

By seven a.m. the building of the Prime Ministry was surrounded by armed soldiers wearing frostflowers on their uniforms and by workers. The victory of the revolution was officially recognized at eight a.m. Archduke Joseph declared to the assembled people the appointment of the President of the National Council as Prime Minister of Hungary.[50] The revolution, though virtually a private venture of the Soldier's Council's rebellious young officers, spurred to action by the citizens of Budapest, had succeeded in bringing Károlyi and the National Council to power. Ernő Garami, a Social Democrat on the National Council gave the best summary of the role of the National Council in the revolution:

> We planned, and the masses, mainly those in uniform, acted.[51]

The victorious revolution seemed to fulfill the requirements for the cessation of conflict according to Wilsonian terms. By the National Council's rise to power, a government was created whose aim was to respond to popular will. Those responsible for the war were eliminated from power. Even the murder of István Tisza on October 31 by some revolutionary soldiers seemed to reflect the popular interpretation of Wilsonism. His death was the death of an individual who symbolized the Old Regime and who was considered personally responsible for Hungary's involvement in the war. His murder by the "general will" became a ritual which was thought to have cleansed the nation of all its guilt.

Károlyi in power fulfilled Wilson's second precondition for peace. His staunch Germanophobia meant the end of German-Hungarian cooperation and precluded the possibility of rapprochement in the near future. By fulfilling the requirements for peace, supporters of the revolution and the government looked forward to a friendly and close relationship with the victorious Allies.

CHAPTER III
THE PEOPLE'S REPUBLIC OF HUNGARY

Károlyi's first task as prime minister was to form a cabinet that would execute the program of the revolution. Cabinet members were to be chosen from the parties in the National Council. During the morning of the thirty-first, the Council moved from its cramped headquarters at the Hotel Astoria to the council chamber at City Hall. It met there until November 11 and then moved into the Parliament Building.

To avoid the problem of dual authority, Károlyi resigned as president of the National Council which promptly elected in his place one of his followers, János Hock, a Catholic priest and a popular orator. The skeleton cabinet that Károlyi formed included another follower, Count Tivadar Batthyány, as Minister of Interior and Márton Lovászy as Minister of Education. The Social Democrats held two cabinet posts: Zsigmond Kunfi was Minister of Welfare and Ernő Garami, Minister of Commerce. Though the Social Democrats were only a minority in the cabinet, their influence on matters of policy was overwhelming. The party's strength was based on its popular appeal coupled with efficient centralized machinery. Its affiliation with the labor unions was also an important asset. In fact, it is safe to say that the government could not have existed without the Social Democrats' cooperation.[1]

The Social Democratic Party's participation in the government removed one of the problems that plagued the March Revolution in Russia: the danger of dual authority. In Russia the investiture conflict between the Provisional Government and the Workers' and Soldiers' Soviet was a source of constant friction which contributed greatly to the Bolsheviks' victory in November 1917. In Hungary, the Soldiers' and Workers' Councils were closely controlled by the Social Democratic Party and, therefore, supported the work of the provisional government.

In Budapest, the Workers' Council began to be organized on the eve of the revolution. Elections to the council were held on October 30 and were conducted by union officials, who made sure that their candidates were acceptable to the socialists. The Workers' Council first met on November 2. It had a total of three hundred and sixty-five members, two hundred and thirty-nine of whom were elected directly as representatives of the factories and one hundred and twenty-six of whom were delegated by the party and union leadership.[2] The council acted as an extension of the Social Democratic Party, rubber-stamping those government measures that the party had approved.[3]

The president of the Workers' Council was Dezső Bokányi, an old Socialist and experienced labor organizer who was the head of the Masons' Union. Károlyi also appointed him chairman of the National Propaganda Committee, a position he was well suited for as the Social Democrats' ablest and most popular orator.[4]

At the time of its inception, the Soldiers' Council was not subject to the control of any other party. Many of its members, however, sympathized with moderate or radical social democracy. In order to forestall a challenge to authority from this source, the Soldiers' Council was reorganized on November 3. Its new president was József Pogány, a former military correspondent of the Socialist newspaper *Népszava* and a trusted Social Democrat. The council came under the strict supervision of the new Minister of Defense, the pacifist Béla Linder. The presidents of the Workers' and Soldiers' Councils acted as a liaison between their respective organizations and the National Council. According to government directives, however, none of the three councils had any executive or legislative powers; instead, their role was defined as "advisory."[5]

The important position of Minister of Nationalities was given to the noted sociologist, Oszkár Jászi, who represented the small Radical Party which he founded just before the outbreak of the war. Like the Social Democrats, the Radical Party had no representation in Parliament, but during the war years it had gained increasing prominence because of its avowedly pacifist platform. It was the one principle that gave unity to the party, which otherwise embraced a wide variety of views ranging from Marxism to laissez-faire liberalism.[6] It was more akin to a political debating society than a close-knit political party like the Social Democratic Party. Most of its support came from the relatively small Hungarian middle class; its intellectuals were mainly Jewish, with whom the "historic class" felt nothing in common. For this reason not a single aristocrat was among Jászi's followers.[7]

The serious problem of the nationalities fell on Jászi's shoulders. Before the war, he had been a leading critic of Hungary's nationalities policy. He considered the suppression of ethnic minorities to be a national shame, indicative of the bankruptcy of the whole system. In a discussion of the ineptitude of public administration in areas inhabited by ethnic minorities, he noted:

> I do not discuss certain specific problems, since the crux of the matter can be found in the whole system, which is based on imprecise laws, on force and on class consciousness.[8]

Because he attributed the minorities' ills to economic exploitations, he believed that the granting of cultural and linguistic liberty would satisfy them.[9] In an essay entitled "The Future of the Monarchy, the Collapse of Dualism and the Danubian United States," written in the middle of 1918, Jászi suggested the organization of a "pentarchy." By this he meant a confederation of the five nations in the Monarchy that had a separate historico-political identity—the Magyar, Polish, Czech, Croat and Serb nations. Jászi saw confederation as the solution because he believed by 1918 that small, isolated states had become an anachronism. If they did not unite, he reasoned, they would have to lean on the Great Powers, and then they would be nothing but impotent buffer states. Within a confederate system he saw Hungary as a kind of eastern Switzerland. He thought the Magyar nation, by means of a natural economic and cultural hegemony, would be able to stimulate effective cooperation with the other nationalities if it would give up its feudalism and its senseless policy of assimilation.[10]

After the collapse of the Dual Monarchy, Jászi's book was reprinted under the revised title, "The Future of Hungary." The text itself was unchanged, because basic principles, he asserted, remained the same.[11]

As Minister of Nationalities in the Károlyi government, Jászi believed that, since the new system was a democratic one, it would be possible to keep the nationalities within the ancient borders of Hungary. With his rational, scientific mind, he did not grasp that the feeling of nationalism defies all rational theories. He also disregarded the fact that the leaders of the various nationalities were already committed to secession. Jászi's plan for an "eastern Switzerland," however, appealed to all parties in the

National Council. The Károlyi Party, perpetuating the liberal democratic traditions of 1848, saw Jászi's plan as an updated version of Kossuth's projected Danubian Confederation. The Radicals gave their leader their undivided support. The Social Democrats backed Jászi's plan because it was international in scope, for Jászi envisioned his "eastern Switzerland" as part of a larger Danubian Confederation, which in turn would be a member of a future United States of Europe.[12] No doubt there was added to all these rational explanations an irrational reverence for borders that dated from "times immemorial."

Jászi's plan may have appealed to the patriotic Hungarian National Council, but it did not appeal to the national councils of the successor states. The latter were demanding large chunks of Hungarian territory. Regardless of their justification, their claims raised new, insolvable problems. Demands overlapped, but none of the new successor states was willing to moderate them in order to arrive at a just and amicable solution.

The Foreign Minister of the Czechoslovak Government, Eduard Beneš, declared on November 5, 1918 in *Matin*, that the Czechs would have to occupy Slovakia in its entirety because Bolshevism threatened Hungary and could spread from there to the West. He also suggested that northwestern Hungary should also be occupied by the Czechoslovaks in order to connect Bohemia with Yugoslavia. He argued that this way a strong barrier would be built between the Germans and the Hungarians. Beneš also claimed that the Czechoslovak cordon would insulate the West from the threat of Bolshevism. Beneš closed his argument by claiming that through Czechoslovakia the Allies were to become the masters of *Mitteleuropa* in place of Prussia.[13] Though the United States and Great Britain were not willing to become active participants in east-central Europe, France needed little prodding to make the area a French *Mitteleuropa*. Beneš' success in this respect was later acknowledged by the French High Commissioner in Hungary, Fouchet, who claimed that "the Quai d'Orsay was entirely in the hands of Beneš."[14]

The Hungarians saw the calls for occupation of Hungarian territories under the pretext of the Bolshevik menace as camouflage for imperialistic nationalism. Under such circumstances, Jászi came increasingly to believe that renunciation of territorial integrity meant betraying the country to "all kinds of exaggerated imperialistic intrigues."[15]

The portfolio of foreign affairs was taken by the Prime Minister himself. This was a very different arrangement from the cabinets of the other former Central Powers. In the new Germany Max von Baden or Ebert, and in Austria Renner were never their own foreign ministers. In the new Austria Otto Bauer occupied the Foreign Ministry. This gave these nations valuable flexibility at home and abroad. Károlyi's decision could be faulted because it made the prestige of the government dependent on Allied support.[16]

The truth is, however, that in late October and early November, when the treaties of Brest-Litovsk and Bucharest came under fire from several sources, no Hungarian government could have attracted popular support if it had not aimed to preserve Hungary's traditional borders. The Magyars, who were the most numerous and powerful of the nationalities in Hungary, believed that their only need for concern was the victorious Great Powers, which could perpetuate the permanent dismemberment of Hungary. For this reason, most people accepted the idea that the best way for Hungary to obtain favorable treatment was to be represented by a man whom the Allies knew to sympathize with the Entente. No one better fitted the role than Count Károlyi. His decision was therefore realistic and popular. The Budapest evening paper *Az Est* editorialized:

> The Entente does not know and could not know anything about the new Hungary. It only knows that Mihály Károlyi is Hungary's leader. It knows that Károlyi was always the knight in shining armor fighting for peace, justice and the rights of the nationalities and the Socialists. Now that it sees Hungary in his hands, it trusts Hungary as he hastens to establish the rule of justice and mutual respect.[17]

The fact that the socialists cooperated with the "moderate" Károlyi and did not decide to form a purely Socialist cabinet was closely tied to the belief that Karolyi was the man who could liquidate the consequences of the war in the most painless fashion. Karolyi's weight as prime minister thus depended from the very first on his success as foreign minister.

Karolyi's actual involvement in the Ministry of Foreign Affairs was very vague indeed, and was to serve as so much window-dressing for the revolution. The actual work of organizing the new ministry and the day-to-day conduct of policy was the responsibility of the Secretary of State, József Diener-Dénes. Diener-Dénes, a socialist, had little experience in foreign affairs, but his acquaintance with foreign socialist leaders was considered an important asset. His deep-seated prejudices and suspicious attitude toward his colleagues made him a poor choice for such an important post. His foreign-policy program, which was endorsed by Károlyi and the cabinet, called for a territorial settlement to be negotiated at the Peace Conference. Unlike other government officials, he was opposed to the use of military force to preserve territorial integrity until the settlement was reached. He thought that territorial incursions by neighboring states would be strongly condemned by the Peace Conference and saw no need to fight intervention.[18]

On the afternoon of October 31, accompanied by the members of the new cabinet, Károlyi went to the Royal Palace to take the oath of office before Archduke Joseph. It soon became evident, however, that the populace wanted a republic. At mass meetings in Budapest speakers demanded that the Government retract its oath. The November 2 issue of *Népszava* published a declaration from one of these meetings, which protested against the fact that "the government should start its business based on an oath given to the King." It also claimed that the sovereign power of the National Council was founded on the support of the workers and soldiers and did not need royal sanction.[19]

In response to popular pressure, the socialist members of the cabinet decided to retract their oath, but Károlyi and other members of his party in the cabinet refused to follow suit. Out of a deep sense of honor these men offered their resignation rather than break their oath of allegiance. Thus, on November 1 the new cabinet had its first crisis. Its collapse within twenty-four hours of its inauguration was prevented by Archduke Joseph. In response to a deputation consisting of Minister of the Interior Tivadar Batthyány and Minister of the Nationalities Oszkár Jászi, the Crown's representative agreed to intervene and advise the king to release Károlyi and his cabinet from their oath of allegiance. The king acceded, but no republic was yet proclaimed as Károlyi thought that this could be settled only by an elected assembly.[20] A fitting conclusion to the allegiance crisis occurred on November 2, when Archduke Joseph and his son went before the National Council to volunteer their oath of allegiance to this organ.

Following the crisis, the new government's task was to implement the pre-revolutionary program of the National Council. Its first objective was to end the war and reach an armistice agreement with the Allies. As early as October 28, the Chief of the Austro-Hungarian General Staff, General Artur Arz von Straussenburg, ordered his subordinates to begin direct negotiations with the Italians on an immediate armistice. On the morning of November 1, the Allies communicated their conditions. They included an immediate cease-fire and evacuation of Austro-Hungarian forces from certain areas which, in general, were identical with those promised to Italy under the Treaty of London. The Allied Supreme Council gave considerable freedom to the Italians, who pushed their own interests, partly at the expense of the Serbs. Besides this agreement, the Allies reserved the right to occupy "such strategic points in Austria-Hungary at such times as they may deem necessary to enable them to conduct military operations to maintain order."[21]

The armistice was finally concluded on November 3 at Padua. It was signed by the military representatives of the defunct Dual Monarchy. During the Padua negotiations, the Károlyi government protested and, fearing betrayal of Hungary's interest, claimed that only the representatives of a responsible government could negotiate with the chief Allied representative, the Italian General Diaz.[22]

As early as November 1, the Hungarian government had denied the Dual Command's right to negotiate on Hungary's behalf. The new Minister of Defense, Béla Linder, in line with Károlyi's pacifist pro-Allied foreign policy, had even ordered the immediate recall of Hungarian troops from all fronts. The order further instructed all Hungarian units in Hungary or elsewhere to lay down their arms.[23] In spite of all protests, however, the Allies considered the Armistice of Padua to be binding on both Austria and Hungary.

The second phase of Károlyi's program emphasized internal reform. Promised democratic laws were now promulgated. On November 16, the government issued a Hungarian "Bill of Rights." This document included a new voting law, prepared with an eye on the forthcoming elections for a Constituent Assembly, which was to meet early in 1919.[24] Suffrage was extended to all males over twenty-one, who also had the right now to be elected to any public office. The same franchise was given to women over twenty-four. Another law, promulgated on the same day, introduced an eight-hour workday and a forty-eight-hour week.[25]

The government prepared a series of tax reforms. On November 8, a government spokesman, Pál Szende, declared that the country's tax burden was to be borne by the "capitalists." Excise taxes on petroleum, sugar, and wheat were reduced with the prospect of complete repeal in the near future. Szende also mentioned the introduction of progressive inheritance taxes.[26] His program was widely applauded, and two weeks later the Radical Party official was appointed Secretary of State in the Ministry of Finance.

Organizing the Ministry of Finance required special gifts. New machinery had to be set up because formerly financial affairs had been conducted by a joint Austro-Hungarian ministry. In spite of his great talent and seemingly inexhaustible energy, however, Szende was never appointed minister of finance because of his Jewish background. Another Jew, Welfare Minister Kunfi, opposed Szende's promotion on the grounds that, with two Jewish ministers in the cabinet, there would be too many Jews in high position.[27] It is not clear whether Kunfi's opposition to more Jewish ministers was motivated by external or internal considerations, or by both.

The fact that in March 1919 the Magyars accepted an almost wholly Jewish leadership may indicate that Hungarian public opinion had no specific objection to Jews in power so long as they were doing what was expected of them. There is no indication that Kunfi as Commissar of Education in the Béla Kun cabinet ever protested against its Jewish majority. It is more likely, therefore, that discrimination against Jewish Magyar leaders occurred primarily to please the Allies. It was in line with the basic objective of Hungarian foreign policy—to project the image of Hungary that would be most pleasing to the West. The repeated humiliation of Hungarians of Jewish background by Allied officials was proof that Kunfi's cares were not unfounded.

Anti-Semitism was on the upsurge in 1918-1919 in the West, where it often identified with anti-Bolshevism.[28] Though it was not voiced as openly and in such justifiable fashion as anti-Bolshevism, anti-Semitism was embraced by many Allied officials. Even such a prominent statesman as Winston Churchill could later speak of a Jewish-Bolshevik conspiracy. At the time of the Polish-Russian crisis he accused the Bolsheviks of bringing about an "international of Russian and Polish Jews."[30] White Russian refugees in the West, with a tradition of anti-Semitism, helped to perpetuate this fear of an international Jewish and Communist conspiracy.

Well-publicised witch-hunts, such as the Overman Judiciary Subcommittee hearings of the United States Senate, helped to give substance to that fear even in America. In February 1919, witnesses testified to the subcommittee that the Russian revolution had been directed by East-Side Jews.[31]

To keep Jewish participation in the Hungarian government to a minimum was difficult. If the best minds of Hungary were to be enlisted in government service, many of them had to come from the assimilated Jewish intelligensia. The two social groups that were best educated in Hungary were the Hungarian aristocracy and Hungarian Jewry. The suspicious attitude of the revolution toward the discredited aristocracy meant that many of the best-educated were excluded from government service. Indications of counter-revolutionary activities by such aristocrats as Andrássy and Windischgraetz deepened suspicions. The liberal and often radical tradition of the Jewish intelligentsia made this group especially welcome to the government. Because of the ever-increasing role of the Jews, French diplomats came to refer to the Hungarian capital as Jewdapest (Youdapest).[32] The Foreign Office was also kept informed of the large Jewish participation in the Hungarian government. Sir Horace Rumbold, the British Ambassador in Switzerland, had even predicted the outbreak of violence and pogroms in Budapest as a protest against the Károlyi government. Similarly, a French agent informed his War Ministry that Károlyi had no policy of his own and that he was a puppet of Jewish socialists.[33]

Land reform presented a special problem, because there existed no clear consensus on how the land should be divided: whether it should be given to the peasantry outright or merely rented out to them by the state. The Social Democrats with traditional Marxist suspicion of the peasantry were mainly responsible for the fact that no land reform law was promulgated until February 16, 1919.

The law proclaimed the state's right to nationalize all estates over 700 acres in area. The former owners were to be compensated on the basis of the table values of 1913. In areas where the peasants were particularly short of land, the government reserved the right to nationalize properties larger than 280 acres. Priority in the distribution of land was given to poor farm hands, laborers and war veterans. The new owner was given the choice of leasing the land from the state in perpetuity or of buying it outright over a period of 50 years at five percent interest. The complicated law, drafted by the Radical Arnold Daniel and the Socialist Jenő Varga,[34] contained 70 paragraphs. Its execution was the responsibility of the newly established Land Commission. Symbolically, the first and almost the only large estate divided up was Mihály Károlyi's own. The hectic situation in March prevented more thoroughgoing implementation of the land reform, while about sixty large estates were seized by local initiatives.[35]

There was no nationalization plan for industry as there was for agriculture. Faced with coal and raw-materials shortages and resultant unemployment, even the Social Democrats were reluctant to initiate such industrial reform. Before starting nationalization, they preferred to have normal production restored, arguing that the government should not take over "scrap metal."

It is remarkable that the Frostflower revolution was virtually bloodless and did not "demand its victims." The only exception was, of course, the murder of István Tisza. His death had a salutary effect on the course of the revolution, for it seemed to relieve tensions. A contemporary writer, Arpád Pásztor, summed it up eloquently:

> The masses demanded a sacrifice. Now he lies dead, like
> a hero of Greek tragedy.[36]

The aftermath of most revolutions—jacqueries and looting—accompanied the Frostflower revolution as well. As Károlyi later confessed, Linder's order to disarm had much to do with the uneasy internal situation. Károlyi hoped to prevent the return of armed men who might have become marauders and outlaws. This, in turn, might have threatened the stability of the government and occasioned Allied intervention.[37] To prevent looting in Budapest, the Social Democrats organized union workers into "people's guards"—another indication of the power of the socialists. The guards were dissolved by the end of November as order in Budapest was reestablished.[38]

All through the early days of November there was steadily mounting popular pressure to proclaim a republic without calling an election. Telegrams from all over the country gave evidence of the strength of the republican movement. Many local national councils called for the establishment of a socialist republic.[39]

The only obstacle standing in the government's way was King Charles. The Hungarian government, however, was reluctant to end the monarchy without a popular vote. It was wary lest such a unilateral act trigger a legitimist counterrevolution. So a delegation was sent to the king to seek his abdication. The king, who had earlier renounced his rights to the Austrian throne, was willing to do the same for Hungary. On November 13, by the Eckartsau Declaration, Charles "renounced participation" in the affairs of state, declaring that he recognized in advance whatever form of state Hungary might in the future choose to be.[40]

On November 16, both houses of Parliament, which had not met since the outbreak of the revolution, reconvened and "voted" to dissolve. On the same day the formal declaration of the republic took place in front of the Parliament Building. Nationalism and internationalism were symbolized by the Hungarian tricolor flying alongside the red flag. The mixture of ideas present in the new system was reflected in the official name of the new state: The People's Republic of Hungary.

The proclamation of the republic was greeted by an immense crowd in Parliament Square. Only a few representatives of the Ruthenian, Slovene and German minorities were present; the largest nationalities, the Slovaks and the Rumanians were conspicuously absent.[41] Among the celebrants was a veteran of 1848. The keynote speaker, János Hock, beckoned him to the platform and declared:

> That which you fought for seventy years ago. . . Hungary's independence, has been won.[42]

CHAPTER IV
FOREIGN REACTION TO PEACE AND REVOLUTION

The victory of the Frostflower revolution brought to power Mihály Károlyi, whose basic program included ending the war and introducing policies based on the tradition of the revolution of 1848. Part of the revolutionary program, however, took shape in spite of the revolution. The armistice was signed by the representatives of a defunct Empire, without the participation of revolutionary Hungary. The nationalities problem was likewise solved by the nationalities themselves, who in both halves of the Empire were no longer disposed to bargain with their former rulers.

The formation of various national councils by ethnic groups in Hungary pointed the way to a final solution of the nationalities problem and the establishment of a *modus vivendi*. As early as October 27, a Rumanian National Council was set up in Arad and issued a declaration claiming self-determination.[1] The Croat National Council, the *Narodno Vijece*, led a successful revolution in Zagreb. On October 29, the Slovene Anton Korešec, the Croat Ante Pavelić and Serb Svetozar Pribičević, leaders of the National Council, solemnly declared the independence from Austria and Hungary of all the Serbs, Croats, and Slovenes. The new government formed by the council aimed to effect the union of Croatia with Serbia and Montenegro.[2]

On October 30, a Slovak National Council met at the town of Turocszentmárton (Turčiansky Sv. Martin) and called for independence and union with the Czechs:

> The Slovak nation is a part of the Czecho-Slovak nation,
> united in language and in the history of its culture. . .[3]

This declaration, regarded as a valid expression of Slovak will, was specious in two respects. False information, originating with Beneš and Masaryk and relayed through Prague, was foisted on the council, which was told that, unless the Slovaks declared themselves part of the "Czechoslovak" nation, the Allies would leave them under Hungarian rule.[4] This threat forced the hand of even so extreme a Slovak nationalist as Hlinka, who, as he later admitted, "spread sails to the prevailing winds" and supported the declaration.[5] Also the original declaration was soon superseded by a new draft which omitted the clause affirming the Slovak's right to send a delegation to the Peace Conference. When this falsified version of the declaration was printed, several delegates protested but to no avail.[6]

On October 31, in the wake of the victory of the Hungarian revolution, Károlyi telegraphed the fraternal greetings of the Budapest National Council to the Slovak National Council. The Slovaks' reply of November 2 declared that "the Slovak National Council, having joined Czecho-Slovakia, would welcome collaboration with the Magyar People's Republic on an international basis."[7]

For Hungary it seemed that, like Kossuth's liberal 1849 nationality program, Károlyi's similar solution had come too late. By 1849, the Hungarian revolution had been vitiated by Austria's skillful manipulation of the ethnic minorities in accordance with its traditional policy of *divide et impera*. The 1918 Frostflower revolution was similarly weakened by the nationalities' opposition to Károlyi's aim of preserving Hungary's integrity. In 1849, Hungary was suppressed by the joint efforts of Austria and Russia. In 1918 the fate of the revolution was decided by the Allies.

The news of revolutionary tension and the subsequent victory of the revolution in Hungary was received with great apprehension by Allied observers. To some, the revolution seemed to be far to the left, heavy with the "seeds of Bolshevism." From Switzerland, which served as the Allied window on Central Europe, the U.S. Minister to Berne, Pleasants A. Stovall, sent back anxious accounts of the situation in Budapest. On November 2, in a telegram to Lansing the Minister informed the Secretary of State that, besides the National Council, Workers' and Soldiers' Councils were being set up and bore a striking resemblance to the Workers' Soviets in Russia. He concluded:

> To summarize, I greatly fear that we may witness a rapid movement towards extreme socialism, which will sweep away not only present forms of government and the dynasty but which will become a clearly defined Bolsheviki movement.[8]

The "semiofficial" organ of the French government,[9] *Le Journal des Débats*, was also sharply critical of the rise of Károlyi. Though it conceded that as a man he was sincere, it believed that as a politician he was as hotheaded and chauvinistic as the other members of the aristocratic oligarchy.[10]

Seton-Watson's *The New Europe,* which had an influence far out of proportion to its circulation, especially on British and American policy-makers,[11] was very apprehensive of the implications of the revolt for the nationalities. The editors feared that Hungary might be considered a "liberated" state by the victors, and the territorial claims of the "oppressed nationalities" ignored. *The New Europe* therefore warned the Allies that the Hungarian revolution was no more than a maneuver without real substance.[12] The article adverted that the revolution was generated by the Magyars, whose responsibility for the war was second only to that of the Prussians. The tone of the article, an ironic tirade against Károlyi's new Hungary, reflected the fears of the exiled leaders of the non-Magyar nationalities, especially the Czechs. With some justice, Masaryk and the other Czech leaders considered *The New Europe* their propaganda organ.[13]

Károlyi had the reputation of being a political leader who had consistently opposed the war. On the other hand, the Czech and other nationality leaders in exile unflaggingly supported the war because they realized that only an unconditional Allied victory could bring their plan to create Czechoslovakia to fruition. During the Károlyi-Wilson negotiations for a separate Austro-Hungarian peace, the Czech leadership, for example, made feverish efforts to ensure that the negotiation came to naught.[14] As the war neared its end, the Czechs were demanding the severe punishment of Hungary to satisfy their own ambitions of creating a Czechoslovakia.

The victory of the Hungarian National Council and the introduction of its platform were anticipated by Colonel House. On October 29, the chief of *Inquiry,* an official United States organization charged with preparing plans for the Peace Conference, sent to Washington for presidential approval the revised version of the *Fourteen Points.* House reported that Point Ten was no longer valid because the rise of the successor states (Czecho-Slovakia, Galicia, German Austria, Jugo-Slavia, Transylvania and Hungary) was a *fait accompli.* House spoke of Hungary as being independent and very democratic in form, but governed by Magyars whose aim was to prevent the detachment of the territory of the nationalities that would "undoubtedly" join some of the new states.[15]

House further recommended American support for the concept of national unity and independence, and a Confederation of Southeastern Europe. The following day President Wilson approved the program, though he insisted that final details must be ironed out at the Peace Conference. Recognizing the confused situation in Central Europe, Wilson felt that the "admission of inchoate nationalities to the Peace Conference" was most undesirable.[16]

On November 1, House received further instructions from the President on the fate of the former Austro-Imperial Army and its subjection to national authority. He favored the transfer of the respective ethnic units of the Austro-Hungarian Army to Czecho-Slovak and Southern Slav authorities. He thought that such a gesture would show the good faith of the Allies toward the new states. At the same time he called for more caution toward Hungary, though he conceded that even there, local control was preferable to foreign. Wilson's view on developing a sphere of influence in east-central Europe was negative. He favored non-intervention by the United States and hoped that the other great powers would follow the American example.[17]

British policy makers adopted a similar policy. In the middle of November, the Austro-Hungarian specialist of the Political Intelligence Department of the Foreign Office, Lewis B. Namier, outlined a policy of non-interference. He also saw the Hungarian revolution in a salutary light, as it promised agrarian reforms.[18] Balfour accepted Namier's views and on November 22, the War Cabinet approved non-intervention in the affairs of the successor states.[19]

American non-intervention in the former Empire was especially significant as the policy was enunciated while the fear of an outbreak of Bolshevism in central Europe gripped Wilson's cabinet. On November 2, Secretary of War Newton Baker warned Wilson of the Bolshevik threat. Baker urged the President to make it clear to the new states being formed out of the Habsburg realm that the United States did not favor violent revolution, but rather wanted them to "observe orderly processes in these revolutionary days and refrain from acts of violence."[20] Even on election day, November 5, the President's major concern was the threat of revolution and in a conversation with cabinet members Wilson spoke at length about the possibility of rebellions in Europe as a result of Bolshevik propaganda.[21]

This fear of Bolshevism forced Wilson to act. In an appeal to the "peoples of the constitutent nations of Austria-Hungary that achieved liberation from the yoke of an Austro-Hungarian Empire," the President called for order with moderation, so that "violence and cruelty of every kind are checked and prevented, so that nothing inhumane may stain the annals of the new age of achievement." The message was conveyed by Lansing to Stovall in Berne with instructions that it should be turned over to the Director of the Committee on Public Information in Switzerland, Mrs. Vira B. Whitehouse. Further instructions ordered that the appeal should be translated and given the "widest possible distribution."[22]

Wilson's message was delivered to Mrs. Whitehouse on the morning of November 7. It was at once released in four languages: German, Hungarian, Italian and French. The language of the message and Lansing's instructions left little doubt that it was directed equally to all the nations of the former empire.

Its communication to those nations was difficult, however, because of the chaotic condition of the disintegrating Austro-Hungarian foreign-affairs apparatus. Minister Stovall furthermore did nothing to facilitate Mrs. Whitehouse's endeavor. Professional jealousy between the diplomatic corps and the C.P.I. often resulted in such sabotage on the part of professional American diplomats.[23] Transmission of the message through Allied military channels would have been too slow to satisfy Lansing's order, so Mrs. Whitehouse had to look for other means to convey the presidential message. Her choice fell on the recently arrived personal representative of Mihály Károlyi, Róza Bédy-Schwimmer.

Bédy-Schwimmer, as a leader of the National Feminist Association of Hungary, was in Switzerland in order to establish contact with Allied representatives, particularly with the Americans. She went as spokeswoman for the pacifist sentiment of women in Hungary, as early in November it was widely believed that peace negotiations would take place in neutral Switzerland. In anticipation of the arrival of Allied leaders, Bédy-Schwimmer convinced Károlyi that she could also be his ideal representative in search for Allied recognition of his National Council.[24]

Before the war she had gained world renown as a pacifist and feminist. In July 1914 she was living in London, serving as International Press Secretary of the International Suffrage Alliance and special correspondent for many important European newspapers. On July 9, 1914, the Sarajevo crisis had led her to ask for an interview with Lloyd George. At a breakfast meeting with the British chancellor of the exchequer and Liberal leader, the Hungarian lady cautioned that England was taking the crisis too lightly. She warned Lloyd George of the dangers of such an attitude and in no uncertain terms predicted an Austro-Serbian war with Europe-wide consequences. Though at the time Lloyd George dismissed her ominous prophecy, he later came to credit her as the only person he met during the crisis who was aware of the dangers inherent in the situation.[25]

Bédy-Schwimmer was also personally acquainted with President Wilson and with Colonel House. She had met the President for the first time in September 1914, when she presented an international petition urging him to call a Neutral Conference for Continuous Mediation between the belligerents.[26] Bédy-Schwimmer soon afterwards met Mrs. Whitehouse at the American Women's Suffrage Convention, where the American suffragette led the isolationist wing of the movement. Bédy-Schwimmer was instrumental in having the convention adopt a foreign-policy platform demanding peace among the belligerents.[27]

Her reputation as an ardent pacifist had been enhanced in November 1915, while she was on a speaking tour in the United States. At that time she had met Henry Ford, who was appalled by the carnage in Europe. He was determined to stop fighting "where 20,000 men could be killed within 24 hours without changing the position of the armies." Bédy-Schwimmer won Ford over to her idea of commissioning a peace ship with prominent American and international personalities abroad. This ship was to visit European ports at which the notables on board would make appeals to the European nations not in the name of the United States government but as representatives of the people.[28]

Once Ford had espoused her cause, the Hungarian pacifist had another occasion to get in touch with President Wilson. She and the later Nobel Peace-prize laureate, Jane Addams, wanted the President to join with other neutral nations to set up a peace committee in The Hague. Its purpose was to make peace proposals and put pressure on the belligerents until a cease-fire was accepted by all warring factions. Though President Wilson could not officially endorse such endeavors, he privately favored Bédy-Schwimmer's efforts.[29]

For Mihály Károlyi, himself a pacifist, Bédy-Schwimmer was the ideal envoy. Her sincerity could hardly be challenged, while her personal acquaintance with the British Prime Minister, the American President and his personal representative in Paris, Colonel House, especially well fitted her for her mission. Once she had met Mrs. Whitehouse and had shown her credentials as Károlyi's representative, Bédy-Schwimmer was instructed to take Wilson's message back to Hungary. Entrusted with this task, the Hungarian became a C.P.I. agent, even equipped with an official pass.

Her orders included distribution of the message among the nationalities of the former empire. She was to have the message translated and printed in Czech, Slovak, Rumanian, Serbian and Ruthenian in addition to the languages in which it had already appeared. The message was to be transmitted to all newly constituted authorities and to all newspapers.[30]

Bédy-Schwimmer left Berne on the evening of the seventh. After she had arrived in Budapest, Wilson's appeal was sent by courier to the national councils of Vorarlberg, Tyrol, Slovakia, Burgenland, Galicia, Poland, and Croatia. In a telegram to Mrs. Whitehouse, Bédy-Schwimmer reported the success of her mission: "The widest publication has been obtained."[31]

Bédy-Schwimmer's mission was regarded in Budapest as a triumph for the Hungarian National Council which during her absence had elected her to its Executive Committee. It was not known to the Hungarian leaders that Mrs. Whitehouse's initiative was her own: rather, it was thought that the American government was looking on Hungary as a go-between among the successor states. After all, it was reasoned, it was the Károlyi government that had been put in charge of translating and distributing Wilson's appeal, and this indicated that Hungary was to receive preferential treatment, at least by the United States. The Anglo-American leaning of the Károlyi government thus seemingly received early encouragement. Károlyi's blind attachment to Wilsonism was strongly influenced by Bédy-Schwimmer's circumstantial role; Károlyi felt that his belief in Wilson was completely justified and he looked forward to close cooperation with the Allies. For this reason, Bédy-Schwimmer was asked to return to Switzerland as representative of the National Council.

On the very day Lansing cabled Wilson's appeal, Stovall reported new, disquieting news from Hungary. He spoke of Károlyi's cabinet as being extremely radical and thought that a step further to the left "could mean the acceptance of bolshevism."[32]

Károlyi himself was very careful to heed Wilson's call and did his best not to alienate the United States' seemingly favorable attitude toward Hungary. Soon after receiving Wilson's message, the Hungarian government received an appeal from Lenin which applauded the revolutions taking place in the old Austro-Hungarian monarchy. Lenin's appeal to the peoples was a call to reject Wilsonism, which he termed a deception of the American capitalists. He reminded the German, Czech, Hungarian and Croat workers and peasants that the American, British and French forces were engaged "in a criminal war against the workers and peasants of Russia in order to force them to pay for the debts incurred by the Russian bourgeoisie and tsarism." Lenin warned that American promises of bread and butter were only a cover for such "criminal activities," and expressed his belief that Wilsonism would be rejected in favor of a Communist revolution:

> Our unshakable belief is that the Austrian and Hungarian workers will understand that they cannot trust the factory owners, bankers and generals of any state: the laboring masses can be freed only through an International Proletarian Revolution. . . . We call on you, unite with the Russian workers and peasants. . .
>
> You have stepped on the road of revolution, continue on this road fearlessly toward victory![33]

The Károlyi government was asked to print the message and transmit it to Prague and Zagreb. Lenin's message, however, was not released by the Hungarian government. It was only saved from oblivion by social revolutionaries who got hold of the appeal through a contact working at the government wireless receiving station in Csepel.[34]

On the day that the People's Republic was proclaimed, the social revolutionaries dropped leaflets bearing the message from an aircraft into the crowds celebrating in Parliament Square. In the leaflet, Lenin's appeal was preceded by an accusation that the government was guilty of sabotage because "since November 10 it has kept the message secret from the Hungarian workers."[35]

The incident forced the subject to be brought up at a Workers' Council meeting where the government was questioned about the veracity of the leaflet. The government representative had to concede that such a message had been received on the date mentioned, but declared that the authorities had the impression "that Lenin's instructions were satisfied, and because of the existing confusion, the radiogram was not published." He added that the cause of the delay was under investigation.[36]

To Lenin and the Bolsheviks Károlyi looked like a Hungarian Kerensky. They regarded Hungary as the state ripest for a proletarian revolution.[37] As far back as 1913, Lenin saw close similarities between Russia and Hungary, and considered that social and economic conditions were very much alike in both countries:

> It is a well-known fact that Hungary is closest to Russia not only geographically, but because the absolute power of the reactionary landlord exists there also.[38]

The Hungarian Social Democrats were anxious to counter Lenin's comparisons. On the first anniversary of the Bolshevik revolution, *Népszava* congratulated Moscow, but took time out to argue with Lenin that Hungarian conditions were very dissimilar from Russia's. In Russia, its editorial said, the percentage of industrial workers was higher than in Hungary. On the other hand, Russia's peasantry, unlike Hungary's, was politically unaware. For this reason, *Népszava* concluded, the Hungarian peasantry would never submit to political dictatorship by the small industrial working class.[39] *Népszava's* observation later proved to be correct, for the Béla Kun regime was greatly weakened by the hostility of the peasants, who were unwilling to defer to directives from the workers of Budapest.

On November 20, when Lenin's appeal was finally published in *Népszava*, the newspaper's commentator warned readers not to take Lenin's call for a Bolshevik revolution to heart. He reminded them that Bolshevism in Hungary would occasion foreign intervention, which would lead to the triumph of reaction.[40] This prophecy, likewise, later came true.

The Hungarian Social Democrats strove to improve the country's international position through their connections with Western leaders. On October 29, Socialist Party leader Manó Buchinger was sent to Geneva to get in touch with the Czech and Slovak Socialists, who were attending a meeting of the Czechoslovak National Council with Beneš. Buchinger's task was to impress upon the Socialist comrades the need for a less anti-Magyar attitude by the Czechoslovak National Council. The future of Slovakia was also expected to be discussed.

On his way to Switzerland, Buchinger stopped in Vienna to meet the Czech socialist and former *Reichsrat* leader, Vlastimil Tusar, who by October 29 was presenting himself as the agent of the Czechoslovak government. Buchinger failed to persuade Tusar to recognize Károlyi's Hungarian National Council. On the second leg of his trip, in Zurich, Buchinger met other Czech socialists who were no less hostile toward Károlyi. The Hungarian then realized the futility of his mission and returned to Budapest without even reaching Geneva.[41]

The first official foreign-policy statement of the victorious National Council was promulgated on November 2, when a call "to the peoples of the world" reported the victory of the revolution:

> The entire Hungarian people has just completed a pacific and victorious revolution, and, breaking the yoke with which it has been oppressed for centuries, has now formed a democratic and completely independent state. The Hungarian people energetically repudiates all responsibility for the war declared by its oppressors. Listening only to its own cry of conscience, it lays down its arms and desires peace.

The proclamation went on to declare the equality and fraternity of all peoples within Hungary and without. It reminded the West that Hungary for a thousand years had been the "bulwark of Europe and Civilization." It called for just treatment for Hungary and for a guarantee of its territorial integrity.[42]

The declaration was the first intimation to the Allies that Hungary's main foreign-policy concern was to be the preservation of its territorial integrity. It is noteworthy that, unlike statements by other ethnic councils, Budapest's declaration did not speak of Hungary's future role as a "bulwark" against Bolshevism. This may have strengthened the fears of many that the Hungarians sympathized with the Bolsheviks.

While *The New York Times* did not report the National Council's proclamation and *The Times* of London printed it without commentary, *Le Figaro* of Paris paid it more attention. *Le Figaro* catered to the French middle classes and was reputed to reflect Premier Georges Clemenceau's position.[43] In an editorial, the newspaper welcomed the victory of the revolution, but had reservations about the tone of the declaration. It acknowledged that it was easy to understand why the Károlyi regime should identify itself with the liberal revolutionary tradition of Hungary under Kossuth, but then questioned how much had been achieved since that time. It wondered how "the Hungarian people could change the color of their skin from one day to the next and be reborn according to the surest democratic methods." It rejected the notion of Hungary's equality with the other nations "who are still bloody from the war that the Magyars and their allies unleashed with such rare ferocity." The paper said that it was up to the Entente to decide under what conditions the Hungarian people, "who in the course of four years have given the greatest evidence of loyalty to the cause of war," should be absolved of their guilt.[44] The tone of the editorial made it clear that now that the war had been won France was swinging away from the Wilsonian ideals and Hungary could expect harsh treatment from Paris.

Another Paris newspaper close to the government, *Le Temps*, printed the Rumanian National Council's response to the Hungarian declaration. The Rumanians called the Hungarian declaration a pack of lies and claimed that the Magyars were answerable for the war. The statement from Arad demanded the dismemberment of Hungary in accordance with the "ideals of Justice." This statement, too, was printed without comment.[45]

Though no major foreign policy statement on the fate of east-central Europe was issued until late December, it was obvious that France favored territorially strengthening those states that could be counted on as allies. Since power meant territory, this presupposed breaking up Hungary. In contrast, Anglo-American foreign policy favored non-interference and self-determination, which kept alive the possibility that, with plebiscites and elections and with an acceptable nationalities program, Hungary could have been preserved whole.[46] In November, then, foreign policy toward Hungary by the Big Three was becoming polarized.

CHAPTER V
FIRST INTERNATIONAL CONTACTS

The armistice of Padua, which officially ended hostilities for the peoples of the late Austro-Hungarian Empire, did not rule out the possibility of future Allied operations in Hungary against the Germans who were still at war. It seemed likely that the Allied Army of the Orient, under the command of General Franchet d'Esperey would soon enter Hungary in pursuit of the Germans. Such right of invasion, which was set down in the armistice, was viewed with alarm by the Hungarians. The government feared that if Serbian or Czechoslovak troops entered Hungary with Franchet d'Esperey, they would try to occupy and ultimately annex large tracts of Hungarian territory.

To forestall this, the Minister of Defense, Béla Linder, contacted the German Consul in Budapest, Count von Fürstenberg, on the morning of November 5, and demanded the immediate withdrawal of German troops.[1] His initiative was given more urgency by the fact that the Czechoslovaks had cut Hungary off from its sources of coal in Silesia on the pretext that it was permitting the passage of supplies to the German forces on its territory. The Commissioner of Coal, Jenő Vázsonyi, had already warned the government that rail traffic must be reduced because coal stocks were enough to keep the trains running only a day and a half more. When the Ministerial Council met on the same day, Linder suggested that Germany should be given a twenty-four-hour ultimatum to evacuate its troops.[2] His bellicose posture was nothing if not shortsighted, for Linder's orders to disarm had left Hungary with no military force to back up the ultimatum.

The Hungarian government's worries were compounded by the fact that the previous day Marshal Foch had taken over supreme command on all fronts. Italy's important military role was at an end.[3] The Hungarians foresaw a collision between the Italian and French Allies. Captain Francesco Carbone, an officer of the Italian High Command, had already offered Károlyi to occupy Hungary with Italian troops sympathetic to the new government.[4] With hostilities over, Italy seemed to have a common cause with Hungary to curb the territorial aspirations of Serbia.[5]

Italy saw Serbian ambitions as a threat to the promises it had received under the 1915 Treaty of London. In this contest, France supported Serbia. French policy makers wanted to win over Serbia and prevent Italy from making the Adriatic an Italian lake.

Italy's interest in Hungary was inspired by the fact that the Adriatic port of Fiume, desired by both Italy and the Serbs, was Hungarian. The Italians were hoping to make a deal with the Hungarians. Hungary's willingness to support Italy's claim to Fiume at the Peace Conference would have been repaid by Italian help in preventing the South Slavs from taking territory from Hungary.[6]

The Károlyi government was undecided as to what course to take. Above all, it was anxious to sign some kind of military agreement with an Allied party. Such an agreement would amount to *de facto* Allied recognition. The Hungarians' delemma was whom to approach. Should Károlyi treat with the Italian, Diaz, at Padua, or with Franchet d'Esperey, whose forces were already at Hungary's border? The recent appointment of Foch as Supreme Commander on all fronts persuaded the Hungarians to approach the French. The government decided to make representations to Franchet d'Esperey to have him order the responsible national councils south of Hungary's borders to respect its territorial integrity. Rather than seizing Hungarian territory by force, the councils should present their demands for settlement at the Peace Conference. Little did the Hungarian government realize that the Croat Narodno Vijece had already sent delegates to solicit the French general's support in its behalf. Franchet d'Esperey was sympathetic toward their cause and, apparently on his own authority, had promised to lend his backing to the council.[7]

As the Hungarian government set about forming a delegation to send to Franchet d'Esperey, the question of who was to lead it posed something of a problem. Károlyi's moderate ministers advised him to head it himself. This, they reasoned, would ease Magyar apprehension. The socialists, supported by Jászi, objected to Károlyi as chief delegate, lest the embassy's failure weaken the government's position at home. The moderate position finally prevailed. The delegation included Oszkár Jászi and the noted publicist, Baron Lajos Hatvany, representative of the National Council. To prove the democratic character of the new Hungary, a representative of the Soldiers' Council, Captain Imre Csermák, was also appointed as a delegate along with the President of the Workers' Council Dezső Bokanyi.

The delegation's aim was to prevent further Allied incursions into Hungary, and if the French would not agree, to urge that any occupation forces should not include troops from the successor states. The Hungarians left Budapest on November 6 to meet Franchet d'Esperey in Belgrade.[8]

The news of the Padua Armistice brought doubt into the mind of Franchet d'Esperey. He was not sure if it were still appropriate to negotiate with the Hungarians. Orders from Paris, however, made it clear that he was to apply the stipulations of the Armistice to a military convention with Hungary.[9]

On the evening of November 8, the Hungarian delegation was received in Belgrade by the French commander. The envoys, who had expected a warm welcome, were greeted coldly. As Károlyi began to introduce his entourage, the delegates were deeply shocked by the fact that the general made no attempt to disguise his anti-Semitic prejudices toward Baron Hatvany.[10]

Profoundly hurt by the episode, Hatvany commented on it in 1938 when Franchet d'Esperey was elected to the ranks of the forty "immortals" of the French Academy along with two other anti-Semites, Jean Tharaud and Charles Maurras. "I suspect my humiliation was in part responsible for the consecration of this French Ludendorff among the forty immortals," he said.[11]

The presentation of the representative of the Soldiers' Council, who was wearing a revolutionary uniform he had designed himself rather than the former Imperial dress, irritated the general further. No doubt scenting Bolshevism, he became very agitated and exclaimed in horror: "Vous êtes tombés si bas!"[12] The socialist Garami later commented:

> We committed a mistake in the composition of the delegation due to our naive belief that the Soldiers' Council, which symbolized the destruction of Austro-Hungarian militarism, would be as happy news to the French leader as it was to us. It turned out that the general identified himself more with the despised Austro-Hungarian generals than with the democratic military organization that was responsible for the revolution among the belligerents.[13]

In his memorandum to the general, Károlyi emphasized that his government was following the traditions set by Kossuth—an ideology that had been silenced by the old monarchy responsible for the war. Károlyi then asked for fair treatment for his government which, he told Franchet d'Esperey, was the true representative of the Hungarian people. At this point Franchet d'Esperey interrupted him, saying that Károlyi was not the representative of the Hungarians but of the Magyars. It was a clear indication that the Hungarians were not going to find much sympathy for their demands for territorial integrity before the Peace Conference made a decision in their favor. Realizing the Frenchman's attitude, Károlyi attempted to remind him of the Wilsonian principles, but Franchet d'Esperey dismissed the American President with a contemptuous wave of his hand. Károlyi pointed out that since November 1 Hungary had been neutral, resolutely opposed to the old Central Powers' alliance, and an enthusiastic supporter of the concept of the League of Nations. In view of this, Károlyi said, he wanted Franchet d'Esperey to impress upon the Czechs the need to suspend their blockade, for the lack of coal was crippling Hungarian industry and causing hardship among the civilians at the approach of winter. He further asked the general to occupy Hungary, if it was necessary, only with French, Italian or American troops.

At most of the delegation's requests Franchet d'Esperey shook his head. When the poor lighting in the room made Károlyi stumble in reading his prepared text, the general ruefully reminded the Hungarians that their German allies were responsible for the shaky electricity supply in Belgrade.

Before reading his written response, Franchet d'Esperey sarcastically asked the Hungarians if they all understood French. Noting nods of assent, he turned to the President of the Workers' Council and asked: "Even the Socialist?" He went out of his way to remark that this was significant since it would be the fate of the poor to have to accept whatever the new situation was in Hungary; while the dissatisfied rich (an allusion to Károlyi) could always move to Switzerland.[14] Satisfied that his quips about the members of the mission had found their marks, he went on to praise the Francophile Hungarians of the past, such as Prince Rákoczi and Kossuth. However, he reminded the Hungarians, since 1867 their country had been an accomplice of Germany and had supported her "lust for power." For this reason, Franchet d'Esperey said, Hungary could expect stiff penalties. He blamed the Hungarians for suppressing the Czechs, Rumanians, Slovaks and South Slavs and warned the delegates that he could order them to destroy Hungary completely. He added that over the years the Hungarian press had also insulted the honor of France.

At this Jászi could contain himself no longer and in nervous indignation explained that only the chauvinistic press could be accused of impugning French honor. The Frenchman cut Jászi short with a sharp "Enough" and announced that it was too late for the Hungarians to ask for favors. He considered Hungary not a neutral country but a defeated power, he said. He told the mesmerized delegates that the only reason why he was willing to talk to them was out of respect for Károlyi whom he had come to know as an honest man during the war. He urged the delegates to support Károlyi as Hungary's only hope, the only man who could improve the nation's lot. He commended them for coming to see him rather than General Diaz because, he said, it was he alone who had the right to suspend hostilities in his sector.

Franchet d'Esperey's stern and antagonistic tone softened only when he inquired about the wellbeing of "the unfortunate young king." Aware of the general's royalist sympathies, Károlyi made a general reply that carefully avoided the fact that the government was on the verge of dethroning King Charles and declaring a People's Republic. In response the general sighed and exclaimed: "Oh, ce pauvre jeune homme!"

The general audience at an end, Franchet d'Esperey then invited Károlyi and Jászi to follow him into his study next door, leaving the rest of the flabbergasted delegates to themselves. The first to recover from the momentary shock was Dezső Bokányi, who blazed at his colleagues that during the war he had been imprisoned by men whose principles were similar to the general's. Foreseeing a need to stop Franchet d'Esperey's plans by armed force, Bokányi turned to Csermák and told him that under the circumstances the Soldiers' Council was an impossible institution. Soldiers would have to remain soldiers, he acclaimed, and not become civilians as was maintained by that "idiot Linder."[15] Hatvany was equally confounded by the brusque treatment and complained that they had been treated not as representatives of a civilized nation but like envoys from a primitive tribe of natives in darkest Africa.[16]

Meanwhile Franchet d'Esperey was presenting his terms to Károlyi and Jászi. His purpose was twofold. Primarily, he was determined to carry through Clemenceau's order and to march in the direction of Munich.

For this reason he demanded that all strategic points in Hungary should be occupied and all means of communication secured. The secondary purpose of his terms that was also Clemenceau's wish, established a demarcation line that served Serbia's military and political interests. Károlyi and Jászi were handed a map of the Balkans and Hungary with a red line drawn across it. The area that was to come under Allied occupation included the Hungarian territory of the Bánát. On the advice of his Serbian aides, Franchet d'Esperey planned to have Serbian troops occupy the area.[17] Clause 17 of the terms, however, guaranteed that the kingdom of Hungary would be under Hungarian jurisdiction. Since it was established that territorial rearrangements could be decided only by the Peace Conference, the sole clause that caused Károlyi and Jászi concern was one stipulating that, in case of disorder, the Allies had the right to take the areas of disturbance under their own administration. The Hungarians feared that their neighbors might use provocateurs to force disputed areas to be transferred into their own control. Károlyi and Jászi pointed out that the Hungarian government was anticipating unrest and possible outbreaks of violence among the people as a result of the deterioration of economic conditions caused by the coal shortage. Franchet d'Esperey asked what industries in Hungary required coal. Jászi said that among others there were the mills, whereupon the general suggested that Hungary should turn back to using windmills.[18] Despite the sarcasm of his answer, the general deleted the controversial clause about occupation in case of disorders.

Once the terms had been agreed upon, the Hungarians insisted on telegraphing the Supreme Council in Versailles to signal their acceptance of the military convention on condition that, pending the signature of a peace treaty, the frontiers of Hungary, excluding Croatia and Slavonia, were to be respected by the Allies, and that, in case of a German attack, the interests of Hungary would be protected as well.

So, in spite of Franchet d'Esperey's hectoring, the Hungarians were offered reasonably fair terms and provisionally accepted them. The delegation then returned to the Hungarian capital to await the Supreme Council's answer and to have the convention ratified by the National Council. On November 12, Franchet d'Esperey forwarded to the Hungarian government the Supreme Council's reply. Signed by Clemenceau, it declared that Franchet d'Esperey could discuss only military questions with Károlyi, so that the Convention of Belgrade was of a purely military character.[19]

Upon his return, Károlyi was faced with a new military threat by the Czechoslovaks. Profiting from Hungarian disarmament, Slovak leaders with General Milan Štefanik, Minister for National Defense of the Prague government, occupied some districts in western Hungary that were claimed by the Slovak National Council. Accompanied first only by a few legionaires, the Czechoslovak troops met little resistance. As a result of the violation of the armistice agreement the pacifist Minister of Defense, Béla Linder resigned on November 9. The Czechoslovak attempt to impose a military solution on the dispute over territory pointed up the need to reorganize the Hungarian army and to rearm. The execution of such policy was put in the hands of the new Minister of Defense, Albert Bartha. To spare the government the embarrassment of changing cabinet, Linder was named minister without portfolio and ambassador at large. His first duty as ambassador was the official acceptance of Franchet d'Esperey's terms on November 13 in Belgrade.[20]

The final terms of the Military Convention were added as an appendix to the Diaz armistice agreements.[21] The convention required the demobilization of all Hungarian forces with the exception of six infantry divisions and two cavalry divisions destined to preserve internal order. The prescribed demarcation line followed the upper valley of the Szamoş (Somes) river, went through Beszterce (Bistriţa) and Marosvásárhely (Tirgu Mureş) to the Maros (Mureş) river, along it to its union with the Tisza river through Beja, Pécs and along the Dráva river, following the border of Croatia-Slavonia. The area south of the demarcation line was to be evacuated by Hungarian troops within eight days and occupied by the Allies even though it was to remain under Hungarian administration. The Allies retained the right to occupy all points and localities deemed necessary by the Commander in Chief. The convention further stipulated the evacuation of German troops from Hungary and the severance of diplomatic relations with Berlin. In Article 17 the Allies agreed not to interfere in the internal affairs of Hungary, while Article 19, the last, declared an end to all hostilities between the Allies and Hungary.[22]

Since the Belgrade Convention was signed two days after the armistice with Germany, many of its terms were already obsolete. The peace with Germany was a bitter blow to Franchet d'Esperey, whose dream of being the conqueror of Berlin had been dashed. His diary for November 12 clearly showed his unsatisfied yearning for glory. In it he complained that he had been neither advised nor consulted about the Allied-German armistice negotiations, even though his troops were already in Hungary and he had managed the unique achievement of occupying two enemy capitals: Sofia and Constantinople.[23] In his encounter, he claimed to have impressed upon Károlyi that the Magyars must "renounce their hegemony over the nationalties," though he had had some difficulty in getting the point over to Károlyi's entourage. In a letter to a friend, the Academician Charles Freycinet, d'Esperey indicated his distrust of Károlyi's followers but felt that it was a wise decision for Károlyi to be Hungary's foreign minister.[24]

Newspaper reports in Budapest described the Hungarian delegation's discourteous reception in Belgrade, but the press regarded Károlyi's mission as successful in view of the fact that the convention did not curtail the administrative powers of the Hungarian state, thus preserving its integrity for the time being. News of the Belgrade parley was received by the neighbors of Hungary with indignation. The occupation of the entire Bánát by Serbian troops was criticized by the Rumanians, while Hungarian sovereignty over the occupied area displeased the Yugoslavs.[25] The Czechoslovaks were not less hostile to the Belgrade treaty. Even during the negotiations, the Czechoslovak Foreign Minister, Beneš, had attempted to ensure that Czechoslovak interests would not be hurt. As he was in Paris, he immediately contacted Foch, Pichon and Clemenceau to remonstrate against having Franchet d'Esperey discuss political questions.

On November 12, Clemenceau informed the Czechoslovak minister of the content of the telegram sent to Franchet d'Esperey. Learning that the Belgrade agreements had no political significance, Beneš was much relieved—especially of his concern that Hungary might have been granted its existing northern border as permanent political frontier. Apparently, Clemenceau failed to inform Beneš that the telegram to Franchet d'Esperey had been sent at the Hungarians' request and for this reason the Czechoslovak minister counted the nonpolitical character of the Belgrade treaty as a personal triumph.[26]

While in Paris, Beneš sought support for Czechoslovak aims by exploiting the reputation of the Czechs as convinced anti-Bolsheviks. He claimed that in Central Europe the Czechs were the only people able to stop the spread of Bolshevism, the threat of which was "for special reasons" greatest in Budapest. He claimed that Bolshevism would not triumph in Czechoslovakia because the Czechs had made preparations to ensure a smooth transfer of all military, administrative and economic functions in their country. Beneš also claimed that Czechoslovakia was suffering from no shortages that could facilitate the growth of communism.[27] The paradox of the Czech arguments *vis á vis* Hungary was evident. The Czechs presented themselves as champions of anticommunism, but by cutting off coal supplies to Hungary they encouraged the development of discontent there, which could in turn breed communism.

Beneš seemed bent on reformulating the concepts of the Bohemian patriot, František Palacký. The leader of the 1848 Austro-Slav Congress had favored the retention of a multinational Austria to serve as a barrier against German expansion into Central Europe. Palacký believed that, if Austria had not existed to fill this role, it would have been the duty "of mankind to endeavor to create it as fast as possible."[28] In 1918 Beneš justified the creation of a multinational Czechoslovak state to replace Austria as a barrier against the onslaught of Bolshevism. It came to be believed by many that, if no Czechoslovak state existed, it would have to be invented as a bulwark against communism.

On November 1, Stovall transmitted to Washington a memorandum that endorsed this concept. The memorandum was written by the American expatriate, George D. Herron, a former theology professor who had gained considerable stature and influence from earlier efforts to mediate between the Allies and the Austro-Hungarians. Herron expressed regret that during the war he had neglected the Czechoslovaks and now recommended them warmly to Washington. He felt that the Czechs "are a rock upon which the President and our Allies may safely build—may safely base their lost and even despairing hope for Middle and Eastern Europe." The justification for a Czechoslovak state was the anti-Bolshevik stand of the Czechs, who were fighting for the "redemption of Russia" and were "holding back the Bolsheviki madness" that threatened Central Europe and Germany.[29] This anti-Bolshevik position and support for the extreme claims of the Czechoslovaks eventually spelled the demise of the Károlyi government.

Article 17 of the Belgrade Convention was the biggest thorn in the side of the Czechoslovak leadership. Continuing Hungarian administration of historical Hungary meant that Slovakia was still subject to Budapest.

The Czechoslovaks as well as the other successor states feared that their claims to the disputed territories would not be fully satisfied at the Peace Conference, so they were intent on changing the status quo before the conference met.

The Czechoslovaks were the first to embark on military intervention into lands that were under Hungarian sovereignty. When the Czechs moved, Hungarian pacifism went by the board. On November 11 in a major foreign-policy speech Károlyi reported that the Hungarian Army had stopped disarming and was ready to defend the territory of Hungary. He spoke of the threat to the city of Pozsony (Bratislava) posed by armed groups who "act in the name of the Czechoslovak state" with which Hungary was not at war. He said his government's objective was to keep the best possible relations with the "Czech Republic," thus omitting to recognize a Czech-Slovak state. He spoke of a Hungarian policy toward the Slovaks that was founded on Wilsonian principles—in other words, self-determination through plebiscites. As far as territorial readjustments were concerned, Károlyi expressed his confidence that the Peace Conference would respect Hungarian interests because "her cause was justified." The statement was a reiteration of his belief that a democratic Hungary would be able to retain the loyalty of the majority of the nationalities. Károlyi concluded his speech by protesting against the Czech-Slovak military incursions, declaring that the Hungarian government had vowed to defend the country's borders "by military force in order to prevent the occurrence of such attacks, which are not in accord with international law."[30]

Swift military action quickly repulsed the Czechoslovak forces and Beneš had no choice but to ask the French to break the terms of the Belgrade Convention. On November 25 Beneš, who remained in Paris in order to exert maximum influence on the Allies, sent a memorandum to the French Foreign Minister, Pichon, asking for French aid. In a closely reasoned letter he argued that, since France recognized Czechoslovakia within its historical boundaries as an Allied belligerent, it surely could not allow Allied territory to be occupied by an enemy power. Pichon replied two days later and assured Beneš that Paris would send instructions through the Supreme Council to order the withdrawal of Hungarian troops.[31] Thus Article 17 of the Belgrade Convention was unilaterally broken.

Since the Convention of Belgrade was signed in the name of the Allies and not by France alone, it seems that Pichon was wary that the Hungarians would protest, creating possible sympathy for their cause among the British and the Americans. To avoid such an eventuality, he instructed his ambassadors in the Allied capitals and in Switzerland to avoid informing their hosts of the French action. Furthermore, the French representatives were asked to generate anti-Magyar feelings by emphasizing the irregularity of Hungary's recent decision to send a woman ambassador to Switzerland. Pichon claimed that this was an impudent and "ultra-democratic" action, camouflaging the Hungarian aim of enslavement of non-Magyar nationalities. Pichon also wanted to tarnish Károlyi's reputation by claiming that he was primarily responsible for the "perfidious act."[32]

It seems, however, that English and American acquiescence to French policy was basically due to their acceptance of the principle of "primary responsibility." This allowed any Ally to prevail with its policy in an area where it was solely or predominantly active.[33] France's domination over East Central Europe was evident to all and French support for Czech interests was so assuring that Tomas Masaryk in his first address to the Czechoslovak cabinet made a point of the need to retain French orientation: "We must have one friend who will always take our side and this will be the French."[34]

The Serbians were no less eager to break the convention and, as they moved into the Bánát, they drove out the Hungarian administrators. The Serbians demanded that Hungarian officials pledge allegiance to Serbia or to the Croat National Council. The Hungarians refused to comply, giving the Serbians a reason for expelling them. The flow of refugee administrators from occupied areas into Budapest reached such proportions that the Minister of the Interior, Tivadar Batthyány, was forced to issue a government edict to curb it. It ordered the administrators, if under duress, to take the required pledge of them. This, in the prevailing situation, would not be considered disloyalty to Hungary and would not compromise their future position in the Hungarian administration.[35]

The Serbs and Croats looked on the Hungarian government no more kindly than did the Czechs and Slovaks and, like them, would have welcomed its collapse. The Croat National Council's envoy to Budapest, Marko Petrović, castigated Károlyi in a report to Zagreb. He expressed the opinion that it was in the interest of the Serbs and Croats to see the Hungarian government brought down as soon as possible. If this was difficult, then the Hungarian government's effort to retain its territorial sovereignty until the Peace Conference reached its decisions had to be frustrated. "This can be achieved only by the swiftest occupation of ethnic areas, with care, of course, not to threaten our relations with the Entente," wrote the Croat.[36]

Hungary's third neighbor was just as hostile as the two foregoing. The Kingdom of Rumania, which had been trounced by the combined German-Austro-Hungarian forces in 1917 and forced to sign the humiliating Treaty of Bucharest, decided to take the field again. On November 9 Rumania declared war on Germany under the pretext that it had violated the Treaty of Bucharest by increasing its army of occupation beyond the agreed strength.[37] In spite of the fact that the Treaty of Bucharest of 1918 took Rumania out of the Allied camp, Rumanian troops were now sent into Transylvania on the pretext of representing an Allied power.

Rumania's reentry into the war was immediately backed by the French military leaders. The French troops in Rumania were commanded by General Henri Berthelot, who was responsible for the Danube theater, a geographical area that included Rumania, Transylvania and southern Russia.[38] The Rumanians, like the Czechs, Slovaks and South Slavs, pursued a pro-French policy. When French troops entered Bucharest on November 10, Rumanian officials were so elated that they even forgot that the victorious Alliance included powers other than France. The French Ambassador, the Count of Saint-Aulaire, was forced to remind the Rumanians of their negligence and had to insist that "spontaneous demonstrations" should be organized in front of the British, American and Italian legations.[39]

At the time Rumania made its second declaration of war on Germany, it also sent an ultimatum to Hungary with the impossible demand that all German troops should be evacuated from its territory within twenty-four hours. Curiously, the ultimatum was not followed by a Rumanian declaration of war, possibly because the French had given Hungary more than a week to accomplish the selfsame task. On November 13 Hungary received another ultimatum from Rumanian Prime Minister Ioan Brătianu, this time demanding the withdrawal of Hungarian troops from T and Hungarian recognition of the annexation of this territory by the Kingdom of Rumania.[40]

Meanwhile, on November 9, the Rumanian National Council in Arad, representing the Rumanians in Hungary, had notified Budapest that it had assumed control of twenty-three Hungarian counties and partial control of three others.[41] The Hungarian government immediately dispatched a delegation to present its position to the Rumanian National Council. The delegation was led by Jászi, who was eager to present his Danubian Confederation project to a Hungarian nationality group. The president of the Workers' Council, Dezső Bokányi, was included in the delegation because it was known that a number of social democrats sat in the Rumanian National Council, which was led by two former deputies to Budapest, Iliu Maniu and Vasile Goldis. Lajos Biró, Secretary of Propaganda in the Ministry of Foreign Affairs, suggested to Jászi that he ought to take along someone who could bargain with money if reasoning failed. Jászi indignantly rejected such tactic claiming that the era of that kind of diplomacy was past.[42]

In his opening address to the Arad Council, Jászi summarized the history of the nationalities. He then offered autonomy to Transylvania and, within this framework, authority to the Rumanian National Council in those areas where, according to statistics, the Rumanians were in a majority. Maniu in turn strongly criticized the statistics adduced by Jászi, claiming that in Transylvania and the Bánát only the government officials were Hungarian while the rest of the inhabitants were Rumanian. The Rumanian side expressed its dislike of Károlyi and complained that in Hungary only the name of the government changed, the system stayed the same.[43]

With the support of the statistics furnished by Budapest, the Hungarians attempted to prove that the character of the countryside was Magyar. In the heat of the discussion the Hungarian delegates warned the Rumanians that, should they have any intentions of trying to detach any territory from Hungary, they could expect harsh reprisals. Bokányi, who recognized some Rumanian socialists who had once participated in his Marxist seminars in Budapest, turned against them in indignation and exclaimed: "So you have become chauvinists too! Would you rather have the Rumanian king and boyar rule than a democratic Hungary?"[44] Like Jászi he vigorously defended the Hungarian position and threatened to organize the workers of Europe to fight against a union of Transylvania with the "reactionary" Kingdom of Rumania.[45]

The Rumanian National Council finally refused to accept Jászi's proposition on the ground that it was not empowered to make a decision on which the present and future existence of the Rumanian people depended. It promised to submit the question to the Grand National Assembly which was to meet on December 1 in Alba Iulia, but it agreed that, in the interest of public safety, the areas in dispute should remain under Hungarian administration for the time being.

Jászi was disappointed by these delaying tactics and, after restating his position, warned the Rumanians:

> Let us consider the international situation very carefully. One's claims should not be exaggerated under the influence of events. The conclusion of peace depends neither on Foch nor the other generals, such as those whom I saw in Belgrade. None of them differs from the Hindenburgs and Ludendorffs, for all speak with their hands on the sword. Peace will be made by the European Soviet Republic, by the Council of Soldiers and Workers. All the promises made by the various European belligerents will not be binding on this European Republic. The fact that the Hungarian government has just accepted Rakovski as representative of the Russian Soviet Republic is a sign of the times. Rakovski knows better than anyone the situation of the Rumanians and Hungary.[46]

This speech of Jászi's was of great significance, for it expounded an opinion that was shared by many Hungarian officials. It indicated that they were expecting the collapse of capitalism and the rise of socialism in the Allied countries, and implied that, in case of a harsh Allied policy toward the Hungarians, the Magyars were already contemplating switching political alliances. Such a policy subsumed a lenient policy toward the national and international communist movements. Jászi later claimed that his speech was not intended as a threat but was only a prophetic warning that the economic strangulation of Hungary through territorial dismemberment would lead to such chaos as would result in communism.[47] His explanation in the light of later events seems very tortuous and, if his warning was prophetic, it became self-fulfilling.

Jászi's pronouncement and Bokányi's intransigence may also have stirred fears of Bolshevism among the Western diplomats who were the readers of *New Europe*, for the gist of the version printed in it was far from what Jászi had intended to convey. The threat of accepting a Russian diplomatic mission in Hungary was highly unconventional at a time when no Western power wanted to recognize Soviet Russia; the establishment of such ties could only indicate Hungarian-Soviet collusion. In reality no Soviet embassy materialized in Hungary during the Károlyi regime, even though the Council of Ministers did accept Rakovsky's credentials on November 12.[48]

Rather than committing himself to a pro-Soviet policy in November, Károlyi drew a different conclusion from his Belgrade meeting and the Arad encounter. Károlyi's answer to general French hostility and the pro-French policy of the successor states that encircled Hungary was a more urgent attempt to draw closer to Great Britain and, most of all, to the United States.

The anti-Hungarian attitude of France and the anti-Károlyi sentiments of the successor states put the Hungarian government in a dire predicament: It had to pin its faith on United States aid.

After Károlyi's cool reception by the French in Belgrade, new importance was attached to the message that Bédy-Schwimmer had brought to Hungary from Woodrow Wilson. On November 19, Károlyi decided to answer and appeal for American assistance. After enumerating the achievements of the Hungarian People's Republic, Károlyi complained about invasion by "foreign armies" which, he said, was threatening Hungary with anarchy. The message also asked the United States president to intervene on Hungary's behalf to have the Czech coal blockade lifted, because it was causing Hungary to drift toward economic catastrophe.[1]

While Károlyi was trying to elicit a favorable response from the Americans, French Ambassador Jusserand was attempting to win Washington over to the French position. He suggested that Czechoslovakia, Poland and the South Slav state should be treated as the victorious Allies' equals, while Hungary should be dealt with as a defeated foe. France's disregard of the Belgrade Convention was reflected in the ambassador's references to a geopolitical entity that he called "Magyarie," an area "stripped of the Slovaks, the Rumanians in Transylvania and the Croatians." Though such a state had never existed, French policy-makers wanted to make it one of the chief culprits for the war.[2]

Hungary had no diplomatic representation in Washington to present its case, a fact that underlined the need to create a permanent diplomatic apparatus. As early as November 9, the Hungarian Council of Ministers had given permission to Secretary of State József Diener-Dénes to organize a Hungarian diplomatic corps.

The first ambassador to be appointed was Ferenc Harrer, deputy mayor of Budapest, who was sent to Vienna. He arrived in the Austrian capital on November 14, accompanied by Diener-Dénes. The socialist Diener-Dénes was to represent the National Council and the Hungarian government at the funeral of the late Austrian socialist leader, Victor Adler. It was evident, however, that the real purpose of Diener-Dénes' visit was to persuade the socialist leaders of the Austrian government to be cooperative with the "bourgeois" Harrer. By now it was obvious that Károlyi considered the social democrats an important asset in international relations. He hoped that they would build bridges to the socialists to act favorably toward Hungary. As for Harrer, it was hoped that through his participation in the Conference of the Ambassadors of the successor states it might be possible to establish amicable relations. The conference concentrated on common economic problems; territorial questions were excluded from its agenda. Existing conflicts of interest between the participants, however, crushed Hungarian hopes.[3]

The appointment of a Hungarian envoy to Switzerland was much more controversial. Károlyi, much encouraged by Bédy-Schwimmer's earlier success as an "American agent," wanted her return to Berne. The fact that Laborite feminist agitation was gathering momentum in England weighted his consideration of the Hungarian suffragette for the post. Furthermore, England was about to go to the polls and Bédy-Schwimmer thus seemed to have connections with whichever party would win the election.

The majority of Károlyi's ministers did not share his enthusiasm for Bédy-Schwimmer. They argued that Károlyi was taking account of her popularity among the British and Americans without considering the host country. In Switzerland, where women's suffrage was not granted until 1971, the federal government was dead set against giving women the right to vote. The Hungarian Council of Ministers feared that the Swiss government might interpret the suffragette's appointment as a hostile act.[4] The council thus rejected the appointment of Bédy-Schwimmer several times and only a personal plea by Károlyi finally swayed it to accept her nomination on November 18. The Hungarian ministers' fears proved to be justified, for the Swiss government declared Bédy-Schwimmer an undesirable alien and refused to recognize her credentials.[5]

The greatest surprise for Budapest, however, was the apparent American disdain for the appointment of the renowned pacifist. The head of the United States Legation, Pleasants Stovall, frowned at Bédy-Schwimmer because she was Jewish and blamed Mrs. Whitehouse for being responsible for the Hungarian government's act.[6] He also took steps to let the Hungarians know about "American" displeasure. Without instructions from the State Department, he asked the American "unofficial ambassador," George Herron, to talk to those Hungarians in Switzerland who could convey to Károlyi that he "send a real representative." Professor Herron was successful in getting the message through by talking to conservatives such as Lászlo Havas, owner of the Agence Havas, and to radicals such as the Hungarian publicist Ignotus.[7]

The American press at home seemed to reinforce Herron's view. *The New York Times* devoted an editorial to Hungary's decision to appoint the first woman to an ambassadorial post. In a facetious tone it ridiculed Bédy-Schwimmer's past pacifist activities—a sign that, retrospectively, pacifism appealed only to the vanquished and not the the victor. She was, *The New York Times* said, a "mistress of the middle and low diplomacy: an expert in the secret and public, the open and shut," the type of diplomat beloved by "writers of a certain school of fiction." The article censured her role in the ill-conceived Ford Peace Ship expedition and in that context accused her of swindling the automobile millionaire. Bédy-Schwimmer was compared pejoratively to Tallyrand, whose name in the coming age of "open diplomacy" had unflattering connotations. The long editorial concluded sardonically that the art of diplomacy was "likely to learn much from the feminine incursion."[8]

In the face of this criticism the Hungarians decided to send out "semi-official" government representatives to sound out the possibility of closer ties with England and the United States. Count Antal Sigray was sent to Berne to try to establish contacts with the Americans through his brother-in-law, the wartime United States Ambassador to Berlin, James W. Gerard. It was hoped that with the help of such an important connection Sigray would be able to work for a "favorable peace." Though he did not manage to accomplish this, he did supply the Károlyi government with valuable and important inside information about the attitude of the Americans toward Hungary.[9]

Count Mihály Esterházy, on the other hand, had valuable connections in England through his mother, a British peeress. As a son-in-law of the Minister of Interior Batthyány and a former Independence Party parliamentarian, he had the deep trust of the Károlyi government. He was also sent to Switzerland to learn the disposition of England toward Hungary. Though Foreign Office documents do not indicate that he was able to make any important British contacts, he returned to Budapest with a report that had important repercussions. Although Anglo-American policy favored non-intervention in Hungarian political affairs, Esterházy warned Károlyi that the Entente would prefer a more moderate Hungarian government.[10] Closer to the truth, however, was Esterházy's report of Bédy-Schwimmer's unpopularity in diplomatic circles. The life of the Hungarian ambassador to Switzerland was further complicated by the fact that, at Stovall's suggestion, Secretary of State Lansing ordered that only accredited diplomats could have direct dealings with the United States legation in Berne.[11] The effect of this was to close to Bédy-Schwimmer any channel to the State Department.

In view of the hostility toward the Hungarian ambassador to Switzerland, Károlyi began to reconsider his position and thought of sending Diener-Dénes to Berne. This seemed especially timely as Diener-Dénes had just been eased out of his position as secretary of state in favor of Ferenc Harrer, who was recalled from Vienna to take over. Esterházy's report put a damper on this plan as well, for the President of the Swiss Federation had hinted to the count that the socialist Diener-Dénes would not be permitted to enter Switzerland at all.

Esterházy's account of the rising tide of conservatism among the Allies encouraged the majority of the Károlyi party to disassociate themselves from their leader's stand. They, too, considered him too radical. The split between the party leader and the rank and file culminated in Károlyi's censure in January.[12] The majority's disloyalty to Károlyi owed much to the peculiar support he received from his followers. The members of the party came to support him during the war not because of his radical sociopolitical views but because of his anti-German and anti-Austrian position. They continued to support him after Germany's defeat because they believed that they had no other choice since Károlyi enjoyed the Allies' confidence. Now that Esterházy had reported Western suspicion of the Károlyi regime, these men decided to cut their ties with their leader. These developments eventually forced Károlyi to withdraw from his party and try to form a new party with those few who remained loyal to him.

Harrer's recall from Vienna on December 2 was occasioned by the fact that Diener-Dénes proved to be a poor organizer, who also believed that the Czechoslovak intrusions should not be opposed on the grounds that injustices would be put right by the Peace Conference. The public and most ministers took a contrary view.

The establishment of a Hungarian Foreign Ministry became law only on December 15, when People's Law No. 5 was promulgated. This did not precisely define the functions of the minister of foreign affairs and left much leeway in setting up the foreign-policy apparatus. It allowed the enlistment of Hungarian members of the Austro-Hungarian Ministry of Foreign Affairs if they swore allegiance to the People's Republic. This provision was strongly opposed by the Social Democrats who viewed the aristocratic composition of the former diplomatic corps with suspicion. Zsigmond Kunfi feared that they might not be able to understand the sociopolitical aims of the Hungarian government. The socialists thus favored attaching socialists to all embassies to survey the professional diplomats.[13]

Diener-Dénes' replacement, Ferenc Harrer, started work at the new ministry with great zeal, establishing five divisions and appointing a man to head each. The political division was under Count Imre Csáky, public administration under Bertalan Kallós, the legal division under Károly Klusinszky, news and propaganda under Iván Praznovsky and administration under Alfréd Drasche-Lázár.

Difficulties in establishing embassies abroad persisted. Because of the war, Austria-Hungary had suspended diplomatic relations with the Allies, so there was not even a skeleton upon which the Hungarians could build their embassies. Because of the difficulties, Károlyi appealed to President Wilson on November 25, though his message was not received by the president until early January 1919. Károlyi's plans to exchange representatives were, however, not answered.[14] In fact, the only country that established a formal embassy in Hungary during the Károlyi era was the Republic of Austria.[15]

While Károlyi's foreign policy after the middle of November focused on securing American friendship, a new challenge threatened the Western orientation of Hungary's policy makers. In mid-November the Hungarian Bolsheviks returned from Russia and on November 24 formed a Communist Party in Hungary. The party was led by such experienced communists as Béla Kun, József Rabinóvics, Tibor Számuely, Ferenc Munnich and Mátyás Rákosi, all of whom had already distinguished themselves fighting in Russia against Czechoslovak intervention.[16]

The new party accepted into its ranks the loosely-knit Hungarian social revolutionaires whose self-styled leader was the young Otto Korvin. A small handful of extremists from the Social Democratic Party also joined the communists. The number of these former socialists was so small, however, that it can safely be said that the Hungarian Communist Party was distinct from the other European communist parties in that it was not a socialist splinter group. It gathered round organized, Russian-trained core groups that were outside the Social Democratic Party.

The secretary of the new Communist Party was the Hungarian communist leader in Russia, Béla Kun. Kun arrived in Budapest on November 17 with plans previously approved by Lenin, who envisaged his disciple in a role similar to his own opposite Kerensky. The Hungarian communists' aim was to show that Károlyi's foreign policy was bankrupt and that Hungary's salvation could come only from the rejection of Wilsonism and the acceptance of Leninism.

Yet the communists, too, favored the preservation of Hungary's integrity. They held that self-determination could not be achieved in a capitalist society and within a system that had reactionary aims. They argued that capitalism created an international proletariat, thus abolishing the meaning of nations. They reasoned that national self-determination would serve only the interests of the respective national bourgeoisies in their struggle against monopoly· capitalism. They further claimed that the highest stage of capitalism, imperialism, weakened national consciousness even more. Thus a proletarian revolution that would destroy imperialism would also bring an end to the existence of nations.

The communist program was made available to the masses by the party organ, *Vörös Újság* (Red News). This newspaper, first printed on December 7, maintained, for instance, that "there are no Frenchmen, Englishmen, Hungarians or Rumanians, only French proletarians and French bourgeois, Hungarian, Rumanian and English proletarians and Hungarian, Rumanian and English bourgeois." It denied the existence of nations under capitalism on the grounds that "national self-determination is simply self-determination of the ruling bourgeoisie." "Our slogan," the newspaper declared, "can but be the right of self-determination of all proletarians, regardless of language— which means the dictatorship of the proletariat."[17]

The communists, with their attack on self-determination, thus went further in defense of Hungary's integrity than Károlyi who hoped that, given the choice, the nationalities would vote to remain within a democratic Hungary. Károlyi himself did not escape attack from the communists. They called him an honest and straightforward man whose pacifism led him to oppose the war but who "sold the nation to Entente imperialism in place of German imperialism."[18]

Not long after the arrival of the anti-Entente communists from Russia, the French supervisors of the Armistice and of the Convention also arrived at Budapest. The mission was organized in Belgrade by the commander of the French Army of the Orient, General Henrys. It was led by Brevet Lieutenant-Colonel Vix, an officer of General Henrys' staff. The mission consisted of fifty-seven men—twelve officers and forty enlisted men. The mission was sent to Hungary in accordance with the Belgrade Convention of November 13. The orders issued to Vix, however, far surpassed the duties originally intended for a supervisor of the convention. In addition to the supervision of the arrangements of the Armistice and of the Belgrade Convention, Vix was ordered to gather intelligence reports in Hungary. He was to survey the movements of all foreigners. This task included the identification of permanent residents who did not originally come from areas of the former Austro-Hungarian Empire. Vix was to find out the reasons for their permanent status. Movement of these permanent residents abroad also had to be investigated. Vix was also asked to report on Austrian and Hungarian relations with neutral Switzerland. The surveillance of the activities of France's small allies, Serbia and Rumania, was also Vix's chore. Lastly, he was to recruit agents in Hungary, though he was warned that recruitment was to be done with utmost secrecy, since their intelligence work would deal with the activities of the Czechoslovaks and Yugoslavs and with the actions of the Rumanians in Transylvania.[19]

The Vix mission arrived in Budapest on the evening of November 26 and was welcomed by Béla Linder, who was accompanied by a delegation of military officers and by members of the Ministerial Armistice Commission. The Commission was organized by the Council of Ministers and was to act as a go-between for Vix and those ministries that had some responsibility in the fulfillment of the clauses of the Armistice and the Convention.[20]   The Armistice Commission included representatives of ten ministries and the commissioners of coal, and of rail and water transportation. It was presided over by an army staff officer, Colonel Victor Stielly, who was present at the signing of the Belgrade Convention.[21]

On November 30, Stielly approached Vix with the first important communication of the Hungarian government. The Hungarians asked the Allies to occupy Hungary for the sake of avoiding disorder.[22] This request by the Hungarians was consequently repeated several times during Vix's stay in Hungary. General Henrys was receptive to the request and called Franchet d'Esperey in Salonica asking him for Allied occupation. Henrys argued that this move was necessary to avoid a clash between the Hungarians and the Czechoslovaks, who were disregarding the Belgrade Convention by creating border incidents.[23]

Apparently, General Henrys had not yet been informed of the fact that his government in Paris considered the Belgrade agreement as a dead letter. The commander of the French forces in Rumania, General Berthelot was better informed as he just happened to be in Paris at the end of November. On the morning of November 28, he confided to the Italian Ambassador, Bonin, that the Belgrade Convention was due to the clumsiness of General Franchet d'Esperey who was not yet aware of the details of the Diaz Armistice. For this reason the French government considered the Convention of no value and a *de facto* accord with local authorities. Berthelot, therefore, expected the outbreak of hostilities in Hungary over Slovakia and Transylvania.[24]

The order of Hungarian troop withdrawal from Slovakia was transmitted to Vix on December 2. This French note was handed to the Hungarian government the following day. The memorandum protested against the "occupation" of Slovakia by Hungarian troops, who expelled Czechoslovak forces that had briefly occupied the area in the middle of November. On receiving the note from Vix, Károlyi vainly objected that it was the Hungarians who had been driven out in the first place in flagrant disregard of the Belgrade convention.[25] Though Vix was aware of Karolyi's logic, he had no other choice but to follow the instructions of his superiors and demand the Hungarians' withdrawal from Slovakia.[26]

After the delivery of the memorandum, Hungarian public opinion, which until then had been friendly, began to turn against Vix and to regard the French Military Mission with hostility. The Hungarian leaders also came to believe that Vix was a heartless tyrant. This view of Vix was amply expounded in the memoirs of the Hungarian leaders and found its way into secondary works as well. The correspondence of Vix with his superiors, however, indicates that he had considerable sympathy for the struggling Hungarian government.

In addition to his orders concerning Slovakia, Vix also received from Henrys directives that originated in the Ministry of Foreign Affairs. He was informed that the Ministry did not recognize the Hungarian People's Republic and the Károlyi government. A few days later, Vix was ordered to treat the Hungarian government as a mere local authority without international status.[27] These orders from the French government were received by Vix with dismay. He responded to his superiors by explaining the difficulty of his position as an overseer of the Belgrade Convention, which was unilaterally broken over the Czechoslovak question. He was also critical of the Ministry of Foreign Affairs for withholding recognition of a government whose legal status could be justified in more than one way.

Upon the receipt of Vix's protest, General Henrys telegraphed the headquarters of his commander in chief in Salonika explaining the perplexing situation. Henrys complained that, as signer of the Belgrade Convention, he was put in an embarrassing position. He claimed that, in the light of the orders in contradiction of the Convention, the sincerity of the French was rightly being questioned. He further complained that the small allies of France were abusing the privileges accorded to them. He also reminded Franchet d'Esperey that Károlyi would resign if he were aware that his government was not recognized by France. Henrys voiced his belief that as signatory of the Belgrade Convention the Hungarian government could be considered the representative of an internationally recognized successor state. Furthermore, Henrys ominously warned his superior of the dangers that Károlyi's resignation would bring about. He forecast disorders that would force the recall of Vix from Budapest. To avoid such developments, Henrys called for the scrupulous respect of the Convention which would assure Károlyi's authority. In addition, he revived Károlyi's call for Allied occupation of Hungary to avoid conflict between the nationalities.[28]

In reply to the complaints of General Henrys and Colonel Vix, Franchet d'Esperey sent some modified orders on handling the Hungarian question. Though Henrys was ordered not to permit Vix to negotiate with the Hungarians issues unrelated to the Convention, Vix was now authorized to accept Hungarian complaints and other communications, which were then forwarded to the appropriate authorities. Apparently Franchet d'Esperey received instructions on this matter from Clemenceau upon the advice of the Ministry of Foreign Affairs. The ministry soon informed the Allies that France did not recognize the governments of defeated states but it did accept communications from them.[29]

The Allied commander in chief also shared Henrys' apprehension about the possible collapse of law and order in Hungary upon the departure of Károlyi from the government. For this reason he called on Henrys to handle his relations with Károlyi with care and to be careful not to push Károlyi too far. Franchet d'Esperey was careful to explain the impasse in the Czechoslovak-Hungarian border question as he received no specific orders referring to a defined border. He claimed that such decisions had not yet been made in Paris. At the same time he noted that Henrys' request to occupy Hungary was rejected by Foch.[30]

While Paris was still undecided on the outlines of the border question, direct negotiations took place between the Hungarians and the Czechoslovak representative in Budapest, Milan Hodža.[31]

Talks between Oszkár Jászi, Defense Minister Vilmos Bartha and Hodža led to a mutually acceptable demarcation line that followed the ethnic borders of Slovakia and Hungary. As soon as Beneš heard that the Czechoslovak representative was ready to agree to a boundary line that was less advantageous to Czechoslovakia than the one in preparation in Paris, he instructed Prague to disavow the Hodža-Bartha agreement.[32]

Finally, on December 23, the French ambassador in Prague transmitted to Hodža the latest decision of the Supreme Council defining a line of demarcation between the Hungarians and the Czechoslovaks. Vix, who ought to have been informed about the new delimitation, was kept in the dark and Hodža went on to inform the Hungarians without keeping Vix abreast with the new order from Paris. Vix finally learned about the contents of the message from the Hungarians who approached him with vehement protests. Hodža's action infuriated Vix, who considered that it would have been his responsibility to arrange military matters.[33] In accordance with the new order of the Supreme Council, by December 28, Czechoslovak troops occupied Kassa (Kosice) in northeastern Hungary and on January 1, 1919 Pozsony (Bratislava) came under Czechoslovak control.[34]

In spite of the generous decision of the Supreme Council, the Czechoslovaks were still not satisfied with their territorial claims and pushed for a corridor through Hungary to connect the Czechs and Slavs with the South Slavs. Late in December, in an address to the Prague National Assembly, Tomas Masaryk declared that "in Czechoslovak and in Yugoslav circles almost everybody is convinced, above all, that a direct geographical union is necessary."[35]

The Hungarian envoy to Prague, Rudolf Krajcsi reported in mid-January 1919 that the Czechs would demand a corridor at the Peace Conference. In the opinion of Krajcsi, the Czechs wanted to unite "with the United Kingdom of the Serbs, Croats and Slovenes" because they wanted a link with the sea. He said that the Czechs would justify their claim by declarations that a Slav barrier against pan-German and Bolshevik threats was necessary. And indeed, in a memorandum handed to the Allies, the Czechs did justify their territorial demands with arguments based on strategic principles, for the number of all Slavs in such a strip of land would not exceed 25% of the total population. The Yugoslavs seemed to favor the idea as well. An attempt was made to seize part of the area inhabited by Slovenes. An unsuccessful military action was carried out under the command of Captain Erminij Jurišić.[36]

Among the Allies, France vigorously backed the Czechoslovak-Yugoslav claim. The influential French frontier-maker, André Tardieu, thought that the other Allies would also favor it as it was a matter of European interest "favorable to two of our allies."[37]

British and American views were less enthusiastic. Lloyd George, for example, thought that it was a "very audacious and indefensible proposal."[38] In spite of Anglo-American opposition to the idea, the corridor plan was not officially rejected until March 8, when it was brought to the attention of the Peace Conference.[39]

The Czech government itself was determined to establish a power balance strong enough to hold Hungary in check. The continuation of the coal blockade, which was causing economic havoc in Hungary, served as a lever against the Hungarians. Foreign Minister Beneš frankly admitted that Czechoslovakia expected to exploit the coal situation to influence Budapest.[40] The exasperated mayor of Budapest vainly appealed to President Wilson to have the Czechs lift the blockade "which makes public security impossible."[41]

In the south, Hungary was continuing to struggle with Serbia, whose troops had crossed the demarcation line established at Belgrade. They continued to push north until they had occupied Hungary's last remaining important domestic coal mines in the area of Pécs.[42]

The Hungarian government fared no better with the Rumanians. On December 1, the Rumanian National Council of Transylvania decided to unite with the Kingdom of Rumania.[43] As soon as this was announced, Rumania annexed the twenty-six disputed counties of Transylvania and called on the Hungarians to evacuate the area. Like the Czechoslovaks, the Rumanians also used the threat of Bolshevism as a justification for expansion. Bucharest claimed that the Hungarian government was undertaking a Bolshevik conspiracy in cooperation with the Russians. The communist campaign was particularly dangerous to the Transylvanians who were so instigated by the Károlyi government.[44]

On December 15, General Berthelot, using the pretext of the Bolshevik threat gave permission to the Rumanian General Staff to occupy Hungarian territories beyond the limits fixed by the armistice.[45] On the following day, Lieutenant-Colonel Landrot, a liaison officer of Berthelot informed Vix that, according to Allied decisions, the Rumanian troops were to cross the line of demarcation and were to take positions at a new line stretching from Szatmárnémeti (Satu Mare) to Nagyvárad (Oradea-Mare) to Békéscsaba. The justification Landrot gave to Vix for Berthelot's orders was that there was a need to protect the Rumanian peasants in Kolozsvár (Cluj) and in the Maros Valley.

Upon receiving this information, Vix contacted the Hungarians with the new order. He made it clear, however, that his information should not be considered an official order as yet, because he had heard nothing from Belgrade on this matter. He asked the Hungarians to order their troops not to resist Rumanian advances for the sake of avoiding bloodshed, and he promised to call on the Rumanians not to advance for the same reason. Vix also sent a hurried report to Henrys on the situation and expressed surprise that such an important decision was not communicated to him directly. He further protested the injustice of the projected Rumanian advances, claiming that the disregard of the original demarcation lines destroyed the convention and for that reason the mission ought to be withdrawn.[46] On December 18 Vix received further orders from Berthelot, asking the Hungarians to withdraw from Kolozsvár which, as Berthelot alleged, would be occupied by Rumanian troops until French forces became available for the occupation. Vix, who just a few days ago had asked the Hungarians for constraint and had promised a reciprocal act by the Rumanians, was indicating exasperation. He bitterly complained to Henrys about the existence of dual authority in Hungary. He claimed that in addition to receiving orders from Franchet d'Esperey and his subordinate Henrys, he was now being commanded by Berthelot, the commander of the French forces in Rumania and in southern Russia.

Berthelot's additional demands on the Hungarians for one hundred locomotives and fifteen hundred railroad box cars were also protested by Vix as it was not part of the Belgrade treaty. Since Hodža handed the Supreme Council's memorandum to the Hungarians during these difficult days, Vix had also considered Hodža as a threat to his own authority. In his report to Henrys Vix concluded:

> In summary, the Convention of November 13 is nothing more than a scrap of paper (*chiffon de papier*). The attitude taken by our small Allies and by ourselves, the absence of authority capable of redressing abuses, seems to show well that there is one authority: the right of the strongest.[47]

Vix felt that the usefulness of his mission to Budapest would be over unless concerted efforts were made to give the Hungarians demarcation lines that were respected by all. Furthermore, he suggested the occupation of Budapest by French and British forces. Both of these suggestions were out of the question. The French government did not consider it necessary to send more than two thousand troops to Hungary, who were there to provide protection for the Entente mission.[48]

The British government continued its policy of non-intervention, although Berthelot's claims of the threat of Hungarian-inspired Bolshevism did come to the attention of the Foreign Office. Lewis Namier criticized Berthelot's actions and claimed that the French general provided "another example of how the cry of 'Bolshevism' is exploited nowadays by anyone who wishes to obtain a hearing and prejudice the case of his opponents."[49] In spite of such a critical attitude, the British refrained from protesting Berthelot's unilateral action.

Berthelot's harking to Bolshevism was buttressed by the fact that, since November 2, he was the commander of the Allied interventionist forces in Russia. For his activities in Russia, he was directly responsible to the Minister of War, Clemenceau, and to the General Staff. His troops in Rumania and Transylvania, now named the Army of the Danube, however, remained subordinate to Franchet d'Esperey.[50] The division of Berthelot's responsibility indicates that for the French leaders the destruction of Bolshevism in Russia was more pressing than the political and military situation in the Balkans. Berthelot's task in Russia was the progressive invasion of Russian territory, including occupation of the ports of Odessa, Nikolaev and Sevastopol on the Black Sea and Taganrog on the Sea of Azov. Inland his advance was expected to reach the Dnieper and Donets region where Allied detachments were to give advice and material support to the anti-Communist White forces.[51]

French intervention in Russia began on December 18 with the landing of 1,800 French troops at Odessa.[52] In his zeal to find allies for intervention, Clemenceau even supported Rumania's participation in the Peace Conference as a minor ally. This was a *volte face* for the French premier who earlier claimed that he could not accept Rumania as an ally because it signed a separate peace treaty with the Central Powers on May 7, 1918.[53] On December 29 the French foreign minister, Stephen Pichon, announced in the Chamber of Deputies in Paris that the Rumanian Army was being reorganized by General Berthelot and was ready to intervene in Russia. That a territorial bounty had to be paid for Rumanian support was explicit by his call for the creation of a "purely Magyar" Hungary while declaring his faith in Czechoslovakia and in Rumania as faithful allies of France. He declared that France had no intention of accepting the establishment of states in Central Europe on the basis of self-determination, but aimed to follow the traditional policy of having strong Eastern European allies. He justified this position as the victor's right over the vanquished. One of the opposition deputies interjected that Pichon was adopting Clemenceau's dictum: "Let us be strong to be just." Clemenceau applauded Pichon's speech and declared that he pinned his faith on a system of alliances to preserve the peace of Europe.[54]

The alliance Clemenceau was alluding to was the anti-Bolshevik alliance. It was for this reason that Pichon's public statement was preceded by instructions to the French ambassador in Bucharest to express his government's support of Rumania's presence at the Peace Conference as an ally. The Rumanians were being told that the Secret Treaty of Bucharest had been annulled by the Peace Treaty of Bucharest of May 7, 1918. Pichon, however, had promised the Rumanians that the French would ask the Allies to support Rumanian demands based on the Secret Treaty.[55] Still, France's rejection of Rumanian claims in the Secret Treaty of Bucharest was significant, for the Rumanians were in the process of advancing into western Transylvania, an area promised them in the Secret Treaty. The Belgrade Military Convention of November 13, however, had clearly stated that it was for Hungary to administer the area unless the Peace Conference decided otherwise.[56] Rumania's advance was done with the overt support of Berthelot, much to the despair of Colonel Vix. General Berthelot, who visited Vix in Budapest, told the French supervisor of the Convention and the Armistice that he considered the Belgrade agreement as arbitrary and supported the Rumanian advance. To Vix and to his superiors, Berthelot's behavior seemed insubordinate.[57] On January 13, 1919, Franchet d'Esperey lodged a complaint about Berthelot and buttressed it by claiming that Berthelot's actions were weakening central authority in Hungary and would facilitate the progress of Bolshevism there.[58]

General Berthelot, who was aware of the assailability of his actions, tried to gain Clemenceau's support by arguing that Rumania must be treated generously because of her proximity to Russia. Berthelot called the Hungarians the enemies of France and asked for a Transylvanian boundary unfavorable to Hungary which would also make the Rumanians pro-French and a virtual French colony. He also reminded Clemenceau that the Rumanians had re-entered the war and as a result they deserved to be treated as old allies.[59] What Berthelot was really seeking was Clemenceau's explicit support of the Secret Treaty of Bucharest.

The French leader's reply was not long in coming. He expressed the view that the Rumanian Peace Treaty with the Central Powers annulled original Allied commitments to Rumania. She had also cooperated with the enemy with her annexation of Russian Bessarabia. Thus, he concluded, Rumania was treated very fairly when it was invited to the Peace Conference as a minor ally. As for the boundaries drawn by the Belgrade Convention, Clemenceau upheld them as a military demarcation line. In support of General Franchet d'Esperey he called on General Berthelot not to act as a broker for Rumania and either to obey his orders or request his own recall.[60] When Count Auguste Saint-Aulaire, the French Ambassador to Bucharest, came to Berthelot's defense, the angry premier accused the general of sounding like a Rumanian statesman rather than an impartial judge of the Rumanian situation.[61]

Clemenceau reacted to Franchet d'Esperey's complaint by restating his earlier orders delineating the areas of responsibility between Berthelot and Franchet d'Esperey. The latter was in charge of supervising all the armistices in Eastern Europe and was also ordered to see to it that the territorial status quo was not disturbed in Transylvania or elsewhere in Hungary. Clemenceau confirmed that Berthelot was the chief of the Army of the Danube in Rumania, subordinate to Franchet d'Esperey, and in charge of the troops in southern Russia, where he had three French, one Italian and three Greek divisions under him. The Rumanians were to contribute as many troops as Berthelot deemed necessary. As before, Berthelot was directly responsible to Clemenceau and Foch for his activities in Russia, but his supplies for Russia were left in the hands of Franchet d'Esperey, who therefore also had some influence over Berthelot's activities there.[62]

Clemenceau's orders and disciplining of Berthelot indicate that in January, when French intervention in southern Russia was proceeding smoothly, even without Rumanian help, he took Franchet d'Esperey's warning seriously. The threat of Bolshevism and anarchy in Hungary forced Clemenceau to retreat from his position on Rumania, taken just a few weeks ago, which was now seen as causing rather than stopping the spread of communism. Even Berthelot's strange reference to French colonial opportunities seemed to have little impact, but perhaps this was due to a general assumption that the Balkans would fall into French influence in any case.[63]

Clemenceau's attention to problems in Hungary was motivated by developments which could possibly create problems for France. In the wake of hostile French pronouncements in the Chamber of Deputies, Károlyi also gave a major foreign policy address which stressed a pro-American position. A possible involvement of the United States in Hungarian affairs had the potential of disturbing the French. On December 30 the Hungarian premier stated:

> My foreign policy is based on Wilsonian ideals. We have only one ideology: Wilson, Wilson, and for the third time Wilson. I am sure that Wilson will win not only in America but in Europe as well. The role of America is to remake Europe, extirpating the idea of revenge and creating a peace that will not leave people embittered.[64]

Károlyi's hope that the United States would come to Hungary's aid received a boost from Count Sigray. In a letter dated January 2, the unofficial envoy to Switzerland informed Károlyi that the United States intended to abide by the Wilsonian principles and that an American mission was on its way to Budapest. In the same letter Sigray also spoke of the hostile French attitude toward Hungary—news that no doubt surprised no one in Budapest.[65]

In the French press the Hungarians were identified as pro-Communist. Early in January *Le Temps* accused Károlyi of being in league with Lenin, furnishing funds to Russian and Rumanian Bolsheviks to exploit the social problems in Rumania. The French newspaper cited as an example of Hungarian duplicity an alleged Hungarian document captured by the Rumanians. It supposedly instructed the Hungarian commissioner for Transylvania in Kolozsvár, István Apáthy, to print propaganda leaflets against the Rumanian King which were to proclaim that only the Hungarian People's Republic would give land to the peasants.[66] This official and unofficial anti-Magyar policy of France led to Rumania's decision to arrest the Hungarian administrator while the city of Kolozsvár was occupied by Rumanian troops and its citizens were forced to pay 900,000 crowns to the Rumanians in indemnities.[67]

The year of 1919 began with setbacks for Hungary. Much of Hungary's territory was occupied. The Károlyi government was regarded with hostility by its neighbors, who were resolved to make their provisional conquest permanent. French policy was hostile while the other great powers seemed indifferent at best.

The government crisis that erupted in Budapest was certainly a consequence of these accumulating difficulties. The crisis was precipitated by the resignation of Márton Lovászy, the moderate minister of education. Lovászy, who was influenced by Esterházy's report on foreign hostility, resigned in protest against the radical policies of the Károlyi government and decided to organize a bourgeois opposition. He was confident that the government, apparently deserted by the Allies, would eventually have to resign, yielding to an opposition party.[68] In the hope of securing French backing, Lovászy soon paid a visit to Vix. He told Vix of the impending government crisis and claimed that Károlyi would be willing to resign in favor of a bourgeois ministry of Lovászy. Károlyi insisted, however, that any viable government must include the moderates of the Social Democratic Party. Lovászy, aware of Károlyi's popularity among the Hungarians, had an alternative solution. He suggested that his bourgeois government could be popular among the masses even without the participation of the social democrats if Károlyi were to become the president of the republic—a post that could be created with the concurrence of the National Council.

Since Károlyi rejected Lovászy's solution, the former minister of education hoped to gain support for his scheme from Vix and the Allies. He inquired if Vix could find out if the Allies in Paris regarded his project in a favorable light. Vix informed Lovászy that he ought to discount Allied military support for his endeavors and refrained from promising him information on the mood of Paris.[69] Lovászy left Vix without any further comment, apparently in full realization of the fact that he had neither external nor internal support for his ambitious plans.

The fact that Vix clearly indicated Allied aloofness from meddling in Hungarian politics also showed that Esterházy's reports from Switzerland were often fabrications. His report on the desirability of changing the composition of the Hungarian government to please the Allies actually reflected the desires of the right-wing Hungarian aristocrats in their Swiss refuge.

The withdrawal of Lovászy, which split the Károlyi party, made the socialists wary and they began to question the role of the Social Democratic Party in government. At the enlarged conference of the party's Executive Committee on January 7, two courses were considered. The first, advocated by Sándor Garbai, called for the formation of an all socialist government. The right-wing socialist, Ernő Garami, countered with a proposal that the socialists withdraw all support from Károlyi and stay outside the government until election to the Constituent Assembly was held. When a vote was taken, Garbai's suggestion was carried by a slender majority. Because of the close vote, the socialists decided to continue the discussion at the Workers' Council meeting the next day.

At the Workers' Council Garbai announced the previous day's decision, warning his comardes of the risk of continuing the coalition because it might lead to a counter-revolution inspired by the "jealousies of the dispossessed bourgeoisie." He claimed that the socialist government would make it possible to control all sources of counter-revolutionary activity emanating from the military and from the bureaucracy. He argued that, with a coalition government in power, the socialist program to nationalize the economy would be indefinitely postponed. An all-socialist government, moreover, would also mean the end of Bolshevik agitation.

In reply, Garami argued that, with party ranks swollen by increased labor union membership, it was necessary to educate the new members before the socialists could participate in government. Calling again for withdrawal from government, Garami reminded his audience that the party's alliance with the bourgeoisie was a betrayal of traditional socialist strategy and meant accepting the Bolsheviks' radical socialism "in social democratic disguise." This, in turn, threatened the "delivery of the socialist masses" into the Bolshevik fold.

Zsigmond Kunfi, who had the reputation of a conciliator suggested that the socialists ought to remain in the government, because their withdrawal would most benefit the counter-revolution.[70] Kunfi's fear was based on a warning by Károlyi that without the assistance of the trade unions, government would be impossible and that, rather than form a purely bourgeois government, Károlyi would resign.[71] Kunfi also knew that the countryside was not socialist. Without the peasants supporting the socialists in Budapest, the advancing successor-state forces might bring down a socialist government. He therefore favored continued cooperation with Károlyi on the condition that the number of socialist ministers in the cabinet be increased. On the first ballot the council rejected Kunfi's suggestion and voted in favor of Garbai's position by 169 to 101.

Kunfi then took the floor again and warned the council against forming a "pseudobolshevik" regime. In response to Kunfi's appeal Garbai decided to withdraw his resolution rather than chance a party schism. The next vote was 147 to 83 in favor of Kunfi's compromise. In response to Vilmos Böhm's call for unity, however, the council decided to vote for the resolution unanimously. When the final vote was taken, only the communists voted against it.[72]

Because of his party's vote of non-confidence Károlyi decided to resign as prime minister. On January 11 he handed his resignation to the executive committee of the National Council, only to be appointed to the newly created post of President of the Republic. The committee's action was a recognition of the fact that with the all important socialist support behind him, Károlyi was still the best candidate to lead the country.

The creation of the office of the President of the Republic filled a gap that had existed since the declaration of the People's Republic on

November 16. Its establishment was justified by article three of the recently promulgated Public Law of the National Council. This law empowered Károlyi to become temporary chief of state until a constituent assembly decided otherwise. It was now argued that a president rather than a prime minister should represent the highest authority in Hungary. This legal maneuver thus permitted Károlyi to maintain leadership of the government. The official statement of the executive committee called on Károlyi to "attempt to solve existing and possible future governmental crises through the presidency with the help of those individuals whose participation in government he deems necessary." Furthermore, the committee declared that there was no reason why Károlyi could not continue to exercise the "direction of foreign policy" from his new post.[73]

As President of the People's Republic, Károlyi appointed the independent Dénes Berinkey to head the government. Berinkey, the former minister of justice in the cabinet, was not a professional politician but a professor specializing in international law. Károlyi intended to appoint him as the new minister of foreign affairs as well. Berinkey's candidacy, however, was opposed by Harrer on the technical grounds that the President and the prime minister could not both be in charge of foreign policy. Thus, from the middle of January, technically speaking, there was no minister of foreign affairs. Károlyi was still in charge of foreign policy making, while Harrer continued to be in charge of the ministry of foreign affairs in the capacity of ambassador-at-large.[74]

The new cabinet, which finally began functioning on January 18, included five ministers still loyal to Károlyi, one minister from the Radical Party and one minister from the Smallholders Party. Jászi, whose nationality program based on his concept of an "Eastern Switzerland" had been defeated, resigned but was not replaced. The socialists, as a price for their participation in government, received two more cabinet posts, doubling their representation.[75] The composition of the Berinkey government thus indicated a definite shift to the left. The government's policy, however, was not more radical, because the aim of the new cabinet was to implement programs that had already been legislated.

Even though the right wing's abandonment of Károlyi was the cause for the crisis, it was that element that wanted to exploit the cabinet's shift to the left. On January 26, Mihály Esterházy's letter to Sir Horace Rumbold was transmitted to the British peace delegation in Paris. In his letter, Esterházy claimed that the new Hungarian cabinet did not represent the desires of the Magyars. He argued that the cabinet came to power as a consequence of a pact between Károlyi and the social democrats. Since the Social Democratic Party was the only organized party in Hungary, representing the interest of a mere 240,000 workers, the majority of the population was not represented. Thus, he stated that the socialists exercised near dictatorial powers and that Bolshevism could only be avoided with Allied intervention. Esterházy reasoned that only such action would "stop the insane bolshevist and socialist agitation which emanates from Budapest."[76] Since the French did not move during the crisis, and Lovászy was cold-shouldered by Vix, Esterházy tried to convince his readers that Great Britain ought to develop a sphere of influence in Hungary, claiming that "Budapest and the Danube line lie on the line of the London—Persian Gulf."[77]

Lewis Namier, the Foreign Office's Austro-Hungarian specialist, rejected Esterházy's arguments. He compared the Károlyi government to the socialist government in Germany, and was of the opinion that the Hungarian coalition was "the only combination through which Hungary can escape civil war." He went on to assail right-wing intrigues and accused Esterházy of wanting to use British power to execute a *coup d'état* on the behalf of the Magyar oligarchy. Namier considered that socialists represented Magyar national interests claiming that the majority of the Magyars were workers. Moreover, the British specialist saw peasant support for the Károlyi government as it promised land reforms. Namier thus advised his superiors to support the Károlyi government on all issues with the exception of the territorial question. Namier called for an official declaration by his government stating that Great Britain "does not mean to interfere in internal Magyar affairs and entertains no prejudice against the existing Magyar Government."[78] Although no such pronouncement came, it is clear that Britain continued a hands-off policy with respect to Hungary. The British position also reflected the fact that the right wing made little headway in influencing the Allies in its behalf.

The Berinkey cabinet was commissioned on the day the Peace Conference was ceremoniously opened in Paris. The decisions the Conference was to make were to have important consequences for the Hungarian government. The Supreme War Council had been in session since January 12 under its peacetime title of the Council of Ten, but the opening of the conference was postponed so that it would coincide with the anniversary of the declaration of the Second German Empire, promulgated at Versailles on January 18, 1871. The inauguration of the Peace Conference on such a memorable date left its imprint on the negotiations which seemed to be charged with emotionalism directed against old hatreds—and against the new fear, Bolshevism.

The Allies had two weapons to contain this new and dreaded ideology. The first, already being tested in Russia, was intervention. This would mean using occupation troops to fight Bolshevism and, in fact, intervention to this end was already under way in Hungary. The purpose of the occupation of Slovak territories by Czechoslovak forces was to eliminate the threat of Bolshevism, for the Czechs insisted that Bolshevism only threatened from without, not from within. President Masaryk on his way to Prague was eager to prove this. In Paris he declared that the Czechoslovaks were not afraid of communist contagion and cited as an example the fact that of 50,000 Czech troops in Russia only 218 had joined the Red Guards.[1] Rumania claimed that Károlyi was using Bolshevik agents in Rumania to justify its intransigent attitude. The South Slavs, in the process of forming their own state of Yugoslavia, were also considered anticommunist. British, American and French intelligence reports discounted any internal threat of Bolshevism in Yugoslavia and suggested that it existed only as an external danger.[2]

Hungary seemed to be surrounded by states that claimed to serve as defensive barriers against Bolshevism. Their enlargement was argued to be in the Allies' interest. Conversely, the reduction of Hungary's size meant the reduction of Bolshevik danger. It is important to note that for this reason intervention against Bolshevism in Hungary began before the rise of Béla Kun's Soviet Republic. France's policy makers, in particular, favored this course of action, for it strengthened their potential allies in eastern Europe.

The second means to contain Bolshevism in Europe was more favored by the Anglo-Americans. They argued for lifting the Allied blockade, as they believed that it was creating unemployment, preventing economic recovery and fertilizing communism.[3] When the Acting Secretary of State in Washington, Frank Lyon Polk, asked the President to make a public statement against the "growing menace of bolshevism outside of Russia,"[4] Wilson declined, explaining that "the real thing to stop bolshevism is food."[5] The President held that aid ought to be supplied "not only to our friends but also to those parts of the world where it was our interest to maintain a stable government."[6]

The French opposed this view. They feared that economic aid would revive the power of its defeated enemies. France's position was disapproved of by both the British and the Americans, and at one time Lloyd George accused a French representative of ranking with "Lenin and Trotsky among those who spread bolshevism in Europe."[7]

After the Interallied Blockade Council had approved a plan to help the eastern European countries with food and raw materials, the Allies went on to set up an investigating commission to find out what the eastern Europeans' actual needs were. This interallied commission was under the direction of an American, Alonzo E. Taylor, an aide to Herbert Hoover, the chief of the American Relief Administration. Organized in Berne, it included four other Americans, two Frenchmen, and a Briton.

The Taylor mission arrived in Budapest on January 9, just in time for the government crisis. An Allied mission led by an American was thus especially welcome to Károlyi and, in spite of the fact that its purpose was to gather information on the economic situation, the Hungarian leaders aimed to use the visit for political ends. Károlyi was the first to have an interview with the Allied representatives.

Dejectedly Károlyi complained to the mission that he had been put in power in the belief that he could readily get in touch with the Allies but that in the last two months he had been unable to do so. This fact was weakening his position, he argued, and for this reason he was under attack by both extremes. The Social Democrats, whom Károlyi described as leaning toward Bolshevism, were asking for more offices, while the conservatives attacked him for being too radical. Alluding to the fact that

Hungary had not been invited to Paris, Károlyi protested that it was totally unjust for Hungary's new borders to be determined at the Peace Conference without Hungary taking part and told the Allies that on this point he was supported by all political factions. In response, the commission took Károlyi to task because the Hungarian government had taken no steps to arrest communist leaders.[8]

The economic situation was not discussed until an evening reception that was given in honor of the Allied mission. Károlyi reported to the mission members the stringent new measures the government had introduced to save coal. Main-line rail service had to be cut to one train a day, and one train a week on branch lines. As for the food situation, Károlyi explained that in many parts of the country the potato harvest could not be brought in because the peasants had no boots or heavy clothing for outdoor work. The most critical shortage, however, was of fats, Károlyi added.

While the American and, above all, the British delegate Sir William H. Beveridge listened sympathetically to the list of grievances, the French member of the delegation, Emile Haguenin, reproached Károlyi for using the mission for diplomatic purposes. He noted that, since no peace treaty had been signed, Hungary could not be recognized diplomatically. Haguenin dismissed the complaints of shortages, claiming that "whatever Hungary was suffering now, Belgium and northern France had suffered worse."

Károlyi found Haguenin's reply offensive. He dismissed as pedantry the comment that a peace treaty putting a formal end to the war was a prerequisite for diplomatic recognition. He pointed out that as Hungary had disbanded its army, it clearly could not fight in case of an unfavorable peace. Beveridge tried to soften the brunt of Haguenin's remarks by claiming that the Allies had no particular dislike for Hungary and were not making a deliberate effort to underrate it. He ascribed the Allies' lack of interest in Hungarian affairs to the fact that they "had many more important things to think about than the fate of ten million people in Hungary." For this reason, he argued, the Hungarians should wait their turn for the Allies' political attention.[9]

The Taylor mission remained for two days. In its report it held that the food situation was less disturbing in Hungary that it was in Austria. The coal shortage, however, was considered very serious, for it was crippling Hungarian industry and creating umemployment that could make Bolshevik propaganda successful. The report noted Károlyi's pro-American position but warned that his position was weak because of his lack of Allied backing. The report concluded that Allied support had to be given to the Hungarian government to insure its survival.[10]

Sir William Beveridge shared Professor Taylor's view on Hungary. Upon his arrival in Paris Sir William went to see Robert Cecil, the Chairman of the Supreme Economic Council, and a member of the British peace delegation. During Beveridge's interview other British specialists on Austria-Hungary were also present, including Sir E. Howard and Harold Nicolson. In his report to his colleagues, Beveridge recommended lifting the economic embargo on Hungary and favoring an economic union of the east central European states. He also favored official contacts with Hungary and the delegation of a Foreign Office representative to Budapest. Beveridge even volunteered to lead a relief mission to Budapest which had the authority to enter into political negotiations with the Hungarian government.[11]

On January 17, Beveridge sent a memorandum to Lloyd George, reiterating his impressions on the Hungarian situation:

> It seems difficult to avoid the conclusion that in order
> to prevent a collapse of social order comparable to what
> occurred in Russia, the Allies must practically if not formally
> treat the war with all parts of Austria as finished and must
> give positive help in the reconstruction here.

To solve the problems of East Central Europe, the British economist recommended an equitable distribution of food, fuel and raw materials. He also stressed the need of the successor states to exchange supplies "without prejudice of political claims" and "irrespective of any terms of military occupation under the armistice."[12]

The response of Beveridge's superiors to his proposals that implied active support for Hungary was negative. Robert Cecil considered that political ties with Hungary were "altogether wild and injudicious," an opinion which was shared by Harold Nicolson, who was in charge of the Central and Southeast European territorial section of the British Delegation.[13] In his memorandum on this matter, Cecil warned the prime minister that Beveridge's views were "not on the right lines and could not safely be pursued at this juncture." Though there is no record of Lloyd George's position on this matter, it is safe to assume that his influential secretary of the War Cabinet and of the British delegation to Paris, Sir Maurice Hankey[14] spoke for the prime minister when he questioned why Hungary of all enemy countries should have official ties with Great Britain. Hankey favored, however, keeping abreast with Hungarian developments.[15] The prime minister's office thus reflected continued British non-interference in Hungarian politics.

The Hungarians profited little from the visit of the Taylor mission. Optimism in government circles continued since Sigray reported from Switzerland that the Coolidge mission was soon to visit Hungary. Hopes were raised by the fact that the Coolidge mission was an all-American undertaking. Archibald Coolidge was assigned by Secretary of State Lansing to "observe the political conditions in Austria-Hungary and neighboring countries."[16] He was to report back to the American Peace Commission in Paris. Such information from diverse commissions became the basis for American policy. The commissions also served a political function since they were regarded as informal diplomatic missions by their host countries.[17]

On December 26 Coolidge went to Switzerland to organize his team. In Berne he met Count Sigray who informed the American official of Hungary's position on the territorial question. He insisted that territorial solutions should be arrived at only through plebiscites, which should be supervised by countries that had no close interests in Europe, such as Great Britain and the United States. He insisted that France had to be excluded from involvement in them. Sigray told Coolidge that the Belgrade Convention was being flouted by France and the successor states. He mentioned the danger of communism which he said was becoming more popular because of the reversals of Hungarian foreign policy. He pointed out that Hungary had no forces to neutralize communism and that the presence of British and American forces in Budapest would greatly reduce the danger. He bitterly complained about the presence of the French military mission whose hostility to the Hungarians, he said, was conducive to red revolution.[18]

Early in January the Coolidge mission transferred its headquarters to Vienna, and the Hungarian embassy there was informed that it expected to arrive in Budapest on January 15. The embassy, on instructions from the foreign ministry in Budapest, sent back a memorandum on what it believed the Hungarians should stress to Coolidge. Ambassador Oszkár Charmant advised Budapest to lay emphasis on the danger of Bolshevism in Hungary.

> Our position is strengthened by the well-developed fear of the spread of Bolshevism, shared not only by the Entente powers but by the United States, which aims to raise a barrier against its spread by supplying food and consumer goods to the eastern European powers in dire need.[19]

This ambassador's advice was no surprise to the Hungarian government, which was already resolved to impress on the Allies the Bolshevik menace to Hungary. The Hungarians hoped that by reminding the Allies of this very real threat the West would come to the aid of the Károlyi government. Captain Imre Csermák was sent to the neutral Netherlands in an attempt to influence the Allies. John Garrett, the United States ambassador in The Hague, looked on the Csermák mission as a mere publicity stunt, for he wrote to the American mission in Paris that Károlyi's representative had 65,000 florins for propaganda purposes:

> From reliable information. . ., this man is attempting to take a prominent part in efforts now being made to impress the Associated Governments with the gravity of the Bolshevik menace.[20]

The Hungarian leaders were convinced that this emphasis on the Bolshevik danger was the right line not only by the Taylor mission's pre-occupation with communism but also by General Berthelot who visited Budapest in mid-January and inquired in detail about the significance and goals of the Hungarian communist movement.[21]

So important did the Hungarians consider the Coolidge mission that an ad hoc committee was formed to draw up a list of those whom Coolidge should see. The list included politicians and statesmen of every opinion inside and outside the government. It was hoped in this way to inform the Americans of the exact political situation in Hungary.

The Coolidge mission arrived in Budapest according to plan. They were welcomed by large crowds at the railroad station and posters put up by the government with a picture of Wilson that read: "We are for a Wilsonian peace only." When they met Károlyi, the Hungarian leader impressed on Professor Coolidge the American orientation of his government by reading to him the foreign-policy address he had made in December.[22]

Zsigmond Kunfi, who also saw Coolidge, combined the two major possibilities and told Coolidge bluntly that Hungary had "two definite programs, Wilsonism and Bolshevism" and that future developments would determine which was chosen.[23]

In his memoranda to the American Peace Commission in Paris Coolidge reported the economic difficulties Hungary was facing because of the disregard of the Belgrade Convention. He emphasized that further deterioration of the economic situation due to the coal shortage would increase the government's difficulties. He concluded that the resulting unemployment would mean "a great danger of bolshevist revolution against a government which has no armed forces with which to meet it."[24]

On the question of territorial integrity Collidge noted that among politicians of all persuasions "there are almost no differences, except a greater or lesser insistence on the principle of a fair plebiscite and a willingness to abide by the result."[25] Coolidge as an *Inquiry* member was concerned with territorial redistribution and sympathized with the Hungarian position.

While the Coolidge mission was in Budapest, another American visitor arrived—the chief of the Committee of Public Information, George Creel. His mission was to set up wireless receiving stations in Central Europe tuned to the C.P.I. news service in Paris. Arriving from Prague, Creel was welcomed by Károlyi. He listened to the Hungarian's complaints with sympathy and was surprised to learn that the Belgrade Convention was being ignored.[26] Creel was much impressed by Károlyi and at a press club reception given in his honor, endorsed Jászi's pigeon-holed concept of a Danubian Confederation and expressed the opinion that Károlyi would make a better president of such a state than Tomǎs Masaryk.

At another reception, this one in honor of the Coolidge mission, Creel, too was present. Károlyi now approached him with a new complaint about Rumanian incursion at the demarcation line. Creel listened attentively and suggested to Károlyi that Hungary ought to ally itself with Serbia against Rumania. He offered his advice with a view to the fact that Rumania and Serbia were embroiled in a controversy over possession of the Hungarian Bánát. Creel suggested that Hungary should cede the Bánát to Serbia in return from a Serbian pledge to help expel the Rumanians from Transylvania. Károlyi was taken aback by such an unexpected proposition and replied that any offers of alliance had to come from the Yugoslavs since they were the victors in the war. Creel then promised that, when he was back in Paris he would get in touch with the Serbians and urge them to contact the Hungarians on the subject.[27]

During the time he was in Hungary Creel was otherwise busy setting up the wireless station and making arrangements for the establishment of an American propaganda press in Hungary. Because of the shortage of newsprint, however, he realized that the latter plan was impractical and sent instructions to the Prague bureau of C.P.I. to have all the Magyar-language material printed there.[28]

Before he finally left the Hungarian capital, the American newsman sent a report to Paris offering his assessment of the conditions he observed in Budapest. In the report, Creel stressed the seriousness of the Hungarian situation. As a result of his friendship with President Wilson, he later claimed that it was in response to a telegram from him that the Council of Ten called on the successor states to refrain from military conquests and wait for the decisions of the Peace Conference.[29]

On his return to Paris Creel decided to speak to President Wilson on Károlyi's behalf. His interview with Wilson took place on February 2. Creel told him that Károlyi's government was worth saving. He suggested that the President should insist at the Peace Conference that the armistice conditions be respected by all. Creel also suggested that a Presidential letter be sent to Károlyi, inviting him to send a delegation to Paris at the earliest date to present Hungary's case. The chief of the C.P.I. thought these two steps by the President would be enough to bolster the Károlyi government against all challenges, internal and external. Creel's proposals were presented in a written memorandum to President Wilson,[30] but there is no indication that Wilson ever replied. It is clear, however, that the United States never took up Creel's second proposal and it is very likely that Wilson agreed with the American plenipotentiaries in Paris, who termed both proposals "unrealistic."[31]

Professor Coolidge, too, understandingly described the critical position facing the Károlyi government. He emphasized the government's weakness and explained that Károlyi was able to remain at the helm despite the cabinet crisis only because of his immense popularity among the Hungarians. He reported that the new Berinkey government meant a new shift to the left. He also spoke of Hungary's plan of federalizing itself. Like Creel he thought it was in the interest of the United States to strengthen Károlyi's position by declaring that the armistice lines were not political frontiers, which could only be decided by the Peace Conference.

Charles Seymour, the chief of the Austro-Hungarian Division of the American Commission, took measure of Coolidge's reports. He praised Károlyi's federative plans as having great merits which would be in the best interest of Central Europe. He claimed that his opinion was shared by many. Nevertheless, he termed the project impractical noting that in Paris the representatives of the nationalities were hostile to the plan. The only thing the Americans could do, Seymour reported, was "to prevent the complete stripping of Hungary of all the economic resources which she requires."

In the final analysis, he voiced the need of informing Károlyi of the realities. He warned, however, that this could only be revealed in a piecemeal fashion; otherwise it would cause the collapse of the government and the rise of anarchism and communism. One way to wake the Hungarians from their dreams was to invite them to Paris, if not for participation, then for consultation.[32] Seymour rightly assessed that such a traumatic experience would certainly make the Hungarians realize that Paris was not the forum for the international principles of Wilson. Implicitly, it was a recognition that in Paris high ideals lost out in favor of political expediencies. Fifty years later Seymour summed up these actualities:

> But in a dozen spots along the Czech and Rumanian border the Americans were too polite or too timid to quarrel. The Americans were also unorganized as a group, so that their judgment was never effectively concentrated or forcefully exercised. Responsibility for failure in this respect was. . . President Wilson's inability to organize and utilize the brains which were offered to him.[33]

In contrast to the realities of Paris, the Council of Ten's decision on he border issue, coming soon after the departure of Creel and Coolidge, further encouraged Károlyi that his pro-American policy was bearing fruit. To try to improve relations with the Allies and in an effort to find a way to establish direct contact with the United States embassy in Berne, Károlyi recalled the Hungarian envoy, Bédy-Schwimmer, on January 18, the day a new cabinet was sworn in. *The Times* of London saw this as an admission of the Hungarians' failure to win feminist sympathies. Its brief report concluded that Hungary had "conspicuously failed in its object." Bédy-Schwimmer was succeeded by a career diplomat, Baron Gyüla Szilassy, who had been the Dual Monarchy's ambassador to Constantinople. The new envoy was accepted by the Swiss as Hungary's *de facto* representative.[34]

Early in February, Károlyi had another opportunity to display his pro-American stand. The government was eager to be represented at the Peace Conference, so it inquired of the American Commission whether Hungary was to be seated at the conference. In the hope of a positive response, Károlyi offered to let the American Commission choose the Hungarian delegates.[35] Such an offer, which vastly compromised Hungary's sovereignty was wisely rejected by the American plenipotentiaries in Paris.[36]

In the meanwhile, Károlyi went ahead with setting up a committee that would be ready to join the Peace Conference at a moment's notice. The new Foreign Affairs Committee, as it was called, was put under the chairmanship of Oszkár Jászi, who drew up the main lines of Hungary's position to be presented at Paris. Jászi would first put forward the concept of Hungary as an Eastern Switzerland which would be part of a larger Confederation of Danubian States. If the conference rejected this plan in favor of partitioning Hungary, Jászi's alternative was to offer two principles.

The first principle was strict adherence to the results of plebiscites in the disputed areas; the second insisted on the guarantee of freedom of trade between Hungary and its lost territories. If the Allies were to reject this second plan, Jászi advised the government to refuse to sign a Peace Treaty:

> If it is proposed to determine our fate by force, we will refuse to sign, appealing to the Wilsonian principles and to the higher sense of justice of the workers of the world.[37]

Another of Creel's ideas, that of arranging a Yugoslav-Hungarian rapprochement, failed to materialize even though the Hungarians tended toward a pro-Yugoslav policy after Creel's departure. In an address on foreign policy given on February 8 Károlyi declared "that the two democratic nations could live next to each other in friendship and that their democratic spirit could win new strength from mutual help."[38] In attempting to build contacts with Yugoslavia, the Hungarian government found itself on the horns of a dilemma: rapprochment with Yugoslavia risked antagonizing Italy, while conversely, Hungarian friendship with Italy threatened to arouse Yugoslavia's animus.

Of the two countries, Italy showed more willingness to develop closer ties with Hungary. The Hungarian commissioner in Fiume, Lajos Fülep, was informed by the Italian members of the Fiume City Council that in return for Hungarian support the Italians were still prepared to send occupation troops to Hungary to watch over the Hungarian government's interests. The Hungarians, however, were suspicious of any Italian occupation,[39] probably because the Czechoslovak army occupying Hungarian territory was under Italian command.[40] Furthermore, it was known to Budapest that the Italians attempted to woo Rumania by promising her parts of Transylvania that were still in Hungarian hands.[41]

Early in February an Italian representative, the Marquis Tacoli, visited Budapest to offer Hungary a free port in Fiume in return for Hungarian support for Italy's claims to the contested city. The discussion was academic since Hungary had access to Fiume only through Yugoslavia. Nevertheless, Budapest continued these negotiations in the hope that they would secure Rome's support of Hungary on other questions at the Peace Conference.

In reality, Károlyi recognized the importance of ties with Yugoslavia. In a confidential letter to Baron Szilassy, the Hungarian President outlined his intentions:

> In our interest, the only useful orientation is rapproche-
> ment with Yugoslavia. Unfortunately, however, we have
> repeated offers only from Italy.

Károlyi believed that Hungary had nothing to gain from an Italian orientation, which he thought could serve only Italy's interests. He had to admit, however, that all Hungarian overtures to Belgrade had come to naught.[42] However bleak the prospects, Károlyi encouraged his envoy in

Berne to spare no effort to make contact with his Yugoslav counterpart. At the end of February a prominent member of the Yugoslav peace delegation, Kosta Stojanović, finally approached Szilassy in Switzerland. The Yugoslav was highly critical of Hungary's relations with Italy. Claiming to have the approval of his foreign minister, Ante Trumbic, Stojanović offered Hungary economic concessions if it would back Yugoslavia's claim to Fiume. Yugoslav rapprochement with Hungary was facilitated by the former's conflict with Rumania over the Bánát. The Bánát was occupied by the Yugoslavs in accordance with the Diaz armistice agreements and the Belgrade Convention. The Rumanians denounced both treaties and claimed the Bánát for themselves.[43]

To profit from the Yugoslav overture, Baron Podmaniczky, a state secretary of the Ministry of Foreign Affairs was sent to Trieste on a mission. Podmaniczky was to offer a partition of the Bánát between Hungary and Yugoslavia. In exchange for Fiume, the Yugoslavs were to provide free access to the Greek port of Salonica.[44] These proposals were seriously considered by the Yugoslav leaders, but further progress in this direction was frustrated by the collapse of the Károlyi regime in March.[45]

The Coolidge mission was soon followed by a British military mission which, too, had its headquarters in Vienna. The Hungarians, encouraged by the friendly attitude of Messrs. Taylor, Coolidge and Creel, were determined to make a favorable impression on Colonel Cuninghame, the leader of the mission. The British officer reached Budapest on February 5 and was warmly received by the Hungarians. He was rather critical of the fact that the regime was divorcing itself from those whom he considered as moderates and he termed Károlyi's system "pink socialism."[46] He also feared that further economic hardships and hostile attitudes of the successor states would create an air of despair favorable to communism.

Cuninghame as a military man was very suspicious of the Soldiers' Council and for this reason the president of the Council, József Pogány, took special pains to explain the difference between the Russian and Hungarian Soldiers' Councils. He stressed the point that in Hungary the Minister of Defense, Vilmos Böhm, had uncontested authority over the armed forces. At the same time Pogány warned Cuninghame of the communist danger, claiming that, unless there was a change of attitude among the Allies toward Hungary, it would go communist and "would set fire to a blazing trail of communism which would reach France and even Great Britain."[47]

Böhm likewise drew a grim picture of the specter of Hungarian communism. He said that the encroachment on Hungarian territory by the forces of the successor states had weakened the socialists in Hungary to the profit of the communists. He advised Cuninghame that the deterioration of economic conditions and a further advance by foreign troops into Hungarian territory could provoke the declaration of a communist republic. The Briton replied that the rise of Bolshevism in Hungary and its aggression against Allied powers, such as Pogány depicted, would be crushed. In contradiction to the established hands-off policy of his government, Cuninghame ominously warned that if Hungary turned Bolshevik, it could expect no leniency but would be subject to general invasion by successor-state troops supported by the great powers.[48]

When Cuninghame returned to Vienna, he gave his superiors a very grim report. He considered conditions ripe for a communist revolution. Like the Anglo-American visitors before him, he sympathized with Károlyi. The British officer blamed the Czechoslovaks for the chaotic economic state of Budapest. He felt that not only Hungary but Austria as well was headed into a major crisis as a result of Czechoslovak interference. Cuninghame thus feared that the rise of communism in Hungary would spread to Austria. Concerned with the life of the earstwhile emperor in view of what happened to the tsar in Russia, Cuninghame visited Charles at Eckartsau in late February. During his audience with the former king of Hungary, Cuninghame recounted his experience in Budapest and his impression that Hungary would turn communist. He told the king that "there was not a dog's chance" that the Allies would do anything to rescue Károlyi's government.

The British officer, whose sympathies were royalist, warned Charles that communism in Hungary would endanger his life, as he lived so close to the Hungarian frontier, and advised him to move his court to a safer place. To point up the danger, Cuninghame asked Charles how he would feel if communist Hungarian cavalry were to cross the frontier and surround Eckartsau. To his astonishment, Charles replied that he wished it would happen but he doubted it ever would.[49] It thus seems that even to Charles communism was preferable to the destruction of the frontiers of his former kingdom.

The Cuninghame mission, like the previous ones, had no executive power, and even though it prescribed the same cure for the ill of communism in Hungary, the Allies were unable to deliver it. American attempts to pressure the Czechs into selling coal to Hungary came to nothing because the Czechs insisted that coal deliveries to Austria prevented them from supplying Hungary.[50]

While the Czechs were contributing to the rise of pro-communist sentiment in Hungary, they were also interested in preserving their image as Bolshevik-fighters. General Milan Štefánik happened to be in Paris at the time of the Coolidge visit to Budapest. At Beneš request he called on members of the American mission and regaled them with tales of the Czechoslovak's heroic deeds against Magyar prisoners of war released by the Bolsheviks.[51] Just how much harm this kind of lobbying did to Hungarian interests is hard to say, but what is certain is that it did not help Hungary at all.

The blockade of Hungary continued even though Herbert Hoover, the chief of the American Relief Agency and a member of the Supreme Economic Council, expressed his disapproval of it several times, blaming it on the French. Finally on March 12, the Supreme Economic Council advised the Council of Ten to end the investment and heard proposals to set up a special Interallied Commission to deal with Hungary's economic plight. Serious discussion about lifting the blockade did not take place, however, until after the Károlyi government had collapsed. The proposals to establish a special commission for Hungary were rejected by the Supreme Economic Council on March 19.[52]

While Hungarian officials were predicting communist victory to Allied visitors and talking about the international working class saving Hungary, the first attempts were made to enlist Western socialists in support of Hungary. They were made in the wake of the International Socialist Congress, convened in Berne on Feburary 6 and attended by 97 delegates from 26 nations. The aim of the congress was to mend the rift between the socialist parties and to effect a reconcilation. The agenda included discussion of the territorial question.[53] The Hungarian socialists were represented by Manó Buchinger, Dezső Biró, Samu Jászai and Zsigmond Kunfi.

At the meeting of the territorial commission, the Czechs took an altogether uncompromising attitude toward the Hungarians. While Buchinger presented the Hungarian position, which insisted on plebiscites in the disputed areas, the Czech socialist leader, M.V. Bechyně, rejected the plebiscites on the ground that the Slovaks were not mature enough to vote because they were under the influence of the Roman Catholic

Clergy. At the same time Bechyně, who later became a vice-president of Czechoslovakia, also argued that the Slovak intellectuals wanted association with the Czech leadership.

The Hungarians' reasoning drew the support of the British Labour leaders, Ramsay MacDonald and Arthur Henderson, and the final declaration of the territorial commission favored the Hungarian position. The declaration called for the settlement of territorial and nationality questions on the basis of self-determination, either by plebiscite or referendum. It also denied that territorial aggrandisement could be justified as the right of the victor over the vanquished.[54]

While the international congress was taking place in Berne, the Hungarian socialists were holding their own party congress in Budapest. The editor of *Népszava*, Jakab Weltner, explained the support given to the Hungarian socialists by the majority at Berne by the fact that the Hungarians were the only socialists who were not splintered. Because of this unity the workers were always able to "oppose capitalist rule and not betray the principle of class struggle for a moment." Weltner claimed that this factor strengthened Buchinger's position in Berne, as he could declare with assurance that "the English and French comrades can shake hands with the Hungarian workers, as they have never associated themselves with chauvinistic slogans and warmongering."[55]

The declaration of the socialists in Berne was regarded by Károlyi as a victory and great publicity was given to the Hungarian delegates' speeches in all the Hungarian newspapers. On their return the delegates were welcomed at the railroad station like conquering heroes.[56]

The Hungarian government took great encouragement from the socialists' declaration, for it lent weight to the belief of many politicians that, if the Allied leaders abandoned Hungary, the Western working classes would still stick by it. This belief was a chimera and, even if the Hungarians took the Berne congress seriously, the policy makers in Paris certainly did not. After the congress ended on February 10, its executive committee took the socialist declaration to Paris. The committee did not succeed in seeing President Wilson, who left Paris on February 14, but did meet Clemenceau and Lloyd George who were given copies.[57] Clemenceau paid little heed to its contents and advised the socialists to contact the respective territorial commissions and leave it with them.

Not only were the socialists, representing the workers of the West, disregarded by Clemenceau, but Moscow, while claiming to wear the same mantle, also denounced the Berne participants. They called the socialists who endorsed the spirit of Berne "lackeys" and "social obscurantists." The Hungarian communists, likewise, concentrated their attacks on the Hungarian socialists for participating in the congress. They labeled them chauvinists and false internationalists bent on serving their own national interests. The communist journal declared: "The delegations in Berne represented their own states, but nobody represented the international proletariat."[58]

In spite of the communist harangue, the visits of various Allied missions in Hungary and the accomplishment of the Hungarian socialists in Berne seemed to revive the confidence of Hungarian leaders. It rekindled hope that after two months of neglect, the Hungarians would receive positive responses from the Allies.

The communists' violent press attack on the Hungarian socialists' participation at Berne culminated a running feud that had lasted through January and ended with the communists' expulsion from the labor movement.

The communists, deploring the Western orientation of the socialists, mounted ever sharper attacks against them and against the government of which they were a member. Following the Leninist blueprint for revolution, the Hungarian communists aimed to weaken the position of the government by agitating for a system of dual authority. This meant the adoption of the Russian slogan: "All power to the councils!" The government crisis early in January spurred on the introduction of such formulae and on January 8 the ten-man communist faction in the Budapest Workers' Council demanded the transformation of the council from a Social Democratic Party institution into a class organ of the proletariat. They also demanded the organization of a congress of workers' councils and the arming of the workers.[1]

The socialist compromise, intended to strengthen Károlyi's position, was vehemently attacked by the communists as another example of the betrayal of Marxism by the socialists, "who now use their power to support the crumbling structure of the bourgeoisie."[2] The communists also condemned the National Council's appointment of Károlyi as president of the republic. On January 15, *Vörös Újság* declared that Karolyi's policy was bankrupt and his rise to the presidency signaled the end of the first phase of the revolution. His appointment was considered to be an act of the petite bourgeoisie, aimed at the protection of private property but disguised as a revolutionary move.

On the day Berinkey was sworn in as prime minister, the communists published the first of three installments of "Lenin's Article for *Vörös Újság*." In the article Lenin attacked all socialists, "from Scheidemann to Kautsky," who favored constitutional assemblies over the power of the soviets and who justified their position by claiming to be defending democracy against dictatorship. Lenin concluded that the workers and peasants of Germany, Austria and Hungary "will soon understand the betrayal of the Scheidemanns and Kautskies":

> As the rule of the above mentioned leaders becomes stronger, the proletariat will very soon become aware that the bourgeois state can only be changed into a system like that of the Paris Commune through the rise of a soviet state. Only through the councils can the road to socialism be opened. The dictatorship of the soviet will save humanity from the yoke of capital and war.[3]

The Hungarian socialists, who considered the communists' agitation for council power to be dangerous, decided to move. At the January 28 meeting of the Workers' Council Jakab Weltner introduced a resolution demanding the censure of the communist movement and the expulsion of communists from the Workers' Councils and labor unions. The resolution was given nearly unanimous support. Sándor Garbai called for a direct confrontation with the communists, who were jeopardizing the socialists' unity: "We must turn our guns against them! No one should be allowed to attempt to break the unity of the workers except at his mortal peril."[4] The communists present at the meeting declared in turn that they would not abandon their fight. Thereupon all thirteen were physically ejected from the council chamber.

The socialists thus showed their continued determination to support Károlyi.[5] The communists reacted with a violent indictment of the socialists in a pamphlet in which they declared:

> The lackeys of the bourgeoisie, the government socialists, after selling out the proletariat of Hungary, have made a bordello out of the Workers' Council of Budapest.

The denunciation accused the socialists of denying the solidarity of the Hungarian workers with the revolutionary proletariat of Russia and claimed that the socialists were responsible for "bringing in French troops to suppress revolutionary activities in Hungary." It ended: "We stand before them and announce to these lackeys of the capitalists: 'Terror for Terror.' This is our message to the government's socialist mafia."[6]

The response to the communist call for revolutionary violence was swift and on February 9 at the Socialist Party Congress the socialists decided to expel the communists from the labor unions.[7] The communist leadership, fearing that the socialists' reaction could deprive them of labor support, decided to change tactics.[8] New instructions were given to the membership, now 2000 to 4000, to refrain from inciting violence because it might jeopardize the existence of communist cells in the labor unions. This appeal was all the more urgent because, even without communist agitation, the severe economic situation was creating an atmosphere amenable to mob violence.

Apparently, the communists were afraid of a repetition of Russia's July Days of 1917, which had forced the Bolsheviks underground. It may be assumed that the failure of the Spartacists in Berlin and the brutal murder of their leaders in prison just days before, also contributed to their decision.[9]

If the communists decided to moderate their revolutionary agitation, this did not mean that they were relinquishing their attack on the foreign policy of the government. They still aimed to show that Károlyi was selling Hungary to Allied anti-Bolshevism. Colonel Vix, incensed by the communist press attacks insisted that the Hungarians must introduce press censorship.[10] The exasperated Károlyi replied that democracy in Hungary included the freedom of the press for shades of political opinion.[11] Thus the communist publications continued to attack the Károlyi government and the Vix mission.

On February 11 the communists claimed that the French and Hungarian armistice commissions were colluding to channel requisitioned German arms in Hungary to the Poles fighting Russian communist forces. The arms were being shipped to Poland in sealed railroad cars marked with French signs, they maintained. In return, the French military mission was supposed to have promised coal deliveries to the Hungarians. Each wagon-load of arms was said to be repaid with eight wagonloads of coal to Hungary.[12]

Hungarian immobility against the communists was also motivated by the fact that from the middle of December the government was negotiating with the representatives of the Russian Red Cross in Budapest for the mutual repatriation of prisoners of war. Károlyi expected that, with Western cooperation, the Russians would allow the Hungarian prisoners of war to return through Vladivostok.[13] Colonel Vix, however, regarded the Russian mission with suspicion and when in January new Russian envoys arrived in Budapest, the French representative considered the event the beginning of an international conspiracy. Though the avowed purpose of the Russians was to continue negotiations for the exchange of prisoners of war, Vix claimed that, according to an informer, the Russians brought money and propaganda material to the Hungarian and Austrian communists. Bowing to charges of international conspiracy, the Hungarian police arrested the mission on January 7, with plans for their expulsion as undesirable aliens. Before such action could be carried through, two officers of the French mission called at police headquarters and demanded transfer of custody of the Russians. The following evening the Russian Red Cross delegation was taken to the railway station under French military escort and, despite the Russians' vehement protests, they were sent to Salonica for French internment.[14]

On January 20, Vix was able to report that since the arrest of the Russians, there had been a détente in the communist movement in Hungary. He attributed the slack to the communists' lack of money and to the defeat of the Spartacist revolution in Berlin. This view was accepted by Paris with great satisfaction.[15] Though the arrest may have been seen in such salutary light by Vix, the Hungarian authorities were not able to establish any positive connections between the Hungarian communists and the Russian Red Cross mission.[16]

The arrest of the Russians had great significance in another respect, as it could be regarded as an act that made Vix a military dictator in Hungary. Apparently, the great conflict of the period forced him to abandon his neutral position and he acted without first consulting his superiors. The international standing of Hungary also became tarnished as a consequence of the incident. The arrest of foreign nationals on Hungarian soil seemed to affirm the Bolshevik propaganda line that Károlyi was a lackey of Entente imperialism directed against Russia. The Soviet Foreign Minister Gregorii Chicherin indignantly telegraphed to Budapest demanding information on the whereabouts of the Russians and called for their release. Chicherin further threatened the suspension of all negotiations with the Hungarian Red Cross representatives in Russia and their expulsion.[17] The president of the Russian Red Cross used even more ominous threats. After branding Károlyi as an Entente stooge,

Veniamin Sverdlov warned the Hungarian government that the Hungarian Red Cross envoys would be imprisoned in Russia in reprisal.[18]

These open threats caused the Hungarian Armistice Commission to turn to Vix repeatedly with requests to have the Russians sent back to Moscow. The Hungarians warned the French that the fate of one hundred thousand Hungarian prisoners of war was in the balance. They claimed that the French action that prevented repatriation might mean death for many, while others would be "pushed into the arms of Bolshevism."[19] The Hungarians received no reply to their requests, most likely because the arrest of the Russians was considered by the French military as part of a broader policy aimed at stemming Bolshevism. The Soviet threat of severing the exchange of prisoners of war was exactly what the French wanted. The supreme commander of the Allies, Marshal Foch, wanted to prevent the return of Russian prisoners to communist controlled Russia. In his note of January 11, 1919, Foch advised the Allies to retain the Russian prisoners of war found in the defeated countries. He argued that such a policy would prevent the Red Army from reinforcing its regiments. He called for the repatriation of only those Russians who were anti-Bolshevik and who were willing to fight against the communist forces in Poland and in southern Russia.[20] Thus it was in the interest of the French military planners to prevent a deal between the representatives of the Soviets and Hungary which would have allowed Russian prisoners of war to return to the Bolshevik side.

For similar reasons, the French were equally averse to seeing the return of the Magyar prisoners of war from Siberia. According to French and British military reports from Russia, a great number of the Hungarian prisoners of war joined the Bolsheviks and contributed to their military successes.[21] Their repatriation to Budapest would have weakened the Bolshevik effort in Siberia but it could also have aided the communist cause in Hungary at the exact time when Vix noted an eclipse of communist agitation. Their return through Vladivostok via a long sea voyage could have been the solution to the dilemma but, as Clemenceau noted, there were no available ships to do the job. The French alternative was an attempt to pressure the counter-revolutionary government in Omsk to keep the prisoners of war in their camps. When this policy failed, the Allies accepted the British solution which called for improving camp conditions as a way to keep the prisoners where they were.[22]

The declining appeal of the communist threat in Hungary was a false observation. The economic difficulties of Hungary were exploited by the communists. On February 20, the Association of the Unemployed held a communist sponsored demonstration in front of the editorial offices of the socialist newspaper *Népszava*. The aim of the demonstrators was to pressure the socialist members of the cabinet to improve the economic situation. No doubt, the communists expected to profit from the bad publicity of the socialists who could do little to ameliorate the situation.

The socialists, fearing mob violence, decided to ask police protection for their buildings. The expected violence materialized when, for reasons still unclear, the demonstrators clashed with the police. In the ensuing fight four uniformed policemen were shot to death.

This violent episode finally gave the police the pretext they needed to arrest the communist leaders. Unbeknownst to the government, they had closely watched the activities of the communists. Agents had infiltrated the party and furnished detailed reports for a confidential file on party leaders. A certain László Nánássy was in charge of these activities. Reports on the communists' activities were also sent to the Ministry of the Interior.

As early as January the commanders of the Budapest police, Captain Károly Dietz and György Páll, began considering a police crackdown on the communists in the old Buda section of the capital. There a group known as the "sailors," because they wore sailors' uniforms, had reportedly stocked arms for use in the revolution. Dietz and Páll decided to see Károlyi to get his approval for a raid. They went to the presidential office where Károlyi was in the midst of a cabinet meeting. In view of the urgency of the situation Károlyi was called out and given all the details. When the police chiefs asked permission to arrest the "sailors" Károlyi, however, refused, dropping into a chair and exclaiming dejectedly: "But gentlemen, what will the world say if blood is spilt in the streets of Budapest?"

The events of February 20 now gave the police an excuse to proceed since the communists had clearly violated existing laws. The authorities handled the case as a routine process: arrest for incitement to riot and murder. As soon as news of violence reached headquarters, Dr. György Páll sent the dossiers on the communist leaders to the chief prosecutor for examination. The next day they were returned with the chief prosecutor's approval for a police arrest warrant.[23] While the police were moving according to established procedures, an emergency cabinet meeting was held. At the meeting the minister of the interior, Vince Nagy, proposed that the communists be arrested; his proposal was accepted without demur by the whole cabinet.[24]

On February 21 the arrests began. Within two days 48 communists were rounded up, including Béla Kun, József Rabinovics and Otto Korvin. The party's central offices and its printing facilities were seized, while the prosecutor confiscated a freshly printed issue of *Vörös Újság* and a number of pamphlets.

The sympathy of the masses at this point was with the government and the martyred policemen, and a new demonstration under socialist sponsorship was organized to display the workers' solidarity.

The police quickly succeeded in alienating the public. After the arrests, a group of police officers decided to take justice into their own hands. In the courtyard of the detention house, where the communists were being held, Béla Kun was brutally beaten. Rumors began to circulate immediately in Budapest that Kun was dead. When these reached police headquarters, Páll and another police chief, Béla Szentkirályi, set off at once for the detention house to see for themselves what had happened. They were accompanied by Vilmos Tarján, a reporter for *Az Est*, an evening tabloid, who opportunely happened to be there. He offered to go with the police in the hope of getting a scoop story. Páll was only too pleased to have a member of the fourth estate present, as he wanted to make it clear that any manhandling of Kun had not been done with official sanction.

At the detention house they saw Kun in the infirmary where he had been taken after the beating. Kun was much relieved to see such high officials and asked for protection because his life was in danger. While Kun was recounting what had happened, a group of police burst into the room. They were led by an officer whose brother had been killed in the *Népszava* riot. Shouting threats, they proceeded to batter Kun with rifle butts. Páll and Szentkirályi attempted to eject them, afraid that they would surely kill Kun. Finally Szentkirályi succeeded in clearing the room. Surprisingly Kun was not only still alive but had not even lost consciousness. The terrified man must have been seeing the ghosts of Karl Liebknecht and Rosa Luxemburg, the two Spartacist leaders lynched in Berlin, for he implored Páll and Szentkirályi to save him.[25] On February 22 *Az Est* published an eyewitness account of the events,[26] arousing much sympathy for the communists.[27]

The savage treatment of the communist chief occasioned a new cabinet meeting at which Károlyi voiced his utmost disapproval. He emphasized that no man could be prosecuted just for belonging to a particular party, only for committing criminal acts. The socialist, Kunfi, echoed his position, but opposed the request of the policemen's association to drop any investigation of the perpetrators of the beatings because he feared that this would only increase public sympathy for the communists.[28] Károlyi saw to it personally that there was no repetition of the beatings and that the prisoners were humanely treated.[29]

The arrest had international repercussions. Shortly after he was seized, Béla Kun managed to slip a note written on a piece of cigarette paper to a free comrade, Lajos Németi. Németi was ordered to go to Moscow and report to Lenin what had occurred. Hearing of Németi's report, however, Lenin showed no sign of alarm or concern.[30] Perhaps he saw events in Hungary developing according to the blueprint of the Russian revolution. To him Károlyi was another Kerensky and the imprisonment of the Hungarian communists was parallel to the arrest of the Russian Bolsheviks following the disturbances in Petrograd in July 1917. The course of events in Hungary could only make Lenin even more confident about the outcome of the situation. The possibility that Kun and the other communist leaders might be murdered in prison, however, compelled the Russians to put pressure on the Hungarians to stop the maltreatment. High-ranking Hungarian officers who were still in Russian prisoner-of-war camps were taken as hostages for the arrested communists. Russia warned the Hungarian government that if the life or health of the communists suffered, equal retribution would be meted out to the Hungarian officers in Russian custody. The Russians also moved against the Hungarian Red Cross mission, arresting its members in reprisal for the arrest of Kun.[31]

The Russians' forceful protest led Károlyi to call another cabinet meeting. As a result, 29 communists were freed from jail and charges of incitement to murder were dropped against the rest, including Béla Kun. Those still detained were ordered to be treated with traditional deference due political prisoners. The government also issued a statement which ruled out prosecution for membership in the Communist Party.[32]

While the Russians pressured the Hungarians to release the prisoners, Károlyi aimed to woo Allied support by publicizing their arrest in the West. In confidential instructions to Szilassy, he instructed his ambassador to announce the imprisonment of the Hungarian Bolsheviks in the Swiss papers.[33] Since most information from East Central Europe reached the Allies through Switzerland[34] Károlyi's purpose was clearly to generate the widest possible confidence. In the same directive, however, Károlyi also warned his Berne representative not to draw analogies between the communists in Hungary and Russia and to refrain from verbal attacks on the Russian communists. Károlyi seemed to avoid having Hungary identified as anti-Russian: "I see it more useful not to direct the attention of the Soviet government to us."[35]

Károlyi's advice to his ambassador about Russia seemed very significant as it implied that the Hungarian leader was beginning to reconsider his one-track pro-Allies policy, and was looking for accommodation with the Russians. This policy reflected a current of opinion that was becoming more general in Hungary. By the end of February there was widespread resignation to the fact that the Allies were ignoring Hungary's pleas for help. As a result, the nation was ready to turn to the East and, for the first time in Hungarian history, ally itself with Russia.

Entertainment of such policy may explain why the government reacted so swiftly to correct the injustice committed against the imprisoned communist leaders. Significantly, on February 22 the government promulgated a new law to intern those "who threatened the achievement of the revolution."[36] This law was directed mainly against right-wing counter-revolutionaries who wanted to reestablish an aristocratic hegemony and renounce all association with the communists. As a result of the new law, about a hundred retired generals and magnates and one Roman Catholic bishop were placed under house arrest. At the same time the socialists decided to make overtures to the communists to heal the rift in the workers' movement.[37]

It was hoped that this working class unity would parry new injustices against Hungary which, in the mind of the Hungarian leadership, was equivalent of further reductions of the Hungarian perimeter. These fears were justified by continued advances of Rumanian forces which by February 14, 1919 had pushed their front to the line of Máramarossziget (Sighet) through Zilah (Zălău), Csucsa (Cuca) and Nagysebes (Sebeş) to the Szamos (Someşul) river. According to Franchet d'Esperey, their ultimate aim was to occupy lands southeast of the Tisza accorded to them in the Secret Treaty of Bucharest. He saw war between the Rumanians and the Hungarians as being near. The Hungarians fielded

5,000 troops to repel any further advance in the area of Csucsa. To prevent a bloody embroglio, the general requested his superiors to reestablish a demarcation line. To separate the belligerents, he proposed the establishment of a zone occupied by French troops. This was necessary, he reasoned, as the Rumanians' past uncontested advances had whetted their appetite and they were now regarded by the Hungarians as deliberately violating the Belgrade Convention.[38]

The message of the Commander in Chief of the Balkan forces was transmitted to the Peace Conference's "Commission for the Territorial Questions Relating to Rumania."[39] The eight member panel of French, British, Italian and American experts was in the process of examining Rumania's claims on her four neighbors.[40] The members of the committee concurred with Franchet d'Esperey that, in order to avoid conflict before its final decision on the Rumanian-Hungarian frontier, a neutral zone should be set up. The experts of the commission therefore proposed a zone which was to put the Hungarians behind a line running ten kilometers west of Vásárosnamény, the junction of the Kis Kőrős and Nagy Kőrős rivers, Algyő and north of Szeged. The Rumanians were to halt their troops ten kilometers east of Szatmarnémeti (Satu-Mare) Nagyvárad (Oradea) and Arad.

Since the proposed zone was occupied by French forces of the Allies, the proposal was transmitted to the Supreme Military Council in Versailles for further comments. During the deliberations of February 19, General Alby, Chief of the French General Staff, reviewed the military aspects of the zone. He said that in the light of the need to re-establish order, it would be wise to renounce the military convention of Belgrade and to draw a new demarcation line between Hungary and Rumania. He observed that the lines proposed by the Rumanian Commission left in the neutral zone such important rail centers as Nagyvárad, Nagykároly (Carei) and Szatmárnémeti—cities that controlled Transylvania's lifeline. Accepting the standard Rumanian argument that Bolshevism was spreading in Transylvania, Alby argued that the Rumanians must control the communications centers to fight against it. He also claimed that, since French troops were to occupy Arad, they could not occupy the aforementioned cities as Berthelot's troops, who were to do the occupation, would have to be sent to southern Russia. The Rumanian occupation of the rail centers thereby would be necessary.[41]

It has been argued in the past that the French military view of the shape of the neutral zone was an organic part of the military plans of the Allied Supreme Commander, Marshal Ferdinand Foch, who was intent on destroying Bolshevism in Russia.[42] Indeed, while the discussions about the neutral zone were taking place, Foch's plan to destroy Bolshevism was also circulated among the peacemakers. The Allied military chief believed that his plan, if put into use, "would end Bolshevism just as 1918 had seen the end of Prussianism."[43] The first step in this project was to encircle Russia. In the north, this was to be done by organizing a Polish army strengthened by the return of Polish troops from France. In the south, an allied force made up of three French, three Greek, one English, one Italian and two Rumanian divisions would occupy the Ukraine and reconquer the Donets basin from the Bolsheviks. The second step included the organization of a Russian army from prisoners of war found in Germany and from Russian troops in France, Algeria and Macedonia. The last step was to be a general offensive which would enable the White Russian troops to destroy the Red Army before the winter of 1919-1920. The plan concluded with the observation that it was necessary to know how much support the Allied states were willing to give to the venture.[44]

It is evident thus that General Alby's call for Rumanian expansion into Hungarian-held territory was a price the French military planners were willing to pay for Rumanian support of the Foch plan. That Hungarian territory was the price the Rumanians demanded was indicated by the Rumanian Prime Minister, Ion Brațianu's speech to the Council of Ten:

> Rumania, exhausted by war, needs the moral support of
> the Allies if it is to remain what it has been hitherto—a
> rallying point for Europe against Bolshevism. . . . Rumania
> asks to be so placed that it can resist. It asks this not only
> in its own interest, but in the interest of the whole of
> Europe and without exaggeration, of the whole civilized
> world.[45]

The question of the neutral zone in Hungary was put on the agenda of the Council of Ten on February 21, 1919. In the absence of the leaders of the Big Four, the Allied representatives accepted the arguments of the military specialists in Versailles and requested them to work out the final details of the military plan.[46] Foch's invasion plans were put before the council four days later. The two plans complemented each other, since the demarcation line put into Allied hands essential Hungarian railway lines which would contribute to the logistic needs of an invasion army in Russia. The new temporary Hungarian frontier was also strongly reminiscent of the one in the Secret Treaty of Bucharest.

Although upon introduction, the Council of Ten shelved Foch's plan that would have engulfed Europe in a new war, for some reason it failed to see the connection between the Russian invasion plan and the proposed harsh demarcation line in Hungary. On the next day, February 26, the Council of Ten, still in the absence of the four Allied leaders, accepted the outlines of the neutral zone. It is very likely that the Allied representatives, preoccupied with other burning issues of the day, wanted to put an end to Rumanian-Hungarian clashes at any price. Since it was known that the Rumanian army did not recognize the Belgrade Convention,[47] giving in to Rumanian demands seemed the only way to bring peace to Transylvania.

According to the Supreme Council in Versailles, the neutral zone was to be policed by troops of two-battalion strength with some cavalry regiments to maintain order. The limits of the Hungarian withdrawal were a line "leaving the Tisza five kilometers northwest of Vásárosnamény, passing five kilometers to the west of Debrecen to three kilometers west of Devaványa and continuing west of Gyoma, five kilometers west of Hódmezővásárhely and Szeged, rejoining the old frontier south of Szeged." In this area the cities of Szeged and Arad were to be under French occupation. The Rumanians were to have an eastern demarcation line that followed the main road from Arad to Nagyszalonta (Salonta) and the Nagyvárad (Oradea)–Nagykároly (Carei)–Szatmárnemeti (Satu-Mare) railway line. The three rail centers were excluded from Rumanian occupation but "were available for the use of Rumanian troops and Rumanians living in areas controlled by the Allies, for economic purposes." The northern limits of the demarcation line followed the river Szamos (Someşul).[48]

Since the establishment of the neutral zone was a military matter, the decision of the Peace Conference was transmitted by Clemenceau to Franchet d'Esperey on March 1 for execution.[49] On March 5, the Allied Commander in the Orient informed General Berthelot of the Paris decision.

Berthelot was to pass on the military details to the Rumanians but was ordered not to inform the Hungarians. Franchet d'Esperey also requested Berthelot to ask the Rumanians not to act prematurely and to wait for Franchet d'Esperey to give them the date to move forward. Berthelot was asked to supply Franchet d'Esperey with information on the disposition of the Rumanian troops which would move into Transylvania so that he (Franchet d'Esperey) could plan a date for the Hungarian withdrawals to begin. Franchet d'Esperey also saw the need to inform Paris of the date of the execution of the Allied project.

Franchet d'Esperey, weary of Berthelot's tendency to disregard his orders, told him that immediate responsibility for the French troops was with General de Lobit in Belgrade as he was the commander of the French Army of Hungary. It was he who was empowered to handle the final details of executing the plan, which was to be supervised by an officer appointed by Franchet d'Esperey. With this in mind, Franchet d'Esperey warned Berthelot not to send any missions to Hungary which would duplicate the task of General de Lobit.[50]

Franchet d'Esperey seemed to have been disappointed by the generous temporary demarcation line accorded to the Rumanians. It appears that he expected the approval of his proposed neutral zone, pushing the Rumanians back to their old line between Nagybánya (Baia-Mare) and Kolozsvár (Cluj). After all, he did not believe in the Rumanian bogey of Bolshevism in Transylvania and had been opposed to French intervention in Russia from the start.[51]

Having seen Rumania's unauthorized advances legitimized in Paris, Franchet d'Esperey began to assume that the memorandum of February 26 would lead to the permanent award of Transylvania to the Rumanian ally. He also believed that such a development would lead to a war between Rumania and Hungary. Therefore, Rumania had to mobilize for war. He felt that Rumania should organize eight divisions to face the six divisions that were allowed to Hungary under the armistice arrangements.[52]

Franchet d'Esperey's concern with possible war-like response to the Paris decision was not without foundations. Although the Budapest government was not officially advised of what happened in Paris, rumors of the decision appeared in the press immediately.[53] It seems that, in response to these rumors of further dismemberment, the Hungarian government began to think seriously about the reorganization of the army to make it battleworthy. The army was to become a volunteer force of seventy thousand, a size that conformed to the limits set in the Belgrade Convention.[54]

The Hungarian government reacted to the rumors in other ways. It decided that it would call an election to a national assembly in the non-occupied areas.[55] The election was to show the Allies that the non-Magyar nationalities approved the People's Republic and so supported its territorial integrity. The hope that the non-Magyar nationalities would participate in the elections and by their vote support a government ruling from Budapest was not based solely on the vague theoretical justification that Hungary now had a democratic system.

Károlyi and the other leaders took the example of Ruthenia as an indication of the feeling of all the non-Magyar nationalities in Hungary. The Ruthenian National Council, as early as November 9, 1918, had chosen Hungary. It had welcomed the establishment of the new Hungarian People's Republic enthusiastically while it had repudiated all separatist tendencies. It demanded for the Ruthenes "the same right as the republic would grant to the other non-Magyar nationalities," and it asked for social and political reforms. The Hungarian ministry of nationalities met these demands and on December 25, 1918 issued the Autonomy Statute for Ruthenia. The Ruthenian autonomous region was to be known as Ruszka-Krajna; it would enjoy self-government in religious, educational and cultural affairs, and administer its own justice. The common affairs that were to be regulated in conjunction with the Hungarian republic were: foreign affairs, war, finance, private and criminal law, the economy, communications and social problems. A Ruthenian National Assembly would legislate local affairs, while representatives sent to the Hungarian Parliament would join in discussion of common affairs. On January 8, 1919, the minister of Ruszka-Krajna issued a proclamation in which he reassured the Magyars of northeast Hungary that no districts with Magyar majorities would be included in Ruszka-Krajna and that in the autonomous area the rights of all minorities would be respected.[56]

Károlyi, the government, and most Magyars looked forward to a similar solution for the whole nationalities problem. They overlooked, however, the fact that, unlike the other nationalities living in Hungary, the Ruthene intelligentsia had been almost completely "Magyarized." As a result of the liberal Jewish laws of 1867, which, unlike the nationalities laws of 1868, had been respected, a great influx of Jews from neighboring Polish and Russian pales had made them a majority in certain parts of Ruthenia. Most of these Jews were ardent supporters of Hungary, into which they were becoming assimilated.[57] They were unsure about Slovak intentions, while the possibility of Rumanian sovereignty over their communities filled them with fear, for Rumania had always treated its Jewish population as second-class citizenry. Thus the Magyarized Ruthenian intelligentsia, the economically influential Ruthenian Jewry and the Ruthenian Magyars made the situation in Ruthenia unique, though in German-speaking areas of Hungary the nationalities also preferred Magyar to "Slav" rule.[58] That the other nationalities would follow suit was, therefore, wishful thinking on the part of the Hungarians.

Domestic reaction to the news of the election on April 13 was mixed. The socialists were confident that they would receive an absolute majority of the vote thanks to their unrivaled party organization. Their election platform embodied the aspirations of the majority of Hungarians. It called for the speedy implementation of land reform as well as national-ization of heavy industry, mines and public utilities. To speed national-ization, the socialists promised to set up a ministry of socialization. Their foreign policy was based on a peace settlement that called for national self-determination.[59]

The Workers' Council of Budapest, however, opposed the election because it feared that the socialists would not receive an absolute majority. On March 5, the council reluctantly reversed itself but warned that, if the socialists did not receive an absolute majority, it would break up the elected assembly. The deliberations of the Workers' Council were clearly influenced by rumors from Paris, because it called for a reorientation of Hungarian foreign policy on the basis of a Hungarian-Russian alliance. With such a Russian alliance in mind, the members asked for the readmission of the communists to its membership.[60]

Growing dissatisfaction with Allied policy toward Hungary and the reorientation of Hungarian foreign policy toward a Russian alliance were furthered by reports in the Hungarian press of the approach of the Russian Red Army. The March 13 issue of *Vörös Újsdg* had even reported that the Red forces were in Galicia, which was formerly part of the Dual Monarchy. The aim of the Red Army, the newspaper declared, was to reach the borders of Hungary and Rumania.[61] In the meantime, many Magyars identified increasingly the struggle of the Russian communists against foreign intervention with Hungary's struggle against the successor states. This feeling was shared by some senior officers in the Hungarian army. Lieutenant Colonel Tombor, in a memorandum written for publicity, applauded the patriotism of the Russian Bolsheviks fighting against the "predatory imperialism of the Entente."[62] The establishment of closer relations between Hungary and Russia was also indicated by Budapest's request to the International Postal Bureau in Berne. Early in March the Hungarians called on the Postal Bureau to invite the Soviet government to establish radiogram communications with Budapest. Though the request was rejected,[63] its mere appearance indicated Hungary's interest in the amelioration of Hungarian-Soviet relations.

While Entente policies came under fire in Hungary, it is significant to note that Károlyi was not condemned and his popularity among the Hungarians did not wane. When the Workers' Council debated the possibility of a socialist government, for instance, there was no question of Károlyi's position as president. When one council member asked if the socialists would demand his resignation, József Pogány, the socialist president of the Soldiers' Council, dramatically declared that he personally would execute any socialist who did not vote for Károlyi as president.[64]

Károlyi himself felt, however, that the Allies were confronting him with insurmountable problems. On February 26, he confided to his wife that he would not sign any agreement detrimental to Hungary's interest. By April 15 he hoped that Hungary would be able to field a new army and with new allies clear the occupied areas. Károlyi also hoped that with such a victory his plan for a United States of Eastern Europe would be realized.[65] Though Károlyi did not elaborate on what he meant by new allies, it is not unlikely that he meant Russia, Germany and possibly Austria.

Hungary's intention to oppose any dictated peace was made quite clear to visiting military missions as well as to Colonel Vix. On February 28 Cuninghame was in Budapest again to investigate Czechoslovak complaints that the Hungarians were massing armies against the Czechs. Accompanying Cuninghame was Ellis Ashmead-Bartlett, a British news reporter, whom the British colonel considered an ideal agent to spy out the military situation in Hungary.

Ashmead-Bartlett had little sympathy for Károlyi or his government, for he considered that "his ministers and supporters were composed of the lowest elements in the land, mostly little Jews."[66] In spite of such negative attitudes the British journalist was unable to confirm the charges, and reported that they were "entirely invented by the Czechs."[67]

As a news reporter Ashmead-Bartlett was able to accompany Károlyi on an inspection tour of the Sekler Division at Szatmárnémeti (Satu Mare), a town which was claimed by the Rumanians. During the tour Károlyi had occasion to address the troops. He told them:

> If Wilson's principles do not materialize, and instead of
> a peace based on mutual agreement a dictated peace
> demanding territorial dismemberment is offered: I promise
> you, soldiers, I will never sign such peace terms![68]

Károlyi also gave a speech to the worried citizens of the town, reassuring them that the area would remain Hungarian:

> I will never accept the dismemberment of Hungary! The
> world must understand that if the Paris Peace Conference
> decides against the right of popular self-determination based
> on mutual agreements, then as an extreme necessity we will
> liberate our country with arms in our hands.[69]

Károlyi's adherence to self-determination reflected his unshaken belief that the nationalities would choose to remain in Hungary. This belief was reinforced by the fact that on March 2, the same day Károlyi addressed the citizens of Szatmárnémeti, Budapest recognized autonomous Eastern Slovakia as part of Hungary. The law claimed that its borders were to be determined by the Peace Conference. Sovereignty over this territory was in the hands of the Slovak Council (Rada) of Eperjes (Prešov) under the Presidency of Győző Dvorcsák.[70] This assembly of pro-Hungarian Slovaks was even less representative than the pro-Czech Slovak National Council of Turóczszentmárton (Turčiansky Svätý Martin) but it seemed to bear out the hopeful contention that there was no universal desire among the Slovaks to unite with the Czechs.

Károlyi's militant speech given to the Seklers was also significant as, according to Vix, the division had military and moral superiority over the Rumanian troops in Transylvania.[71] Thus it indicated Hungarian willingness to challenge Allied decisions by force. Hungarian exasperation over Allied attitudes was aggravated by exactions made by Vix at the end of the month of February in the aftermath of an incident involving some undisciplined Hungarian soldiers who, acting without superior orders, stopped a munitions train in the northern city of Miskolc. The train was destined for Poland under French supervision, and carried arms that the Hungarian government wanted to exchange for coal. The soldiers fired at the locomotive, disarmed the French guards and refused to let the train pass.

In reprisal for the incident, Vix demanded an immediate indemnity of two million rounds of ammunition.[72] Such an act was indeed contrary to the spirit of the Peace Conference which allowed for reparations but not indemnities. The exasperated minister of defense, Böhm, decided to refuse the demand by handing his resignation to the government.

Colonel Cuninghame, who was in Budapest, was much opposed to Böhm's resignation because he considered him an anti-communist. In an attempt to have Böhm retained in government, Cuninghame went to see Böhm's socialist colleague Garami and asked him to try to talk Böhm out of his decision. Garami agreed but warned that Vix's performance could lead to catastrophe. He told Cuninghame that the Hungarian government, with the support of its constituent parties, might take steps that would be tragic not only for Hungary but for the whole of Europe.[73] Cuninghame promised to intervene on behalf of the beleaguered Hungarians—a promise he reiterated in a letter written to Böhm on March 3. He asked Böhm to stay on as minister and promised to ask Vix to rescind his demand. He assured Böhm that England looked to a just and moderate government in Hungary. Cuninghame asked Böhm to reconsider for this reason, since his departure would be deemed to be a further shift to the left by Hungary.[74] In spite of such promises, Vix did not repeal his order, issued without the consultation of his superiors. Rather, his order was strengthened when, on March 12, a telegram from General de Lobit in Belgrade carried a congratulatory message from Franchet d'Esperey commending Vix for the firmness he had exhibited toward the Hungarians.[75] The train episode therefore underlined a further conflict of opinion by the different Allied representatives in Hungary. Moreover, the congratulatory message not only enhanced Vix's dictatorial posture but encouraged the French colonel to act independently, without waiting for superior command.

Hungarian resistance to Allied demands was dependent on eliminating the rift between the two Marxist parties, the socialists and the communists. An understanding between the two parties was slowly being realized. On March 11, Ignác Bogár, of the Metal Workers' Union was dispatched to conduct talks with the imprisoned Béla Kun. The outcome of the conversations was a memorandum drawn up by Kun outlining the communists' conditions for rapprochement. Kun still demanded that all power should be transferred to the councils of workers and soldiers. He also insisted on thoroughgoing socialization. On foreign policy he called for the abandonment of "the bourgeois concept of territorial sovereignty," Hungary's support for the Third International and a Russian orientation:

> It is my belief that the salvation of the Hungarian proletariat will not be achieved by American food blackmail or by coal bought for munitions supplied to the Polish and Ukrainian lackeys of the Entente, as these acts can only put the Hungarians in bondage. First of all we must look for alliances with the revolutionary Russian, German, Latvian and Ukrainian proletariat.[76]

Thus by mid-March many political leaders were apparently contemplating a decisive change, turning from a sterile pro-Anglo-American policy to friendship with Russia. By March 14 a report was circulating among the right-wing opposition leaders that Károlyi had already composed a draft of a declaration calling for Russian orientation of Hungary. According to the account supplied by an inside informer, Károlyi's declaration was to transfer power from the Berinkey government to a government that was made up of members of a socialist-communist coalition. The new government was to oppose further demands of the Allies in military alliance with the Soviet Russians.[77] Whether such a document existed or not cannot be substantiated, but that Károlyi and other government leaders entertained cooperation with Russia is beyond doubts.

Vis also suspected Russo-Hungarian cooperation in response to Allied demands for the evacuation of Transylvania. Vix received the details of the February 26 decision of the Peace Conference on March 12.[78] The Allied command of the Balkans added the tactical details, whereby Hungarian withdrawal was to start on March 23 and had to be completed in ten days. The document was signed by de Lobit, but was not accompanied by any specific instruction for its delivery. Vix, who was personally experiencing the growing impatience of the Hungarians, believed that transmission of the memorandum was not appropriate at that time because it would bring down the government. He also observed that in northeastern Hungary the Ruthenian corridor between the Czechoslovaks and the Rumanians was left in the hands of Hungary. Vix, who felt that a Russo-Hungarian alliance in defiance of Allied demands was likely, decided to warn his superiors that, through the strategic Ruthenian town of Csap, the Hungarians could be the recipients of Soviet aid. To avoid such possibility, Vix suggested the establishment of a French control commission at Csap, a scheme that soon carried the approval of Franchet d'Esperey.[79] In order to prevent the Hungarians from learning of Rumanian military preparations along the demarcation line, Vix ordered the Hungarians to stop their observation flights along their borders. He claimed that disregard of his request would lead to the blockade of the food supplies being imported.[80]

Though Vix did his best to prepare grounds for the Allied démarche in secret, Károlyi was informed of the events to come. The president's informer was the American military attaché to Bucharest, Halsey E. Yates. While in transit, Lieutenant Colonel Yates stopped in Budapest on March 15. Károlyi, who made it his business to talk to all Allied visitors, took the opportunity to meet Yates too. The Hungarian leader used this meeting to complain to Yates about the Czechoslovak occupation of Slovakia and about the Rumanian advances in Transylvania.[81] Károlyi claimed that, according to military intelligence, the Rumanians were gathering forces and supplies along the borders.[82] Yates told Károlyi in reply that Slovakia was accorded to the Czechoslovaks by the Peace Conference. He also warned Károlyi that Transylvania must also be ceded to Rumania if the Peace Conference so decided. What Yates clearly implied to Károlyi was that rumors of the February 26 decision were true. Apparently Yates was aware of Hungarian willingness to resist such decision and warned Károlyi to accept Allied demands. He claimed that even though the Allies did not have sufficient armies around Hungary to reply in force to Hungarian intransigence, they possessed other means. Yates hinted at Allied intervention in food supplies and in financial settlements.[83] This conversation thus can be construed as the first official notification to Károlyi about the changes in the Transylvanian demarcation line.

During his brief sojourn in Budapest, Yates also visited Lieutenant Philip Goodwin, the representative of the Coolidge mission, and lastly Colonel Vix. Yates described to Vix the substance of his conversation with Károlyi. Yates also indicated his fears about the situation in the Ukraine and expressed his intention of telegraphing to Paris and requesting the suspension of Rumanian advances into Hungary until the Rumanians were strong enough to defeat the Hungarians in case of a conflict. He also thought that along with the French officers Anglo-American officers should be sent to the neutral zone for supervisory purposes.[84] Yates' communication clearly indicated that he favored the postponement of the execution of the memorandum in Vix's hands. Vix was greatly taken aback by what Yates had to tell him. Clearly, Yates was meddling in the affairs of Hungary which raised the specter of dual authority again. Moreover, Vix's secret was out.

The Hungarians, however, failed to protest about the news that Károlyi received. The only sign of Hungarian defiance came from prime minister Berinkey, who challenged Vix's interdiction of spy flights in the vicinity of Csucsa and threatened to resign if Vix cut food supplies to Hungary.[85]

It was not only Yates who was preoccupied with the situation in the Ukraine. The French also became more concerned with the situation. This was occasioned by a sudden turn in the fortunes of the anti-Bolshevik coalition in southern Russia. On March 1, Franchet d'Esperey had informed Clemenceau and Foch that contingents of the Red Army under Colonel A. I. Yegorov were advancing on a front stretching from Troiskaya to Pekatchevo. According to intelligence reports, they were to be reinforced by the 20,000 men of the First Army supported by artillery.[86] Thus at a time when Marshal Foch was looking to Rumanian intervention in Russia, the Red Army was threatening to carry the war into Rumania and recapture Bessarabia.

The change of circumstances in Russia also brought a change in Clemenceau's attitude. When on March 1, General Berthelot formally requested his recall from Rumania, Clemenceau lacked the acerbity of his communications of January. He told Berthelot that the situation in the east had become more delicate and, for this reason, he could not terminate his mission. Rather, he suggested that Berthelot should come to Paris at a convenient time for an interview.[87] Clemenceau's temperate response to Berthelot must have upset Franchet d'Esperey for soon after he went out of his way to discredit Berthelot by blaming the crisis in southern Russia on him. He reported that, at a time when no reinforcements were coming from France and the power of the Allied forces was being reduced by attrition, Berthelot encouraged Rumania's expansion into Transylvania. As a result, there was a shortage of troops in Bessarabia at this critical juncture.[88]

By the time Franchet d'Esperey filed his new attack on Berthelot, the situation in southern Russia had deteriorated further. In February the Allied troops had occupied Tiraspol, Kherson and Nikolaev. On March 10 the pro-Bolshevik forces of Ataman Grigoriev retook Kherson, and by March 14 Nikolaev had fallen. Soon the Reds were advancing on Odessa.[89] To stop the tide of Bolshevik victories, Franchet d'Esperey proposed to his superiors in Paris a new line of Bessarabian defense along the Dniester river. He saw the need to put the Rumanian army and the Allied forces under a unified command and proposed General Berthelot for the job so that he himself could undo the errors he had committed. If Berthelot continued to falter, Franchet d'Esperey nominated General Degoutte to head a single general staff that would include the Rumanian army under its command.[90]

On March 12 Franchet d'Esperey sped another telegram to Clemenceau about the Russian situation. He said that he was aware that Berthelot was directly responsible to Clemenceau for Russia but, according to his orders of January 28, he was in charge of operations in the east and they were being threatened by developments in Russia. The Allied commander stated that it was no longer a question of marauding bands of Bolsheviks but of well-organized and well-disciplined troops under strong command who were imposing order on the chaotic situation in southern Russia. He added that local xenophobia was eroding the morale of the Allied troops. The indigenous population was hostile to them and shot many in the back in Kherson as the Red Army was approaching. He warned that repetition of such incidents in Odessa, a city of 900,000, could have dangerous consequences.[91]

Clemenceau's reply came the following day. He ordered Berthelot to deploy Rumanian troops in defense of the Tiraspol-Razdelnaya-Odessa railway line, which was considered a vital link in Odessa's defense, and promised to send several battalions of French infantry to reinforce the city.[92] On March 14, new directives cancelled Berthelot's intended visit to Paris. Apparently Clemenceau also became convinced that Berthelot's powers should be curtailed. Thus using the pretext of Berthelot's complaint that communications between Bucharest and Paris were poor, Clemenceau relieved him of his Russian command. Provisionally, the French Premier and Minister of War appointed Franchet d'Esperey to command the Allied forces in southern Russia.[93] For the first time, all the Allied forces in eastern Europe were truly under the command of one man.

The new emergency in Russia gave the Rumanians the opportunity to press for the execution of the February 26 Paris decision concerning the withdrawal of Hungarians beyond a new demarcation line. The same day Berthelot lost his Russian command, a member of the Rumanian delegation to the Peace Conference, Victor Antonescu, sent a memorandum to Clemenceau stressing the obvious—the possibility of an attack on the Rumanians by the Bolsheviks. He asserted that, according to Rumanian intelligence reports, the Hungarians had reached an accord with the Bolsheviks in the Ukraine and were about to launch their own offensive against Rumania. This claim was completely baseless, but it provided the grounds to argue that Rumania was now encircled and was the last bastion against Bolshevism. Antonescu therefore requested stronger Allied support for Rumanian needs.

Having identified the Hungarians as allies of the Reds, Antonescu's memorandum went on to complain of Franchet d'Esperey's slow handling of the Peace Conference's decision of February 26. He claimed that while Franchet d'Esperey was looking for a suitable French officer to supervise the Peace Conference's order, the Hungarians were stripping Transylvania and spreading Bolshevik agitation. These charges were also baseless, but they bolstered his request for immediate action *vis á vis* Hungary. Antonescu reasoned that, since the Reds in the Ukraine and the Hungarians were allies, a commander was needed who would be in charge of southern Russia, Transylvania and Hungary. There is little doubt that Antonescu wanted to see Berthelot expand his independent command to Hungary. At this juncture it is evident that Antonescu was not aware of the fact that the Hungarophobe and Rumanophile General Berthelot was relieved of his duties in Russia on the self-same day of the delivery of the Rumanian memorandum. Nevertheless, in the atmosphere of anti-Bolshevik hysteria in Paris, Antonescu's arguments had their effect. That very day Clemenceau sent new orders to Franchet d'Esperey about the February 26 decision. Using almost exactly the same words as Antonescu's memorandum, Clemenceau's new orders referred to the Hungarian scorched-earth policy in Transylvania and urged Franchet d'Esperey to put the Peace Conference's decision into effect without further delay. Clemenceau also proposed to organize a mixed commission of French, Hungarian and Rumanian members to see that his orders were executed.[94]

The reason for Clemenceau's sudden support for Rumania's appeal for the swift implementation of the February 26 decision is clear. In the light of Franchet d'Esperey's reports, it is unlikely that he was taken in by the invention of a Hungarian-Bolshevik alliance. Rather, the French leader wanted to make sure the Rumanians were rewarded for their intended support of the troubled Allies in southern Russia. The price for Rumania's loyalty was the speedy occupation of areas accorded to them by the Peace Conference. Thus while such a lesser American official as Colonel Yates saw salvation in the new crisis in southern Russia through the postpone- ment of the transmission of the February 26 decision, the powerful French leader's solution was to the contrary.

With his new orders from Premier Clemenceau, Franchet d'Esperey proceeded to carry them out. On March 19, the Commander in Chief ordered General de Lobit in Belgrade to transmit the February 26 decision to the Hungarians. At the same time he appointed General de Gondrecourt to deliver the Allied *demarché* to President Károlyi. De Gondrecourt was also put in command of the neutral zone.[95]

The boundaries of the neutral zone troubled Franchet d'Esperey as they troubled de Lobit, who as early as March 7 had proposed extending the zone to the Hungarian frontier in the Carpathians. Their reason was to prevent a Rumanian-Hungarian clash in Ruthenia, above the neutral zone designated by the Peace Conference. Franchet d'Esperey therefore ordered de Lobit to extend the neutral zone all the way to Galicia,[96] including the city of Munkács (Mukachevo), an area claimed by Eduard Beneš for the Czechoslovaks.

Franchet d'Esperey's order enlarging the neutral zone should have been cleared by the Peace Conference first, but there was no time for that. Clemenceau's order brooked no delay. So Franchet d'Esperey asked

Clemenceau to have the change in the neutral zone approved by the Peace Conference *ex post facto*, and make it appear to the Hungarians that it was part of the original Allied demand.[97] In his zeal to execute Clemenceau's wishes and to ensure that Rumanian troops would be available to fight the Russians and not the Hungarians, he wanted Clemenceau to present the Allies with a *fait accompli*. This way it would be the task of the Allies rather than French troops to coerce Hungary into accepting the ultimatum.[98]

Once the order had been issued for General de Lobit to begin putting the provisions of the memorandum into effect, General Franchet d'Esperey embarked on an inspection tour of Odessa on March 19. But his order hit a snag, for General de Gondrecourt was not in Budapest to hand the memorandum to the Hungarians. For General de Lobit time was pressing and rather than allowing time for de Gondrecourt to reach Budapest, he ordered Colonel Vix to transmit the order to the Hungarians. It seems that de Lobit's undue haste was motivated by his assumption that the Yates encounter with Károlyi was leading to the organization of Hungarian resistance. At the same time he ordered Vix to take action he also sent an explanation to Franchet d'Esperey:

> While transmitting the information, I draw your attention
> to the drawbacks of the missions of various nationalities,
> traveling without checks and, as it may be without mandates.
> They forewarn about decisions often in contradiction to the
> will of that authority qualified to give them. In the present
> case, the intervention of Colonel Yates shall have had the
> result of warning the Hungarians in advance about the
> intentions of the Congress of Paris and giving them time to
> prepare resistance and objection.[99]

Subsequently, Franchet d'Esperey approved de Lobit's change in the procedure as he (Franchet d'Esperey) reported to Clemenceau that the American might have given the Hungarians advance notice. When de Lobit ordered Vix to hand the memorandum over to the Hungarians, another order of Franchet d'Esperey was overlooked. Franchet d'Esperey had told de Lobit to extend the neutral zone into Ruthenia, but de Lobit ordered Vix to deliver the original text of the memorandum which defined the neutral zone.[100] Vix was instructed to present the memorandum on March 20, giving the Hungarians forty-eight hours to reply.[101] He was also informed that if the Hungarians refused to accept the decision of the Peace Conference, no immediate war-like acts would be instituted against them.[102]

Upon the receipt of the new orders, Vix immediately contacted all Allied representatives whom de Lobit was so critical about. Vix invited them for a meeting that was to take place on the following morning, the 20th of March. Lieutenant Goodwin, who was just leaving for Paris, could only guess the purpose of the briefing session: rightly, he thought it would be about the neutral zone. When he arrived in Paris on the twenty-second, still unaware of the most recent Hungarian developments, he expressed his opinion that the memorandum's transmissions to Károlyi was inadvisable and warned the American plenipotentiaries of the consequences of the terms of the memorandum:

> The results of this order will be extremely serious. It places a large number of Hungarians under Rumanian domination, and is likely to arouse the national feeling of the people to a greater extent than any other act which has taken place up to the present time.[103]

The only thing that Goodwin failed to perceive was that Vix called the other Allied representatives together in order to have them present when he gave the memorandum to President Károlyi. He claimed that their presence was needed for proof that the decision of the Peace Conference was taken by the American, French, Italian and British governments in unison. Captain Nicholas Roosevelt, the newly arrived representative of the Coolidge Mission in Budapest, however, was uncertain of the propriety of his presence at the transaction. For this reason, he telephoned to Vienna for instructions, but he was unable to reach Professor Coolidge. Being at a loss as to what to do, he finally succumbed to the urgings of his Allied colleagues and went with them to meet Károlyi at ten o'clock in the morning. Captain Roosevelt's final decision thus played right into the hands of Vix, who was now able to parade before Károlyi as a man who had solid Allied backing in his present endeavor.

Vix and the other representatives found Károlyi alone in his presidential office. Upon the receipt of the memorandum Károlyi read it halfway through and then asked Vix if he could send for his minister of war, since the withdrawal was of a military nature. Vix suggested that Károlyi send for his prime minister as well, implying that the pullback had political significance too. At this juncture Károlyi remarked with some rancor that the Allies might make Hungary a French colony or a colony of Rumania or of Czechoslovakia.[104] Károlyi said that the ultimatum was unacceptable for it clearly showed that Hungary was to be dismembered. Any government that signed such a document, he added, would not last a day.

Böhm and Berinkey joined the discussion. With the two ministers present, Károlyi went on to question the sincerity of the memorandum which was to separate the Rumanians and Hungarians while drawing no zone in Ruthenia, where, as Károlyi claimed, the Rumanians and the Czechoslovaks could join forces and press for more Hungarian territory. Berinkey reinforced his president's argument by saying that indeed the Rumanians received the green light to do exactly that.[105]

Apparently Vix was unaware that it was precisely along this Hungarian line that Franchet d'Esperey argued in his request to Clemenceau to extend the neutral zone to the Carpathians. Had Franchet d'Esperey had more time to work out detailed military plans for the neutral zone, the likelihood of the Czechs and Rumanians permanently linking forces in northeastern Hungary would have been reduced, the fears of the Hungarians allayed and the collapse of the Károlyi regime prevented.

The Hungarian Minister of War, Vilmos Böhm, insisted the new line was contradictory to the Belgrade Convention. Vix repeatedly asserted that the new line had nothing to do with the cease-fire line but was a decision of the Peace Conference—though he stressed the decision was by no means final. Böhm, with Károlyi acting as interpreter, declared that the Communist Party would gain 200,000 new members in protest of the Allied demands. When Károlyi asked what happened if the government refused to heed de Lobit's orders, Vix replied curtly "Alors nous ferons nos malles."[106] Since the original responsibility of the Vix mission was to oversee the armistice, the threatened withdrawal of the mission, in the presence of other Allied representatives, was tantamount to the resumption of hostilities. Since Vix was aware that the Army of the Orient was in no position to fight and that, upon the rejection of the memorandum by the Hungarians, he was ordered to do nothing, his threat could be considered as a bluff. At this juncture it is puzzling why Károlyi did not inform Vix that he was aware that the Allies were in no position to start a war against Hungary. Rather than doing that, Károlyi proceeded to threaten Vix with his resignation. Thus a bluff was answered with a bluff. Previously such threats did move the Vix mission to moderation and apparently Károlyi thought that this old routine could move Vix to suspend negotiations and ask for new instructions from Belgrade.

Indeed, according to de Lobit's communication, upon Hungarian rejection of the memorandum, Vix should have followed such procedure. The French officer clearly acted in excess of his instructions.[107] He threatened war with Hungary without indicating that such act required the sanction of the Paris Peace Conference. Before leaving Károlyi, Vix added to his dictatorial posture by reducing the grace period from 48 to 30 hours. Moreover, he insisted that Károlyi had no other choice but to accept or reject the memorandum. This way the de Lobit memorandum became the Vix ultimatum. The encouragement that Vix received from Franchet d'Esperey to act on his own now reached tragic proportions. The limited time that was given to the Hungarians to answer the ultimatum was leading to a new governmental crisis.

That same morning, after the Vix encounter, Defense Minister Böhm called on his two chief military advisors, Colonels Stromfeld and Tombor. He asked them to prepare a map with new borders and to give their advice on how acceptable they were. Within half an hour they suggested the rejection of the Vix ultimatum, claiming that the new borders would result in the complete economic, political and military destruction of Hungary. At the same time Böhm was informed that, if the ultimatum were accepted, the crack Sekler Division in Transylvania would refuse to follow orders. Colonel Tombor added to the collective decision an appeal for an eastern orientation of the nation's foreign policy and for a mass levy to defend the country. He told Böhm that a socialist government capable of organizing the masses had to be formed. He also suggested a compromise with the communists so that there could be cooperation with the Soviet Russian forces in Galicia.[108]

In the afternoon the Social Democratic Party central committee held an emergency meeting to discuss what had transpired. It was Böhm who took the floor first. He unfolded the map prepared by his advisors and reiterated their conclusion. He moved for a socialist take-over of the government on the grounds that the present cabinet would not be able to lead the country in a fight against encirclement. He also advocated an immediate understanding with the communists to avoid "a stab in the back."[109] His proposals were discussed but the committee decided to postpone a decision until after the emergency cabinet meeting that was to take place that evening. Meanwhile, one of the socialists' leaders, Jenő Landler, was sent to Kun's prison to find out the communists' reaction to the Vix ultimatum and their position on the possible establishment of a socialist dictatorship.[110] Landler considered his mission of utmost importance and, with Kun, began to negotiate a socialist-communist understanding.[111]

At the emergency cabinet meeting Károlyi stated his position, which was similar to that of the socialists. He spoke of the need to form a socialist cabinet in place of the coalition. He admitted that his pro-American policy had been defeated and emphasized the necessity to marshal forces that would save the country. He called on his socialist ministers to come to an understanding with the communists, since a life-and-death struggle for the country was about to take place against the imperialist powers. He volunteered to remain as president until the situation had stabilized. Böhm endorsed Károlyi's proposals but made the formation of a socialist cabinet contingent on the communists' support for the socialists. Kunfi, on the other hand, suggested that the coalition should remain in power and should make a final attempt to open the Allies' eyes to the consequences of the Vix ultimatum. Ernő Garami reminded the ministers of the failure of their Western policy and saw no justification for putting any further effort into appeals to the Allies. The President of the National Council, János Hock, in the name of the Károlyi Party announced the party's withdrawal from the cabinet in order to make it easier for the socialists to come to an understanding with the communists. The other nonsocialist ministers were also willing to resign in favor of the socialists. The council finally decided on the rejection of the ultimatum and the resignation of the cabinet. In place of the coalition a socialist ministry would be formed under Károlyi.[112]

The news of the Vix ultimatum was greeted with defiance by the populace. On the morning of the twenty-first, a meeting at the industrial suburb of Csepel of representatives of the biggest factories of Budapest demanded an immediate change of Hungarian foreign policy and an alliance with Russia. Representatives of soldier councils were also present at the meeting. They also supported the resolution. As a sign of defiance some soldiers began to drag cannons to the top of St. Gellert Hill, a nine hundred foot high mountain in the middle of Budapest. Such an act was an sanctioned by the government, even though the Soldiers' Council that met at three in the afternoon approved the action.

Crowds on the main thoroughfares of Budapest participated in spontaneous demonstrations and many of the civilians carried rifles and other weapons ready to defy Allied authorities. The powerful metallurgical union started to fulfill Böhm's stark warning of the previous day as 30,000 of its members voted to join the Communist Party.[113]

The socialists also met in the morning to consider the cabinet's decisions. With the exception of a few moderates the overwhelming majority of the party's central committee accepted the proposals for a socialist government and for unity with the communists. During the committee's discussion, Jenő Landler was able to report that the communists did not oppose union with the socialists. In the wake of Landler's report a five-man delegation was set up to return to prison to continue talks with the communists. The delegation consisted of Kunfi, Landler, Pogány, Weltner and Haubrich.[114] The communists were represented by Kun, Rabinovics, Vágo, Vantus, Seidler, Jancsik and Chlepko.

Their meetings were extremely brief. The socialists explained the government's predicament and claimed that the situation could be solved only by unity among the workers' parties and by their joining the Third International. The communists accepted the socialists' offer and a joint communiqué was drafted. It was agreed that the newly united party would temporarily take the name of the Socialist Party of Hungary until the Third International had decided on a final name for it. Communists were to receive posts in the government while the "dictatorship of the proletariat" would be assured through the workers' and soldiers' councils. The plans for a national election were abandoned. The concluding sentence of the joint communiqué pointed to what the government's new foreign policy was to be: "For the assurance of proletarian rule in the struggle against the Entente imperialism, a complete military and ideological alliance must be achieved with the Soviet Russian government."[115]

It is likely that in addition to the written agreement the communist and socialist leaders decided to make their take-over really "revolutionary" by removing Károlyi. The purpose of this would be to dispel any notion that the socialist take-over was merely a cabinet shake-up without socio-political consequences. It is also likely that foreign-policy considerations played a part, for it was known that the Russians considered Károlyi a lackey of the Allies. The likelihood is strengthened in the light of the fact that when the cabinet met at five o'clock the socialist ministers informed neither their colleagues nor Károlyi that the socialists and communists had succeeded in coming to an understanding as has been suggested.

They evidently refrained from telling Károlyi about the accord because they did not wish to let him know that his dismissal was part of it.[116] Since only the previous evening Károlyi had declared his intention of remaining president, the socialists may have feared that he would refuse to step down. The cabinet's resignation became effective at six o'clock, when the time allotted in the Vix ultimatum expired. Károlyi then officially informed the French representative that the cabinet had chosen to resign rather than accept the ultimatum. The last order issued by his ministers came from Sándor Juhász Nagy, the minister of justice, who ordered the chief prosecutor, Albert Váry, to free Béla Kun and the remaining imprisoned communists. With the written resignations in his hands, Károlyi turned to Zsigmond Kunfi to form a socialist cabinet. Kunfi still failed to apprise Károlyi that the power to appoint a new prime minister was no longer in his grasp.[117]

At six o'clock the Workers' Council met also. It was urged to accept the cabinet ministers' resignations. Originally it had been hoped that the council would nominate Kunfi as prime minister, a decision that would then be handed to Károlyi who was waiting for it at his office in the Sándor Palace. The council meeting was opened by Sándor Garbai, who declared:

> The imperialists of the Entente took democracy and national self-determination as their slogans, but since victory they have acted differently. Our hope for peace was destroyed by the ukase from Colonel Vix. There is no longer any doubt that those gentlemen in Paris wish to give us an imperialist peace. . . . From now on we must look to the east for justice, as it has been denied to us in the west.[118]

Garbai then informed the delegates of the fusion of the two Marxist workers' parties. The purpose of the union was the formation of a socialist government which could identify itself with the interests of the Bolsheviks' government of Lenin and which could offer and gain a military alliance with Soviet Russia.[119]

The resistant mood of the Workers' Council was reflected by the enthusiastic reception of Garbai's speech. The council, which only weeks before ejected its communist members, now applauded the newly-welded Marxist unity. Moreover, with its newly recovered legislative authority, the council called for the establishment of the Hungarian Soviet Republic.

National indignation over the Vix memorandum thus turned the delegates into supporters of Bolshevik internationalism. The meeting was closed with the words of the Socialist Dezső Bokányi who noted that the decision of the council was "the greatest and most sacred goal of the proletariat."[120] In the light of the above discussion, however, Bokányi's words had a hollow ring to them.

After the Workers' Council had decided to create a new governmental system, the telephone rang in Károlyi's residence. His secretary Henrik Simonyi answered it and, as if following prearranged plans, rushed into Károlyi's study and handed him a typewritten sheet, asking him to sign it without delay. The document was Károlyi's resignation. Károlyi refused and asked who had written the document since he had not done so. Simonyi then admitted that it was he who had drawn it up in collaboration with the socialist journalist, Pál Kéri. He justified his action by saying that he wanted to avoid an intraparty fight at the Workers' Council meeting between Károlyi's supporters and the others.[121] Károlyi still refused to sign. Simonyi then left Károlyi's study but returned a few minutes later saying that the morning papers were already on the streets and wall posters had been pasted up announcing the resignation and the proclamation of a proletarian dictatorship. Faced with a well-organized coup, Károlyi accepted the *fait accompli* and signed "his" resignation rather than risk causing worse confusion.[122]

That same evening at nine o'clock Kun, now at liberty, met with the other communist and socialist leaders in the office of the now defunct Social Democratic Party secretariat. They proceeded to form a provisional Revolutionary Governing Council. The new cabinet had two communist commissars. To counter-balance the socialist majority, the other commissars' assistants were also communists.[123] The direction of the new government's foreign policy was made evident by the appointment of Béla Kun as commissar of foreign affairs. The other communist commissar was Károly Vantus, who was commissar of agriculture. The inclusion of the minister of Ruszka-Krajna, Oreszt Szabó, in the cabinet, now also with the title of commissar, indicated the determination of the socialist-communist union to continue Hungary's fight for territorial integrity.

On the morning of March 22 a communiqué of the Revolutionary Governing Council informed Hungarians of the changes. Printed on posters under the slogan "To Everybody," the communiqué declared that "the country could be saved from collapse and anarchy only by socialism and communism." It explained that with the borders proposed in the ultimatum Hungary would have been economically strangled. A dictatorship of the proletariat was therefore necessary to save the Hungarian revolution. The manifesto called for iron discipline and promised death to looters and counter-revolutionaries. As far as the foreign policy of the new government was concerned, the manifesto declared:

> It [the government] will organize a gigantic proletarian army that will strengthen the dictatorship against the Hungarian capitalists and magnates as well as the Rumanian boyars and Czech bourgeois.

> It [the government] declares complete ideological unity with the Soviet government and offers the proletariat of Russia a military alliance. It sends brotherly greetings to the workers of England, France, Italy and America and urges them not to permit villainous military intervention against the Hungarian Soviet Republic by their capitalist governments.[124]

The new leaders' appeal was a mixture of nationalist desperation and Marxist ideology, and as a result even those with little sympathy for Marxism declared in favor of the socialist dictatorship. The bourgeois daily *Nyugat* best summed up the reaction of the majority of Hungarians to the Vix ultimatum: "Not that! Rather Bolshevism a thousand times over!"[125] The communist paper *Vörös Újság* gave an ideological justification for preserving territorial integrity in an article entitled "The Entente against the Proletariat":

In power the Hungarian petite bourgeoisie could not answer the Vix ultimatum. They were forced to recognize that only the proletariat could oppose imperialism victoriously. The territorial integrity policy of these petite bourgeois parties, which aimed to protect their markets, gave way to the right of self-determination of the proletariat.[126]

The first cabinet meeting of the new government took place on March 22. The cabinet decided to notify Russia of the changes that had taken place in Hungary and to ask for a military alliance.[127] At the same time Vix was ordered put under close surveillance. The order was issued in response to a telegram that Vix sent to Belgrade allegedly requesting General Franchet d'Esperey for 15,000 troops to crush the revolution. The cabinet also ordered the telegrapher who cooperated with Vix by sending the telegram over Hungarian government cables to be court-martialed.[128]

The ministry of foreign affairs was occupied by Kun on March 22, though the formal transfer of office from Harrer to him did not take place until March 24. An aid to Kun, Ernő Por, pointed up the magnitude of the change to Harrer by comparing Kun's arrival at the ministry to Trotsky's arrival in the Russian revolution. Kun was less fulsome and told Harrer that they would have occasion in the future to cooperate. This promise went unfilled, but Kun did have occasion to work with the former foreign minister, Mihály Károlyi.

On March 26, the day the Vix mission left Hungary, Kun contacted Károlyi, asking him to transmit a Hungarian offer to the Allies. Kun asked Károlyi to go to Vienna to contact the allies. Kun wanted to make a deal with them. In return for a guarantee of Hungary's integrity, Kun volunteered to mediate differences between the Allies and Russia. Kun also pledged that Hungarian forces would not link up with the Russian Red Army and the government would not disseminate propaganda abroad. For their part the Allies were to promise that plebiscites would be held in the disputed areas and food aid would be given to Hungary. Károlyi accepted the mission and left for Vienna on March 30. He accomplished little as the Allies were busy assigning a representative to go to Hungary to investigate the new situation.[129]

The Allies were very preoccupied by events in Hungary. On March 25 the Council of Four met to discuss them. President Wilson was at a loss as to how the Allies should deal with the socialists in Hungary, a country he considered friendly. Clemenceau vehemently denied that the Hungarians were friends of the Allies. He argued that, while the other Austro-Hungarian peoples had fought against the Allies in spite of themselves, the Magyars and their leaders, including Tisza, were directly responsible for the war.[130] Two days later President Wilson criticized the interventionist policy of the French and suggested that the Allies should keep their hands off Hungary if "Bolshevism" was to be contained within its borders. He was supported by Lloyd George, who was against intervention on the grounds that few countries in Europe needed a social revolution as badly as Hungary.[131]

Later, on March 29, when the Hungarian problem was on the agenda again, the British prime minister asked why the Magyars and Croats should not receive the same treatment when they had fought against the Allies with equal vigor. He said that Clemenceau was wrong in declaring that the Magyar electorate was limited. Now, months too late, Lloyd George wanted the Allies to establish relations with Hungary:

> We maintain relations with the Croats and the Slovenes although they have on their conscience the death of innumerable Allied soldiers. Why not make contact with the Magyars as well?[132]

Thus Allied recognition, which had been withheld from the Károlyi regime, was now proposed by the Anglo-Americans for the Kun regime. On March 31, Lansing even admitted that the Allies had a certain responsibility for what had happened in Hungary. It seemed as though diplomatic contact with Kun was to be an atonement for the mistakes of the past. Even at this stage, however, the French were against any dealings with Hungary. Pichon was at pains to remind his colleagues that "Béla Kun was the friend and accomplice of Lenin."[133]

On March 31 the Council of Four decided to send South African General Jan Christiaan Smuts to Hungary to investigate the situation. At last an emissary of the Big Four was to visit Budapest. But even before he was appointed to head the mission to Hungary, Smuts had pinpointed the reasons for the collapse of the Károlyi regime when he wrote to Lloyd George:

We cannot be blind to what has just happened in Hungary. Károlyi was favorable to us and endeavouring to work with us, but found no encouragement. Rumania and Serbia had to be placated with Hungarian territory. Result: Hungary is now joining hands with Bolshevist Russia. . . .[134]

Smuts' observation justly summarized the cause for the Hungarian crisis. The revived hopes of mid-February that the Allies would finally pay some attention to Hungary's cause gave way to despair in March. Abandoned by the West, the Vix ultimatum served to count out the Frostflower Revolution. Kunfi's ominous warnings that Hungary could choose between Lenin and Wilson were borne out. Thus it was no mere accident that this Hungarian Cassandra was one of the leaders to institute Hungary's *volte face*. The Hungarians felt that their ideals were betrayed by Wilson—they turned to Lenin for deliverance.

CONCLUSIONS

The October revolution of 1918 was born out of the defeat of an oligarchy which had pinned its hopes of survival on what turned out to be a lost war.

Military defeat and Allied insistence on the establishment of representative government as a precondition for peace assisted the revolutionary forces in Hungary in their quest for power. The revolutionary government of Mihály Károlyi aimed to liquidate the quasi-feudal remnants of an outmoded order. It promised universal suffrage, agrarian reforms, tax reforms and the division of large estates. Károlyi counted on Allied support and sympathy once the armistice was signed. He expected the United States to play a major role in bringing Hungary back into the community of nations.

The democratic ideals of Wilson, his calls for new diplomacy and internationalism were eagerly embraced by the Hungarian revolutionaries. Moreover, Jászi's plan for an "Eastern Switzerland" as a solution for the century-old nationalities problem was a further illustration of Hungary's willingness to attempt novel solutions.

The expectations of the supporters of the revolution were disappointed. Hostility greeted the People's Republic of Hungary. Serbian, Rumanian, and Czechoslovak armies flouted the Belgrade convention of November 13, 1918 with the open support of France. At the same time, the Hungarian republic received little encouragement from the other great powers: England and, more importantly, the United States.

It is evident that President Wilson remained loyal to his foreign policy directive of November 1, 1918, which kept the United States out of direct involvement in East Central European affairs, especially those of Hungary. Visiting American missions recommended measures to ease Hungary's economic and political crises. These suggestions, however, never took concrete shapes. The numerous letters of Hungarian leaders sent to President Wilson remained unanswered. The lone enthusiastic pro-Károlyi voice of George Creel in Wilson's immediate entourage failed to move the American leader to action.

Jászi's plan for a federated Central Europe fell on deaf ears. The cry for national sovereignty had drowned the call for reason. Thus nation states were created in an area where they never existed before and where there-fore a federal system had some rudimentary basis as a Habsburg heritage.

Outright hostility and hands-off attitude toward Hungary were largely the outcome of the emotional atmosphere that affected all those who found themselves on the side of the victors at the end of the war. The fear of Bolshevism forced the hands of even those Allied policy-makers who seemed determined to remain objective and impartial. Effective participation in the Russian Civil War by Hungarian prisoners of war later became a stigma that had to be borne by the whole People's Republic. Internal democracy, permitting the Hungarian communists to function in Hungary in an orderly fashion, was interpreted by many Allied officials as a government conspiracy to spread Bolshevism.

Racial prejudices, the anti-Magyarism and anti-Semitism of many of the diplomats working outside the limelight also contributed to the Allies' unfriendly attitude toward Hungary. At her post in Switzerland Bédy-Schwimmer was avoided by the American ambassador because she was a Jew while her feminist sympathies were offensive to the host country. Her recall in January 1919 was symbolic of Hungarian failure.

American and British aloofness caused Hungarian policy to be redirected toward Soviet Russia, whose leader Lenin had indicated as early as November 1918 the willingness of Russia to support Hungary. The Hungarians warned the Allies from that month on that the lack of recognition of Hungary would prompt Budapest to turn to Moscow for help. This was the message of Jászi's Arad speech, in Kunfi's stern warning to Coolidge, Garami's plea to Cuninghame and Böhm's appeal to Vix. When their pleas remained unheeded, the Károlyi regime collapsed to be replaced by Béla Kun's Soviet Republic. His pro-Russian policy brought about a veritable diplomatic revolution for Hungary. Not since the projects of Peter the Great was there an instance when Hungary was in alliance with Russia.

It is significant to note that a reorganization of Hungarian foreign policy toward Russia was an implicit part of Károlyi's policy. A switch of Hungary's international relation did not come about earlier because it was hoped that the aims of the Frostflower Revolution could be perpetuated with Allied support. As Károlyi's pro-Western policy met with continual failure and the Bolsheviks seemed to be on their way to victory in Russia, the establishment of a Soviet Republic seemed to be the best way to preserve the accomplishments of the revolution. The socialists who dominated the Károlyi government agreed with the communists on social policy. It was on the question of the political leadership where the two Marxist parties differed. While the Social Democrats hoped to achieve socialism through evolution within a liberal parliamentary system the Communist Party opted for a dictatorship.[1] The failure of Károlyi's pro-Western policy healed the rift between the two Marxist parties at the expense of social democracy.

Béla Kun, the leader of the Hungarian Soviet Republic, like Károlyi before him, received his mandate for leadership as a result of his explicit attitudes in the area of foreign policy. Being a pupil of Lenin, he was most likely to attract the support of the Russian communists. As a commissar of foreign affairs of the republic, however, Kun did not change the basic aim of Hungarian foreign policy—the preservation of Hungary's territorial integrity. He rejected the new Allied terms presented to him by General Smuts; a "new armistice line that was running further east than Colonel Vix's line."[2] The new demarcation line was to be declared a military boundary with no effect on the decisions to be made at Versailles. The South African also promised Kun his support for Hungary's invitation to the Peace Conference. In return Hungary had to observe the armistice agreement and stop rearming. These favorable conditions ought to have been accepted without delay, but were rejected by Kun on the grounds that they would lead to a second Brest-Litovsk.[3]

The birth of the communist republic gave the neighbors of Hungary the pretext they wanted to launch an invasion. It further gave them the excuse to dispense with the notion of plebiscites in the contested areas, claiming that the communist danger prevented them from following democratic practices.[4] By the end of April, the Rumanian Army was near Budapest. To stem the advance, class instinct merged with national pride and half the working population of Budapest enlisted in the newly formed Hungarian Red Army. This force was led by Vilmos Böhm and staffed mainly by former Imperial and Royal Army officers. The Red Army had several successful encounters with the invaders, but in the long run the odds proved to be overwhelmingly in favor of the aggressors.[5] All attempts by the Russian Red Army to link up with the Hungarians were frustrated by the sharp fighting taking place in the Ukraine between Red and White forces. As a consequence of the setbacks the Reds suffered at this time,

Commissar of War Trotsky's plan to form a separate Russian liberation army had to be abandoned.[6] Rather than having the Russians save the Hungarian revolution, the contrary seemed to be the case. As a result of the Rumanian intervention in Hungary, all the Rumanian interventionist forces were withdrawn from the Russian front, which reduced the pressures on the Red Army.

On August 1 the leaders of the Hungarian Soviet Republic resigned and fled the country. The right-wing socialist, Gyula Peidl, disassociating himself from his earstwhile allies, formed a new government that was overthrown within a few days by István Friedrich, who had the backing of the Habsburg Archduke Joseph. On November 14, 1919, the Rumanians occupying Budapest retreated from the Hungarian capital, taking as much loot as they could on the way. A few days after the Rumanian evacuation, the counter-revolutionary National Army, organized in Rumanian-occupied Szeged under French tutelage, entered Budapest with Admiral Miklós Horthy at its head.[7]

The months following the fall of the Soviet Republic were a period of "White Terror" during which thousands perished. Those suspected of communist sympathies were rounded up by terrorist gangs, beaten, tortured, and murdered. Jews especially were the victims of the terror as they were accused of being the major disseminators of communism.

In November the Friedrich government was replaced by one that was led by the clerical Károly Huszár with the support of Horthy's troops. In January 1920, under Allied pressure, elections were held for seats in the National Assembly. Social democratic candidates, however, were arrested as a danger to public safety, so the party boycotted the elections. The communists were legally barred from participating. Voting was supposed to be on the basis of universal suffrage, but the continued existence of the terror made a mockery of such principles.

The newly elected National Assembly, meeting in the Parliament building under the watchful eyes of the National Army, was forced to "elect" Admiral Horthy as Regent of the Kingdom of Hungary, over which he ruled until 1944. During his "reign" most social reforms introduced by the two republics were repealed and power was returned to those privileged classes who shared it before 1918. The recognition of this government by the Allies was the last example of the betrayal of the ideas of Wilson. If there was any segment of the Hungarian people that could be considered as culprits of the war, it was the ruling class which now had power again. Admiral Horthy as the wartime commander of the Austro-Hungarian Navy symbolized a leadership that Allied war pronouncements promised to destroy. Thus the Allies made it possible for the partial fulfillment of the war aims of the prewar oligarchy—the perpetuation of their socio-economic privileges.

If justice was served at Trianon, where Hungary was reduced to one-third of its prewar size, it was only because the harshest of all the peace treaties was accepted by men who were responsible for the war. This would have meant that the second part of their war aims—the continued exploitation of the nationalities was frustrated. The new Hungary for the first time in its thousand year history was ethnically almost purely Magyar with over two million compatriots living outside its borders. The truth, however, was that the Horthy leadership refused to accept the Treaty from the moment it was signed. This intransigence doomed all hopes for international stability in East Central Europe.

NOTES

CHAPTER I

1. Oszkár Jászi, *A nemzeti állomok kialakulása és a nemzetiségi kérdés* [The Evolution of the Nation States and the Nationality Question] (Budapest: 1912), p. 349. Hereafter cited as *A nemzeti állomok kialakulása.*

2. Robert William Seton Watson, *A History of the Czechs and Slovaks* (New York: Hutchinson and Co., 1943), p. 278.

3. Victor S. Mamatey, *The United States and East Central Europe 1914-1918* (Princeton: Princeton University Press, 1957), p. 16.

4. Milan Hodža, *Középeuropa országutján* [On the Highway of Central Europe] (Bratislava, Eugen Prager, 1938), p. 29.

5. Mátyás Unger and Ottó Szabolcs, *Magyarország története* [The History of Hungary] (Budapest: Gondolat, 1965), pp. 256-258.

6. Erzsébet Andics, (ed.), *A Magyar nacionalizmus kialakulása és története* [The History and Development of Hungarian Nationalism] (Budapest: Kossuth, 1964), p. 180. Hereafter cited as *A Magyar nacionalizmus.*

7. Regina Donáth, *A Tisza István elleni 1912-i merénylet a hirlapirodalom tükrében* [The Attempt Against the Life of István Tisza as Seen through the Journals] (Budapest: 1935), p. 5.

8. Aladár Mód, *400 év küzdelem az önálló Magyarországért* [Four Hundred Years of Stuggle for Independent Hungary] (Budapest: Szikra, 1951), p. 367; László Remete, *Barikádok Budapest utcáin 1912* [Barricades on the Streets of Budapest-1912] (Budapest: Kossuth, 1972), pp. 271-273.

9. Donáth, *op.cit.*, pp. 11-13.

10. *Ibid.*, pp. 92-96.

11. Oscar Halecki, *Borderlands of Western Europe: History of Eastern Europe* (New York: Ronald Press, 1952), p. 353.

12. Joachim Remak, *Sarajevo* (New York: Criterion Books, 1959), pp. 33-34.

13. as quoted by Mod, *op.cit.*, p. 263.

14. Norman Stone, "Hungary and the Crisis of July 1914," *Journal of Contemporary History,* III (1967), 159.

15. Gusztav Grátz, *A dualizmus kora* [The Age of Dualism] (Budapest: Magyar Szemle, 1934), II, 298.

16. Michael Károlyi, *Memoirs of Michael Károlyi, Faith Without Illusion* (New York: E. P. Dutton, 1957), p. 47. Hereafter cited as *Memoirs.*

17. Lajos Kossuth, *Válogatott munkái* [Selected Works] (Budapest: Lampel Robert, 190?), p. 252.

18. Archives of the Department of State Relating to Internal Affairs of Austria-Hungary, file no. 864.00. National Archives. Hereafter cited as *Papers on Internal Affairs of Austria-Hungary.* Mihály Károlyi, *Egy egész világ ellen* [Against the Entire World] (Budapest: Gondolat, 1965), pp. 77-88.

19. Oscar Jászi, *The Dissolution of the Hapsburg Monarchy* (Chicago: University of Chicago Press, 1961), p. 364. Hereafter cited as *The Dissolution.*

20. Luigi Albertini, *The Origins of the War of 1914* (Oxford: Oxford University Press, 1957), II, 127.

21. Károlyi, *Egy egész világ ellen*, p. 138.

22. Zsuzsa L. Nagy and András Zsilák, (eds.), *Ötven év. A Nagy Oktober és a Magyarországi forradalmak. Tanulmányok* [Fifty Years. The Great October Revolution and the Hungarian Revolutions. Essays] (Budapest: Akadémiai Kiadó, 1967), p. 125.

23. *Ibid.*, p. 118.

24. *Ibid.*, p. 119.

25. Tibor Hajdu, *Az Őszirózsás Forradalom* [The Frostflower Revolution] (Budapest: Kossuth, 1963), pp. 30-35. Also, Tibor Szamuely, *A Kommunisták Magyarországi Pártjának megalakulása és harca a proletárdiktaturáért* [The Organization and Fight of the Hungarian Party of Communists for the Proletarian Dictatorship] (Budapest: Kossuth, 1964), pp. 57-72.

26. John Reed, *The War in Eastern Europe* (New York: Charles Scribner's Sons, 1919), p. 84.

27. József Kristóffy, *A királyságtól a kommunizmusig* [From Monarchy to Communism] (Budapest: Kultura, 1920), p. 75.

28. Leo Viliani, "Italian-Austro-Hungarian Negotiations in 1914-1915," *Journal of Contemporary History*, III, (1967), 113.

29. István Tisza, *Összes Munkái* [Collected Works] (Budapest: Franklin Társulat, 1926), III, pp. 365-366; also in Victor Regnier (ed.), *Lettres de guerre 1914-1916* (Paris: Les Oeuvres Représéntatives, 1931), p. 184.

30. Ivo J. Lederer, *Yugoslavia at the Paris Peace Conference* (New Haven: Yale University Press, 1963), p. 23.

31. Thomas Garrigue Masaryk, *The Making of a State* (New York: F. A. Stokes Company, 1927), p. 96.

32. Zoltán Szviezsényi, *Hogyan veszett el a Felvidék?* [How Was Ruthenia Lost?] (Budapest: Franklin Társulat, 1921), p. 64; also in Harrison Thomson, *Czechoslovakia in European History* (Hamden: Archon Books, 1965), p. 307.

33. *The New York Times*, August 29, 1916, 1:7.

34. United States Department of State, *Papers Relating to the Foreign Relations of the United States: The World War 1917*. Hereafter cited as *FRUS-WW 1917* (Washington: Government Printing Office, 1933), Supplement I, p. 8.

35. Alexander Dallin, *et.al., Russian Diplomacy and Eastern Europe 1914-1917* (New York: King's Crown, 1963), p. 80.

36. Ray Stannard Baker and William E. Dodd (eds.), *The Public Papers of Woodrow Wilson* (New York: Harper and Bros., 1927), I, 132-135.

37. United States Department of State, *Papers Relating to the Foreign Relations of the United States: The World War 1918* (Washington: Government Printing Office, 1933), Supplement l, I, 9. Hereafter cited as *FRUS-WW 1918*.

38. *Ibid.*, pp. 29-30.

39. Arthur J. May, *The Passing of the Hapsburg Monarchy 1914-1918* (Philadelphia: University of Pennsylvania Press, 1964), II, 684. Hereafter cited as *Hapsburg Monarchy*.

40. Károlyi, *Egy egész világ ellen*, p. 157.

41. Mód, *op.cit.*, p. 388.

42. as quoted in May, *Hapsburg Monarchy*, II, p. 694.

43. *Révai Nagy Lexikona*, "A választójog története" [The history of Franchise Laws] XVIII, Tarjan-Var 732-33, (Budapest: 1925); Pál Schönwald, *A magyarországi 1918-1919-es polgári demokratikus forradalom állam és jogtörténeti kérdései* [The Constitutional and Legal Questions of the Bourgeois-Democratic Revolution of 1918-1919] (Budapest: Akadémiai Kiadó, 1969), pp. 242-243.

CHAPTER II

1. C. A. Macartney and A. W. Palmer, *Independent Eastern Europe, A History* (New York: St. Martin's Press, 1966), p. 84.

2. Victor S. Mamatey, *The United States and East Central Europe 1914-1918. A Study of Wilsonian Diplomacy and Propaganda* (Princeton: Princeton University Press, 1957), p. 243.

3. Robert L. Lansing, *War Memoirs of Robert Lansing* (Indianapolis: Bobbs-Merrill Co., 1935), pp. 269 ff.

4. as quoted in Mamatey, *op.cit.*, p. 269; Joseph P. O'Grady (ed.), *The Immigrants' Influence on Wilson's Peace Policies* (Lexington, Ky.: University of Kentucky Press, 1967), p. 166.

5. James R. Mock and Cedric Larson, *Words that Won the War. The Story of the Committee on Public Information 1917-1919* (Princeton: Princeton University Press, 1938), p. 230.

6. *Ibid.*, p. 306.

7. L. Nagy and Zsilák, *op.cit.*, p. 206.

8. Emma Iványi (ed.), *Magyar minisztertanácsi jergyzőkönyvek az Első Világháború korából* [Minutes of the Council of Ministers from the Era of World War One] (Budapest: Akadémiai Kiedő, 1960), p. 398; József Lengyel, *Visegrádi utca* in *Lengyel József összegyüjtött munkái* [Visegradi Street in the Collected Works of Jozsef Lengyel] (Budapest: Szépirodalmi Könyvkiadó, 1966), p. 74; Márton Farkas, *Katonai összeomlás és forradalom 1918-ban* [Military Collapse and Revolution in 1918](Budapest: Akadémiai Kiadó,, 1969), pp. 119-121.

9. Béláné Kun, Mrs., *Kun Béla (Emlékezések)* [Béla Kun, Memoirs] (Budapest: Magvetö, 1966), p. 75.

10. Hajdu, *Az Öszirózsás Forradalom*, p. 48.

11. United States Department of State, *Papers Relating to the Foreign Relations of the United States: Russia* (Washington: Government Printing Office, 1932), II, 131. Hereafter cited as *FRUS-Russia*.

12. C. K. Cumming and Walter W. Pettit, (eds.), *Russian-American Relations March 1917-March 1920, Documents and Papers* (New York: Harcourt, Brace and Howe, 1920), pp. 177-188.

13. Ray Stannard Baker, *Woodrow Wilson, Life and Letters* (Garden City: Doubleday, Page and Co., 1939), VIII, 389.

14. Lawrence E. Gelfand, *The Inquiry, American Preparations for Peace, 1917-1919* (New Haven: Yale University Press, 1963), p. 212.

15. United States Department of State, *FRUS-WW 1918*, Supplement 1, I, 816.

16. as quoted in Macartney and Palmer, *op.cit.*, p. 85.

17. Great Britain, Foreign Office, "Alleged negotiations between Count Karolyi and Baron Sonnino in Switzerland." June 11, 1918, 371/3136, Public Record Office, London. Hereafter cited as *F. O.*

18. United States Department of State, *FRUS-Russia*, II, 254-255.

19. "Robert Cecil's Conversation with Benes," May 18, 1918, *F. O.* 371-3443.

20. Great Britain, War Office, "The Czecho-Slovak Army in Siberia, by Dr. Beneš," August 15, 1918, 106/684, Public Records Office, London. Hereafter cited as *W. O.* Estimates of the number of Hungarians fighting in the Russian civil war quote 100,000 officers and soldiers. See Rudolf L. Tőkés, *Béla Kun and the Hungarian Soviet Republic* (New York: Praeger, 1967), p. 70.

21. "The History of the Czecho-Slovak Army in Russia," September 9, 1918, *W.O.* 106/683.

22. United States Department of State, *FRUS The Lansing Papers 1914-1920*, II, 382.

23. Mock and Larson, *op.cit.*, p. 231.

24. See page 21.

25. Károlyi, *Egy egész világ ellen*, p. 87.

26. Károlyi, *Memoirs*, p. 138.

27. *Ibid.*, p. 199; Hugh R. Wilson, *Diplomat between Wars* (New York: Longmans, Green and Co., 1941), p. 41; United States Department of State, *FRUS-WW 1917*, Supplement 2, I, 322-325.

28. Sir H. Rumbold to Lord Bertie, December 7 (?) 1917, *F. O.* 800/161.

29. Memorandum of Edward Drummond to Foreign Office, December 10, 1917, *F. O.* 800/200.

30. United States Department of State, *FRUS-WW 1918*, Supplement 1, I, 341.

31. Mihályne Károlyi, Mrs., *Együtt a forradalomban Emlékezések* [Together in the Revolution, Memoirs] (Budapest: Europa Konyvkiadó, 1967), p. 261.

32. United States Department of State, *FRUS-WW 1918*, Supplement 1, I, 367.

33. Károlyi, *Egy egész világ ellen*, p. 327.

34. United States Department of State, *FRUS-1918*, Supplement 1, I, 368.

35. Magyar Képviselőház, *Képviselőházi Napló* [Diary of the House of Representatives] (Budapest: 1918), XLI, 276-284.

36. *Ibid.*, pp. 294-295.

37. József Breit Doberdoi, *A magyarorszdgi 1918-1919 évi forradalmak és a vörös háboru története* [The History of the Revolutionary Movements of 1918-1919 and the Red War] (Budapest: Magyar Királyi Levéltár, 1925), I, p. 15.

38. Magyar Szocialista Munkáspárt Központi Bizottságának Párttörténeti Intézete, *A Magyar munkasmozgalom történétének válogatott dokumentumai* [Selected Documents to the History of the Hungarian Labor Movement] (Budapest: Kossuth, 1956), V, 266, hereafter cited as *MMTVD*: Károlyi, *Az egész világ ellen*, pp. 352-354.

39. Károlyi, *Memoirs*, p. 106; Hajdu, *Az Öszirózsás Forradalom*, pp. 90-91.

40. Árpád Szélpál, *Les 133 jours de Béla Kun* (Paris: Artheme Fayard, 1959), p. 24.

41. Gusztav Grátz, *A forradalmak kora* [The Age of Revolutions] (Budapest: Magyar Szemle Tarsasag, 1935), p. 17.

42. *Ibid.*, p. 17.

43. *Ibid.*, p. 18; Oszkár Gellért, (ed.), *A diadalmas forradalom könyve* [The Book of the Glorious Revolution] (Budapest: Legradi, 1918), p. 171.

44. Tibor Számuely, *op.cit.*; p. 115. Farkas, *op.cit.*, p. 337.

45. Sándor Juhász Nagy, *A Magyar Oktoberi Forradalom története* [The History of the Hungarian October Revolution] (Budapest: Cserépfalvi, 1945), p. 222.

46. Grátz, *A forradalmak kora*, p. 18.

47. Károlyi, *Memoirs*, p. 118.

48. Oscár Jászi, *Revolution and Counter-Revolution in Hungary* (London: S. King and Son, 1924), p. 32. Hereafter cited as *Revolution and Counter-Revolution*.

49. Empress Zita later claimed that Charles did order Lukachich to resist. See Gordon Brook-Shepherd, *The Last Habsburg* (New York: Weybright and Talley, 1968), p. 189.

50. Hajdu, *Az Őszirózsás Forradalom*, pp. 170-174; Károlyi, *Az egész világ ellen*, pp. 370-397; Károlyine, (Mrs.), *op.cit.*, p. 282.

51. Ernő Garami, *Forrongó Magyarország* [Seditious Hungary] (Leipzig: Pegazus, 1922), p. 30.

CHAPTER III

1. Arno Mayer, *Politics and Diplomacy of Peacemaking: Containment and Counterrevolution at Versailles, 1918-1919* (New York: Alfred A. Knopf, 1967), p. 524, hereafter cited as *Politics and Diplomacy*; Számuely, *op.cit.*, p. 157.

2. Gyula Hevesi, *Egy mérnök a forradalomban* [An Engineer in the Revolution] (Budapest: Europa Kk., 1959), p. 171.

3. The existence of dual authority and its close parallel with the Russian situation is claimed by Tibor Hajdu, *Tanácsok Magyarországon 1918-1919-ben* [Councils in Hungary in 1918-1919] (Budapest: Kossuth, 1958), p. 41 and Tőkés, *op.cit.*, p. 8g Elek Bolgár, *Válogatott tanulmányok* [Selected Essays] (Budapest: Kossuth, 1958), p. 172 and Ferenc Harrer, *Egy Magyar Polgár Élete* [The Life of a Hungarian Bourgeois] (Budapest: Gondolat, 1968), p. 357 disagree and affirm that the problem of dual authority did not exist in Hungary.

4. Jolán Kellen and Gyula Barabás, *A Néptribun Fejezetek Bokányi Dezső életéből* [The People's Tribunal—Chapters from the Life of Dezső Bokányi] (Budapest: Kossuth, 1964), p. 201.

5. *MMTVD*, V, pp. 319 and 402.

6. Jászi, *Revolution and Counter-Revolution*, p. 3; Gyula Mérei, *A magyar oktoberi forradalom es a polgári pártok* [The Hungarian Revolution of October and the Bourgeois Parties] (Budapest: Akadémiai Kiadó, 1969), pp. 20-21.

7. Andics, *A magyar nacionalizmus*, p. 243; Lee Congdon, "History and Politics in Hungary: The Rehabilitation of Oszkár Jászi," *East European Quarterly*, IX, No. 3, 315-318.

8. Oszkár Jászi, *A nemzeti államok kialakulása*, p. 3.

9. *Ibid.*, p. 497; Gábor Vermes, "The Agony of Federalism in Hungary under the Károlyi Regime, 1918/1919," *East European Quarterly*, VI, No. 4, 490.

10. Béla K. Király, "The Danubian Problem in Oscár Jászi's Political Thought," *The Hungarian Quarterly*, V (April-June, 1965), 127-129.

11. *Ibid.*, p. 134.

12. Jászi, *Revolution and Counter-Revolution*, p. 38.

13. "Extract from the Matin 5 Novembre 1918," *F.O.* 371/3136; for a similar declaration of the Czecho-Slovak National Council see November 7, 1919, *F.O.* 371/3134; Jenő Horváth, *Magyarország és a nemzetiségi kérdés, 1815-1920* [Hungary and the Nationality Question, 1815-1920] (Budapest: Pfeifer, 1920), p. 80.

14. Great Britain, Foreign Office, May 21, 1921, *F.O.* 800/155.

15. as quoted in László Kővágó, *A magyarországi délszlávok 1918-1919-ben* [The South Slavs of Hungary in 1918-1919] (Budapest: Akadémiai Kiadó, 1964), p. 70.

16. For a critical appraisal see Mayer, *Politics and Diplomacy*, pp. 525-526.

17. as quoted in Ferenc Göndör, *Vallomások könyve* [Book of Confessions] (Vienna: A szerző kiadása, 1922), p. 53.

18. Harrer, *op.cit.*, p. 379.

19. Számuely, *op.cit.*, pp. 178-179.

20. Károlyi, *Memoirs*, pp. 128-129; Garami, *op.cit.*, p. 39; Jászi, *Revolution and Counter-Revolution*, pp. 51-52.

21. Francis Deák, *Hungary at the Paris Peace Conference. The Diplomatic History of the Treaty of Trianon* (New York: Columbia University Press, 1942), p. 9.

22. Károlyi, *Memoirs*, p. 130.

23. Dominic Kosáry, *A History of Hungary* (Cleveland: Benjamin Franklin Bibliophile Society, 1941), p. 381.

24. Számuely, *op.cit.*, p. 180.

25. *Ibid.*, p. 179.

26. Juhász Nagy, *op.cit.*, p. 297.

27. Garami, *op.cit.*, p. 36.

28. E. Malcolm Carroll, *Soviet Communism and Western Opinion 1919-1921* (Chaptel Hill: University of North Carolina Press, 1965), pp. 12-14.

29. Charles Seymour, *Letters from the Paris Peace Conference* (New Haven: Yale University Press, 1965), p. 132; James T. Shotwell, *At the Paris Peace Conference* (New York: Macmillan, 1937), p. 108.

30. Carroll, *op.cit.*, p. 13.

31. Robert K. Murray, *Red Scare: A Study of National Hysteria, 1919-1920* (New York: McGraw-Hill, 1964), pp. 94-95.

32. Comte de Saint-Aulaire, *Confession d'un vieux diplomate* (Paris: Flamarion, 1953), p. 483; the disproportionate Jewish participation in the revolution is attributed to Jewish "messianism" by István Deák, "Budapest and the Hungarian Revolutions of 1918-1919," in *Slavonic and East European Review*, Vol. XLVI (January 1968), 139.

33. Rumbold to Balfour, January 4, 1919, *F.O.* 371/3541; Ministère des Affaires Etrangères, Correspondance des Affaires Politiques, Compte Rendu, L'Agent 337-A, January 4, 1919, Hongrie, Vol. 27, Archives des Affaires Etrangères. Hereafter cited as *CAP*.

34. Following the rise of the Hungarian Soviet Republic, Varga became Commissar of Finance and Chairman of the Supreme Economic Council. He worked out directives for a planned economy that were utilized by Russian economists devising the First Five-Year Plan. Varga gained world-wide renown as the Director of the Institute of World Economics and World Politics of the Soviet Academy of Sciences (1927-1947).

35. Károly Mészáros, *Az Öszirózsás forradalom és a Tanácsköztársasdg paraszt-politikája* [The Agricultural Policy of the Frostflower Revolution and of the Soviet Republic] (Budapest: Akadémiai Kk., 1966), pp. 65-66. Vera Szemere, *Az agrárkérdés 1918-1919-ben* [The Agrarian Question in 1918-1919] (Budapest: Kossuth, 1963), p. 92.

36. Oszkár Gellért, *op.cit.*, p. 103.

37. Mihály Károlyi, *Válogatott irásai* [Selected Works] (Budapest: Gondolat, 1964), p. 29.

38. Számuely, *op.cit.*, p. 168.

39. *Ibid.*, p. 179.

40. Károlyi, *Memoirs*, p. 139.

41. Juhász Nagy, *op.cit.*, p. 31.

42. Károlyi, *Memoirs*, p. 144; For a brief history of the revolution, see Gábor Vermes, "The October Revolution in Hungary: from Károlyi to Kun," *Hungary in Revolution*, ed. Iván Völgyes (Lincoln: University of Nebraska Press, 1971), pp. 31-60.

CHAPTER IV

1. Macartney and Palmer, *op.cit.*, p. 92.

2. Lederer, *op.cit.*, pp. 41-43.

3. Mamatey, *op.cit.*, p. 339.

4. Wenzel Jaksch, *Europe's Road to Potsdam*, translated by Kurt Glaser (New York: Frederick A. Praeger, 1963), p. 192; Mary Barbara Fuchs, *The Problem of the Hungarian-Czechoslovak Frontier, November 3rd 1918 to November 15, 1920* (New York: Ph.D. dissertation at St. John's University, 1942), pp. 35-36.

5. Stephen Bonsal, *Suitors and Supplicants, The Little Nations at Versailles* (New York: Prentice-Hall, 1946), p. 161.

6. Jaksch, *op.cit.*, p. 193.

7. Michael Hodža, *Federalism in Central Europe* (London: Jarrolds Publishers, 1942), p. 72; Macartney and Palmer, *op.cit.*, p. 93; for texts of the message and reply see Ivan Thurzo: *O Martinskej deklaracii* [The Martin Declaration] (Kniznica Miestneho odgoru Matice slovenskej v Martine, 1968), II, 75.

8. *FRUS-WW 1918*, Supplement 1, I, 447.

9. John E. Howard, *Parliament and Foreign Policy in France* (London: Cresset Press, 1948), p. 142.

10. *Journal des Débats*, November 3, 1918.

11. Harry Hanak, *Great Britain and Austria-Hungary during the First World War. A Study in the Formation of Public Opinion* (London: Oxford University Press, 1962), p. 269; Arthur J. May, "R.W. Seton Watson and British Anti-Hapsburg Sentiment," in *The American Slavic and East European Review*, February 1961, XX, 53.

12. *The New Europe*, October 31, 1918.

13. Masaryk, *op.cit.*, p. 82.

14. Stefen Osusky, "The Secret Negotiations between Vienna and Washington," *The Slavonic Review*, IV (1926), 658; H.R. Wilson, *op.cit.*, p. 45; Masaryk, *op.cit.*, pp. 305-306; O'Grady, *op.cit.*, p. 167.

15. Charles Seymour, (ed.), *The Intimate Papers of Colonel House* (Boston: Houghton Mifflin Co., 1928), IV. 198-199.

16. *FRUS-WW 1918*, Supplement 1, I, 421.

17. Ray Stannard Baker, (ed.), *Woodrow Wilson, Life and Letters* (New York: Doubleday, 1939), p. 542.

18. Namier to Tyrrell, November 11, 1918, *F.O.* 371/3134.

19. Great Britain, War Cabinet, Minutes of Meeting, November 22, 1918, CAB 23-B, Public Record Office, London.

20. N. Gordon Levin, Jr., *Woodrow Wilson and World Politics: America's Response to War and Revolution* (New York: Oxford University Press, 1968), p. 188.

21. David F. Houston, *Eight Years with Wilson's Cabinet* (Garden City: Doubleday, 1926), pp. 321-324.

22. *FRUS-WW 1918*, Supplement 1, I, 470.

23. Walter Lippmann to Sidney Mezes, September 5, 1918, Mezes Mss., Columbia University Library.

24. Rósa Bédy-Schwimmer to Mihály Károlyi, October 28, 1918, Róza Bédy-Schwimmer Papers, Box A 125, New York Public Library Manuscript Division, (Hereafter cited as Bédy-Schwimmer Papers); Róza Bédy-Schwimmer to Colonel House, November 3, 1918, Bédy-Schwimmer Papers, Box A 126; Vira B. Whitehouse, *A Year as a Government Agent* (New York: Harper and Brothers, 1920), p. 420.

25. Rósa Bédy-Schwimmer to David Lloyd George, October 3, 1917, Rosika Schwimmer Papers, Box 1, Hoover Institution Archives; International Committee for World Peace Prize Award to Rosika Schwimmer, *Rosika Schwimmer World Patriot* (New York: 1938), p. 2; David Lloyd George, *War Memoirs* (Boston: Houghton Mifflin Co., 1933), I, 50; Burnet Hershey, *The Odyssey of Henry Ford and the Great Peace Ship* (New York: Taplinger Publishing Co., 1967), pp. 62-69.

26. International Committee. . . , *op.cit.*, p. 3.

27. Whitehouse, *op.cit.*, p. 238.

28. *The New York Times,* November 26, 1915, p. 4.

29. Seymour, *Intimate Papers*, II, p. 96; Mark Sullivan, *Our Times, The United States* (New York: Charles Scribner's Sons, 1933), V, pp. 162-183.

30. Whitehouse, *op.cit.*, p. 251.

31. Copies of Wilson's declaration in various languages are in Bedy-Schwimmer Papers, Box A 127; Whitehouse, *op.cit.*, p. 261; Slovak language version printed in K.A. Medvecký, *Slovenský Prevrat* [Slovak Revolution] (Bratislava, 1931), Vol. IV, pp. 12-13. In this publication Bédy-Schwimmer was identified as a C.P.I. agent.

32. *FRUS-WW 1918*, Supplement 1, I, p. 474.

33. *MMTVD*, V, 345; *Pravda*, November 3, 1918.

34. Lengyel, *op.cit.*, p. 76.

35. Ervin Liptai, *A Magyar Tandcsköztársaság* [The Hungarian Soviet Republic] (Budapest: Kossuth, 1965), p. 37; *Sarlo es Kalapacs* (Moscow), March, 1932, p. 54.

36. *MMTVD*, p. 345.

37. *Ibid.*, p. 363; Aladár Mód, *Válaszutak 1918-1919* [Alternatives, 1918-1919] (Budapest: Magveto, 1970), p. 173.

38. Vladimir Ilyich Lenin, *Lenin Magyarországról* [Lenin about Hungary] (Budapest: Kossuth, 1974); László Réti, *Lenin és a magyar munkásmozgalom* [Lenin

and the Hungarian Labor Movement] (Budapest: Kossuth, 1970), p. 21; Erzsébet Andics, *Munkásosztály és nemzet* [Workingclass and Nation] (Budapest: Szikra, 1949), p. 83.

39. Jakab Weltner, *Forradalom, Bolsevizmus, Emigráció* [Revolution, Bolshevism, Emigration] (Budapest: Weltner, 1929), p. 69; Réti, *op.cit.*, pp. 105-106.

40. Weltner, *op.cit.*, pp. 76-77.

41. Mano Buchinger, *Tanuvallomás: Az Oktoberi forradalom tragédiája* [Testimony of a Witness: The Tragedy of the October Revolution] (Budapest: Nepszava, 1936), p. 82.

42. *The Times* (London), November 5, 1916.

43. George Bernard Noble, *Policies and Opinions at Paris, 1919* (New York: The Macmillan Co., 1935), p. 12.

44. *Le Figaro*, November 4, 1918.

45. *Le Temps*, November 6, 1918.

46. The likeness of British to American foreign policy toward Eastern Europe is described in Seth F. Tillman, *Anglo-American Relations at the Paris Peace Conference of 1919* (Princeton: Princeton University Press, 1961), pp. 210-216. For a recent Hungarian analysis of British policy toward Hungary, see: Lajos Arday, "Angol-Magyar viszony a polgári demokratikus forradalom idején az angol levéltári források tükrében" [English-Hungarian Relations during the Bourgeois Democratic Revolution as Reflected in English Archival Sources] *Történelmi Szemle*, 1975, XVIII, no. 2-3, 271.

CHAPTER V

1. Jenő Horváth, *A trianoni békeszerződés megalkotása és a revizió útja* [The Construction of the Peace Treaty of Trianon and the Course of Revision] (Budapest: Magyar Tudományos Akadémia, 1937), p. 25. Hereafter cited as *a revizió utja.*

2. *Ibid.*, p. 8.

3. Alfred D. Low, *The Soviet Hungarian Republic and the Paris Peace Conference* (Philadelphia: The American Philosophical Society, 1963), p. 13.

4. Horváth, *a revizió utja*, p. 8.

5. Otto Bauer, *The Austrian Revolution* (London: Leonard Parsons, 1925), p. 120; Mamatey, *op.cit.*, p. 314.

6. Lederer, *op.cit.*, pp. 66-67; Zsuzsa L. Nagy, *A párizsi békekonferencia és Magyarország 1918-1919* [The Peace Conference of Paris and Hungary 1918-1919] (Budapest: Kossuth, 1965), p. 60.

7. Lederer, *op.cit.*, p. 57.

8. Károlyi, *Memoirs*, p. 133; Mihály Károlyi, *Az uj Magyarországért* [For the New Hungary] (Budapest: Magveto Konyvkiadó, 1968), pp. 415-417. Hereafter cited as *Magyarországért.*

9. Bogdan Krizman, "The Belgrade Armistice of November 1918," *Slavonic and East European Review*, XLVIII (1970), No. 110, p. 76.

10. Károlyi, *Memoirs*, p. 132.

11. Lajos Hatvany, *Urak, polgárok, parasztok* [Lords, Citizens, Peasants] (Budapest: Révaj, 1947), p. 106.

12. Károlyi, *Memoirs*, p. 132; Jerome et Jean Tharaud, *Quand Israel est roi* (Paris: Plon, 1921), pp. 155-157.

13. Garami, *op.cit.*, p. 45. The cruel treatment of the Hungarians at the hands of Franchet d'Esperey was immortalized in Ezra Pound's magnum opus: *Cantos*. In it he praised the ideals of the Hungarian revolution and contrasted them with the ideals of the *Ancien Régime*, represented by Franchet d'Esperey. See Ezra Pound, *Cantos* (New York: A New Directions Book, 1965), Canto XXXV.

14. Paul Azan, *Franchet d'Esperey* (Paris: Flamarion, 1949), p. 230.

15. Zoltán Szende, "Count Michael Károlyi at Belgrade," *The Hungarian Quarterly*, V (1939), No. 3, pp. 425-437; later, the embittered Károlyi in exile, recalled the Belgrade meeting and wrote to Jászi that Franchet d'Esperey was an "idiot." Oscar Jaszi Papers, Jan. 8, 1920, Columbia University Library.

16. Tharaud, *op.cit.*, p. 157.

17. Jean Charbonneau, (ed.), *Franchet d'Esperey maréchal de France* (Paris: Cahiers Charles de Foucauld, 1956), p. 64; Krizman, *op.cit.*, pp. 72-74.

18. Károlyi, *Memoirs*, pp. 132-135.

19. Vilmos Böhm, *Két forradalom tüzében* [In the of Two Revolutions] (Budapest: Népszava Kk., 1946), p. 61; Farkas claims that the convention turned the Károlyi government into a servant of Entente counter-revolution, *op.cit.*, p. 406.

20. Tivadar Batthyány, *Beszámolóm* [My Account] (Budapest: Athenaeum, 1931), II, 26; Low, *op.cit.*, p. 25.

21. Ministerio degli affari esteri, *I Documenti diplomatici italiani* (Rome: Istituto poliografico dello stato, 1956), I, 6 ser., 168.

22. Francis Deák, *op.cit.*, Document 2, pp. 339-362.

23. Azan, *op.cit.*, p. 235.

24. Charbonneau, *op.cit.*, pp. 149-150.

25. C. A. Macartney, *Hungary and Her Successors: The Treaty and Its Consequences 1917-1937* (London: Oxford University Press, 1937), p. 105; L. Nagy, *op.cit.*, p. 12.

26. Eduard Beneš, *My War Memoirs* (Boston: Houghton Mifflin Co., 1928), p. 427. The same faulty interpretation is given by Piotr S. Wandycz, *France and Her Eastern Allies 1919-1925: French-Czechoslovak-Polish Relations from the Paris Peace Conference to Locarno* (Minneapolis: University of Minnesota Press, 1962), p. 20.

27. *Journal des débats*, November 6, 1918.

28. Hans Kohn, *The Habsburg Empire, 1804-1918* (New York: Van Nostrand, 1959), p. 120.

29. Mamatey, *op.cit.*, p. 354.

30. Juhász Nagy, *op.cit.*, p. 304.

31. Minute, Pichon to Clemenceau, *CAP*, Tchécoslovaquie, Vol. 44; Beneš, *My War Memoirs*, p. 477.

32. Pichon to French embassies, November 29, 1918, *CAP*, Hongrie, Vol. 44; Reference to Pichon's telegram is made in György Litván, "Az első világháboru és az 1918-19-es forradalmak magyar vonatkozású anyagai a francia levéltárakban" [French Archival Materials Relating to Hungary during World War I and during the Revolutions of 1918-19] *Történelmi Szemle*, (1973), No. 1-2, p. 270.

33. Mamatey, *op.cit.*, p. 352; Ferenc Boros; *Magyar-Csehszlovák kapcsolatok 1918-1921-ben* [Hungarian-Czechoslovak Relations in 1918-1921] (Budapest: Akadémiai Kiadó, 1970), p. 39.

34. Quoted in Wandycz, *op.cit.*, p. 21.

35. Batthyány, *op.cit.*, I, 298.

36. Quoted in Kővágó, *op.cit.*, p. 71.

37. R. W. Seton-Watson, *A History of the Roumanians* (Cambridge: Cambridge University Press, 1934), p. 535.

38. Azan, *op.cit.*, p. 241.

39. Saint-Aulaire, *op.cit.*, p. 476.

40. Eugene Horváth, *Transylvania and the Rumanians: A Reply to Professor R. W. Seton-Watson* (Budapest: Sárkány, 1935), p. 85; Sherman D. Spector, *Roumania at the Paris Peace Conference: A Study of the Diplomacy of Ioan I. C. Bratianu* (New York: Bookman, 1962), p. 65.

41. Macartney and Palmer, *op.cit.*, p. 119.

42. Károlyi, *Válogatott írásai*, II, 320.

43. Louis Varjassy, *Revolution, bolchevisme, reaction: L' Histoire de l'occupation française en Hongrie (1918-1919)* (Paris, 1934), pp. 22-23; Miron Constantinescu and Ştefan Pascu, eds., *Unification of the Roumanian State, the Union of Transylvania with Old Romania* (Bucharest: Academy of Romania, 1971), pp. 244-247.

44. Kellen and Barabás, *op.cit.*, p. 203.

45. Varjassy, *op.cit.*, p. 22.

46. Octavian Goga, "The Achievement of Rumanian Unity," *The New Europe*, IX, No. 116 (January 2, 1919).

47. Jászi, *Revolution and Counter-Revolution*, p. 59.

48. L. Nagy, *op.cit.*, p. 239, footnote 80, Tibor Hajdu, *Az 1918-as magyarországi polgári demokratikus forradalom* [The Bourgeois Democratic Revolution of 1918] (Budapest: Kossuth Könyvkiadó, 1968), p. 190. Hereafter cited as *demokratikus forradalom*; the Hungarian offer is judged "progressive," while Jászi's speech is labelled as scare tactic in, Zoltán Szász, "Az erdélyi román polgárság szereplése 1918 öszén" [The Role of the Transylvanian Rumanian Bourgeoisie during the Fall of 1918], *Szdzadok*, No. 2, 1972, p. 325.

CHAPTER VI

1. United States Department of State, *Papers Relating to the Foreign Relations of the United States, Paris Peace Conference 1919* (Washington, D. C.: Government Printing Office, 1942), II, 193. Hereafter cited as *FRUS-PPC.*

2. *FRUS-PPC*, I, pp. 348, 366.

3. Ferenc Harrer, *op.cit.*, pp. 359-368.

4. Garami, *op.cit.*, p. 84; Károlyi, *Magyarországért*, p. 471.

5. Schweizerisches Politisches Deparment Ableilung für Auswärtiges, November 28, 1918, Box A 129, Bédy-Schwimmer Papers; Dutasta to Pichon, November 26, 1918, *CAP*, Hongrie, Vol. 44; *The New York Times*, December 12, 1918.

6. Whitehouse, *op.cit.*, pp. 264-265.

7. Stovall to Herron, December 9, 1918; Herron to Stovall, December 12, 1918; Havas to Herron, December 13, 1918, The George David Herron Papers, Hungary, Czecho-Slovakia, Hoover Institution Archives; Havas to Bédy-Schwimmer, December 14, 1918, Box A 133, Bédy-Schwimmer Papers.

8. *The New York Times*, November 26, 1918.
9. Ludwig Windischgraetz, *My Memoirs* (Boston: Houghton Mifflin Co., 1921), p. 331; Batthyány, *op.cit.*, II, 169-171.
10. *Ibid.*, p. 72.
11. *FRUS-PPC*, II, 206-207.
12. Batthyány, *op.cit.*, p. 77.
13. L. Nagy, *op.cit.*, p. 28.
14. *FRUS-PPC*, II, 204-205; *Woodrow Wilson Papers*, Library of Congress, Series 5B, January 18, 1919. Acting Secretary of State Frank Polk in Washington acknowledged the Hungarian note and sent it to the American mission in Paris for decision.
15. Harrer, *op.cit.*, pp. 384-388.
16. Számuely, *op.cit.*, p. 211.
17. *Vörös Újság*, December 25, 1918.
18. *Ibid.*
19. Ministère de la Guerre, Etat-Major de l'Armée, Archives historiques, Vincennes, Paris, Campagne contre Allemagne (1914-1918), carton 106, dossier 2, hereafter cited as *CCA*; for an account of the activities of the Vix mission to Hungary see Peter Pastor, "The Vix Mission in Hungary, 1918-1919: A Re-examination," *Slavic Review*, XXIX (1970), No. 3; Sándor Vadász, "Vix és Károlyi," *Hadtörténelmi Közlemények* XVI (1969), No. 2. For a history of French military activities in Hungary and the Balkans based solely on material of the Archives historiques, see Jean Bernachot, *Les armées françaises après l'Armistice de 1918*, Vols. I and II (Paris: Imprimerie Nationale, 1970).
20. Vix to Henrys, November 28, 1918, *CCA*, carton 106, dosier 3.
21. Schönwald, *op.cit.*, pp. 159-161.
22. *Ibid.*
23. Henrys to Franchet d'Esperey, November 30, 1918, *CCA*, carton 106, dossier 2.
24. *The Sonnino Papers*, University Microfilms, Ann Arbor, Michigan, Reel 20, Bonin to Cabinet, November 28, 1917. Hereafter cited as *Sonnino Papers*.
25. Henrys to Franchet d'Esperey, December 9, 1918, *CCA*, carton 106, dossier 2; Böhm, *op.cit.*, p. 97.
26. Beneš, *My War Memoirs*, p. 478; *FRUS-PPC*, II, 379.
27. Henrys to Vix, December 2, and December 8, 1918, *CCA*, carton 106, dossier 2; Litván, *op.cit.*, p. 270.
28. Henrys to Franchet d'Esperey, December 9, 1918, *ibid*.
29. French Embassy to Foreign Office, December 31, 1918, *F.O.* 371/3514; Pichon to Clemenceau, November 29, 1918, *CAP*, Hongrie, Vol. 44.
30. Franchet d'Esperey to Henrys, December 13, 1918, *CCA*, carton 106, dossier 3.
31. István Borsody, *Magyar-Szlovák Kiegyezés* [Hungarian-Slovak Understanding] (Budapest: Officiana, 1946), p. 59; Boros, *op.cit.*, p. 45.
32. Wandycz, *op.cit.*, p. 63; Boros, *op.cit.*, pp. 46-47.
33. Vix to Henrys, December 23, 1918, *CCA*, carton 106, dossier 3.
34. József Doberdoi Breit, *op.cit.*, I, 80; Wandycz, *op.cit.*, p. 71.
35. As quoted, Kővágó, *op.cit.*, p. 116.
36. *Ibid.*; Boros, *op.cit.*, pp. 54-57.

37. *FRUS-PPC*, VII, 608; none of Tardieu's examined work explains his stand. Andre Tardieu, *La Paix* (Paris: Payot, 1921); *L'épreuve du pouvoir* (Paris: Flammarion, 1931); *L'heure de la décision* (Paris: Flammarion, 1934).

38. David Lloyd George, *The Truth About the Peace Treaties* (London: Victor Gollancz, 1938), II, 930.

39. Kővágó, *op.cit.*, p. 116.

40. Wandycz, *op.cit.*, p. 92.

41. *Woodrow Wilson Papers*, Series 5B, December 27, 1918.

42. Low, *op.cit.*, p. 26.

43. The German Saxons of Transylvania formed a National Council of their own at the same time as the Rumanians. The Saxons adopted a wait and see position and on January 21, 1919 voted to join Rumania. Macartney, *Hungary and Her Successors*, p. 277; a recent Rumanian publication calls the Saxon response "definite and prompt," Constantinescu and Pascu, *op.cit.*, p. 305.

44. Rumbold to Balfour, December 9, 1918, *F.O.*, 371/3141.

45. "Secret Report from French Source," December 27, 1918, *F.O.*, 371/3139.

46. Vix to Henrys, December 16, 1918, *CCA*, carton 106, dossier 3.

47. Vix to Henrys, December 23, 1918, *ibid.*

48. Hajdu, *demokratikus forradalom*.

49. December 30, 1918, *F.O.*, 371/3139.

50. Clemenceau to Berthelot, December 31, 1918, *CCA*, 20 N 731.

51. *Ibid.*; "Instructions pour les Generaux Franchet d'Esperey et Berthelot," January 21, 1919, *CAP*, Roumanie, Vol. 19; John M. Thompson, *Russia, Bolshevism and the Versailles Peace* (Princeton: Princeton University Press, 1966), pp. 58-59; John Bradley, *Allied Intervention in Russia* (New York: Basic Books, 1968), p. 137; John Silverlight, *The Victors' Dilemma: Allied Intervention in the Russian Civil War* (New York: Weybright and Talley, 1970), pp. 102-108.

52. Bradley, *op.cit.*, p. 152; Silverlight gives December 17 as the day of the landing, Silverlight, *op.cit.*, p. 107.

53. Saint-Aulaire, *op.cit.*, p. 484; Raymond Poincaré, *Aux service de la France, Vol. X, Victoire et Armistice 1918* (Paris: Plon, 1933), p. 457; Jules Laroche, *Au Quai d'Orsay avec Briand et Poincare* (Paris: Hachette, 1957), p. 73; For telegram of Clemenceau requesting information on number of troops the Rumanians could spare in southern Russia, see Clemenceau to Berthelot, December 27, *CCA* 20 N 731.

54. *Le Temps*, December 31, 1918.

55. Pichon to Saint-Aulaire, December 30, 1918, *CAP*, Roumainie, Vol. 32.

56. Krizman, *op.cit.*, p. 86.

57. Henrys to Franchet d'Esperey, January 13, 1919, *CCA*, carton 3830-696-70 E.

58. Franchet d'Esperey to Clemenceau and Foch, January 15, 1919, *CAP*, Roumanie, Vol. 47.

59. Berthelot to Clemenceau, January 9, 1919, *CAP*, Roumanie, Vol. 32.

60. Clemenceau to Berthelot, January 15, 1919, *CAP*, Roumanie, Vol. 32.

61. Clemenceau to Berthelot, January 24, 1919, *CAP*, Roumanie, Vol. 32; also in Roumanie, Vol. 42.

62. "Instructions pour les Generaux Franchet d'Esperey et Berthelot," *op.cit.*

63. "Raport fait au ministre. Analyse," March 23, 1919, *CAP*, Serbie, Vol. 25.

64. *MMTVD*, V, p. 391.

65. Batthyány, *op.cit.*, II, 191.

66. *Le Temps*, December 31, 1918.

67. Breit, *op.cit.*, pp. 209-210.

68. Garami, *op.cit.*, p. 84; Mérei, *op.cit.*, pp. 107-112.

69. Henrys to Franchet d'Esperey, January 6, 1919, *CCA*, carton 106, dossier 2; Bernachot, *op.cit.*, Vol. 1, 28.

70. *MMTVD*, V, pp. 453-454.

71. Károlyi, *Memoirs*, pp. 147-148.

72. Tőkés, *op.cit.*, pp. 115-116; Mayer, *Politics and Diplomacy*, p. 531. Since Mayer could not rely upon the minutes of the Workers' Council, (f. n. 51) his details are imprecise.

73. Juhász Nagy, *op.cit.*, p. 411.

74. Harrer, *op.cit.*, p. 391.

75. The government included: minister of defense, Vilmos Böhm (socialist); minister of agriculture, Barna Buza (Károlyi Party); minister of justice, Sándor Juhász Nagy (Károlyi Party); minister of commerce, Ernő Garami (socialist); minister of education, Zsigmond Kunfi (socialist); minister of public supplies, Ferenc Nagy (Károlyi Party); minister of interior, Vince Nagy (Károlyi Party); minister of economy, István Nagyatádi Szabó (Smallholders' Party), minister of welfare, Gyula Peidl (socialist); minister of finance, Pál Szende (Radical Party); minister of religious affairs, János Vass (Károlyi Party).

76. Memorandum of Namier, February 17, 1919, *F. O.*, 371/3514.

77. *Ibid.*

78. *Ibid.;* Although this author considers Namier objective, Arday came to the conclusion that the British official was too critical of the Károlyi government's actions. See, Arday, *op.cit.*, pp. 251-252.

CHAPTER VII

1. *Le Temps*, December 6, 1918.

2. Lederer, *op.cit.*, p. 72.

3. Herbert Hoover, *The Ordeals of Woodrow Wilson* (New York: McGraw-Hill, 1958), p. 151.

4. *Woodrow Wilson Papers*, Series 5B, Polk to Lansing, January 6, 1919.

5. *Ibid.*, Series 5B, Wilson to Lansing, January 10, 1919.

6. S.L. Bane and R.H. Lutz (eds.), *The Blockade of Germany After the Armistice, 1918-1919* (Stanford: Hoover Institute Press, 1942), p. 216.

7. *Ibid.*, p. 218.

8. *FRUS-PPC*, XII, pp. 232-233.

9. Lord William H. Beveridge Papers, "Diary of Visit to Vienna, Prague and Budapest, December 1918-January 1919," Box JI lg, London School of Economics, hereafter cited as *Beveridge Papers*; Lord William H. Beveridge, *Power and Influence* (New York: The Beechhurst Press, 1955), pp. 155-156.

10. *FRUS-PPC*, XII, pp. 232-235.

11. *The David Lloyd George Papers*, Robert Cecil to Lloyd George, January 16, 1919, Austria, Series F, Box 197, folder 5, in the Beaverbrook Library, London. Hereafter cited as Lloyd George Papers.

12. *Ibid.*, Interim Report, January 17, 1919; *Beveridge Papers*, Box JI lc; Lord Beveridge, *op.cit.*, pp. 376-377.

13. Harold Nicolson, *Peacemaking 1919* (London: Constable and Co., 1944), p. 240.

14. John Connel, *The Office* (New York: St. Martin's Press, 1958), p. 22.

15. Robert Cecil to Lloyd George, January 16, 1919, *Lloyd George Papers*, Series F, Box 197, folder 5.

16. Harold J. Coolidge and Robert H. Lord, *Archibald Cary Coolidge—Life and Letters* (Boston: Houghton Mifflin Co., 1932), p. 196.

17. Mayer, *Politics and Diplomacy*, p. 370.

18. *FRUS-PPC*, II, pp. 221-224.

19. As quoted in L. Nagy, *op.cit.*, p. 51.

20. *Woodrow Wilson Papers*, Series 5B, January 11, 1919.

21. Liptai, *op.cit.*, p. 75.

22. Coolidge and Lord, *op.cit.*, p. 211.

23. *Ibid.*

24. *FRUS-PPC*, XII, pp. 372-374.

25. Coolidge and Lord, *op.cit.*, p. 211.

26. George Creel, *How We Advertised America* (New York: Harper and Brothers, 1920), p. 421. Neither Creel's published writings nor his private papers at the Library of Congress describe or discuss this meeting.

27. Károlyiné, *op.cit.*, pp. 450-451.

28. Creel, *op.cit.*, p. 424.

29. Creel, *op.cit.*, p. 421; for the decision of the Peace Conference, see *FRUS--PPC*, I, 415.

30. *Woodrow Wilson Papers*, Creel to Wilson, February 3, 1919, Series 5B.

31. *FRUS-PPC*, XI, 34.

32. Seymour to Coolidge, Seymour to Tyler, February 14, 1919, *House Mss.*, Drawer 29, file 186, Yale University Library.

33. Seymour, *op.cit.*, p. XXX.

34. Harrer, *op.cit.*, p. 387.

35. Coolidge and Lord, *op.cit.*, p. 202.

36. *FRUS-PPC*, XI, 34.

37. Jászi, *Revolution and Counter-Revolution*, p. 91; Oscar Jaszi Papers, Diary.

38. C.M. Storey to A.C. Coolidge, February 10, 1919, Document 184.01102/76, National Archives; Daily Report on Austria-Hungary, February 26, 1919, *House Mss.*, Drawer 29, file 132. The Storey report included the speech in full, while the Daily Report which was to inform the American plenipotentiaries is merely a summary.

39. L. Nagy, *op.cit.*, p. 60.

40. See p. 70

41. Confidential report in Daily Report on Austria-Hungary, February 10, 1919, *House Mss.*, Drawer 29, file 132, Yale University Library.

42. L. Nagy, *op.cit.*, p. 64;–, "Az olasz érdekek és Magyarország 1918-1919-ben" [Italian Interests and Hungary in 1918-1919] in *Történelmi Szemle*, no. 2-3, 1965, 262.

43. Report of General Badoglio, January 29, 1919, *Sonnino Papers*, Reel 26.

44. Confidential report in Daily Report on Austria-Hungary, March 5, 1919, *House Mss.*, Drawer 29, file 132.

45. *Ibid.*, March 18, 1919.

46. Thomas Cuninghame, "Between the War and Peace Treaties: A Contemporary Narrative," *Hungarian Quarterly*, V, No. 3, 1939, 412-413. Hereafter cited as "Between the War."

47. Thomas Montgomery Cuninghame, *Dusty Measure* (London: John Murray, 1939), p. 317.

48. Cuninghame, "Between the War," p. 422; Robert Graham to Lord Curzon, February 27, 1919, *F.O.*, 371/3514.

49. Cuninghame, *Dusty Measure*, p. 320.

50. *FRUS-PPC*, XII, 237-239; Beneš, *Nemzetek Forradalma*, III, 204-205.

51. Stephen Bonsal, *op.cit.*, p. 151.

52. *FRUS-PPC*, IV, 204, 269, 522; *Ibid.*, X, 66; Bane and Lutz, *op.cit.*, p. 271.

53. Mayer, *Politics and Diplomacy*, pp. 387-389; Rózsa Köves and Tibor Erényi, *Kunfi Zsigmond életutja* [The Life of Zsigmond Kunfi] (Budapest: Kossuth, 1974), pp. 104-106.

54. Buchinger, *op.cit.*, pp. 103-109.

55. *Ibid.*, p. 107; Weltner, *op.cit.*, p. 115.

56. Buchinger, *op.cit.*, p. 112.

57. Mayer, *Politics and Diplomacy*, p. 405.

58. *Vörös Újság*, February 11, 1919.

CHAPTER VIII

1. Hevesi, *op.cit.*, p. 171.

2. *Vörös Újság*, January 11, 1919.

3. *Ibid.*, January 18, 21, 23, 1919.

4. Számuely, *op.cit.*, p. 296.

5. Tőkés, *op.cit.*, p. 117; *Vörös Újság*, January 30.

6. Frank Eckelt, "The Rise and Fall of the Béla Kun Regime in 1919," Ph.D. dissertation presented at New York University, 1965, p. 254.

7. Weltner, *op.cit.*, p. 131.

8. *MMTVD*, V, 547-548.

9. Marxist historiography assumes the opposite hypothesis. Marxist historians claim that socialist attacks on the communists were due to the fact that they were encouraged by the German example. See Számuely, *op.cit.*, p. 296; Society for Dissemination of Scientific Information, *Hungarian-American Relations, 1918-1960* (Budapest: Pannonia Press, 1960), p. 9; Liptai, *op.cit.*, p. 75.

10. Vix to de Lobit, December 26, 1918, *CCA*, carton 106, dossier 3; Vix to de Lobit, December 27, 1918, *CCA*, carton 106, dossier 3.

11. Böhm, *op.cit.*, pp. 99-100; Tharaud, *op.cit.*, p. 179.

12. *Vörös Újság*, February 11, 1919.

13. "Radiogram Aux Gouvernements des Etats Alliées, Washington, Paris, London, Roma, Belgrade, Moszkva et Tokio," December 20, 1918, *Sonnino Papers*, Reel 22.

14. *MMTVD*, V, p. 451.

15. Vix to de Lobit, January 20, 1919, *CCA*, carton 106, dossier 2; Pichon to French ambassadors in London, Rome, Bern and to French minister in Prague, January 25, 1919, *CAP*, Hongrie, Vol. 27.

16. Stielly to Vix, January 21, 1919, *CCA*, carton 3830-696-70 E.

17. "Sürgöny Tchicherintől, Moszkva," February 9, 1919, *ibid.*

18. *MMTVD*, V, p. 452; *Pravda*, February 4, 1919.

19. Stielly to Vix, February 20, 1919, *CCA*, carton 3830-696-70 E; Hungary, *Fegyverszüneti Bizottság* [Armistice Commission] Hoover Institute Archives, p. 341.

20. The Ray Stannard Baker Papers, "Note in regard to the Russian Prisoners now interned in Germany," January 11, 1919, Box 8, Princeton University Library, Princeton, New Jersey; British Armistice Commission, Spa. "Notes," January 14, 1919, *W.O.*, 144/8.

21. Janin to Clemenceau, November 17, 1918, *CAP*, Russie, Vol. 49; British Embassy to Ministry of Foreign Affairs, March 19, 1919, *CAP*, Russie, Vol. 49.

22. Clemenceau to Pichon, November 13, 1919, *CAP*, Russie, Vol. 49; Pichon to British Embassy, March 27, 1919, *CAP*, Russie, Vol. 49; *Sonnino Papers*, February 1, 1919, Reel 26.

23. George Páll, personal interview with the author, at Columbia University, New York, September 16, 1968.

24. Vince Nagy, *Oktobertől-Oktoberig* [From October to October] (New York: Pro Arte Publishing Co., 1962), p. 102.

25. Páll, *loc. cit.*; the triumvirate of police leaders included Károly Dietz and his two assistants, György Páll and Béla Szentkirályi.

26. Partial photographic reporduction of an article in Kelen, *op.cit.*, p. 81. parts reprinted in, László Remete, (ed.), *Rengj csak, Föld!* [Let's have Earthquake!], (Budapest: Kossuth, 1968), pp. 294-297.

27. Kunné, *op.cit.*, pp. 121-123.

28. Tibor Hajdu, "A KMP vezetőinek 1919 Február 21-i letartoztatása a Minisztertanács elött" [The February 21 Arrest of the Leaders of the Hungarian Communist Party before the Council of Ministers] *Párttörténeti Közlemenyek*, II (1965), 173.

29. Károlyi, *Memoirs*, p. 148.

30. Borbála Szerémi, (ed.), *Nagy Idők Tanui Emlékeznek* [Witnesses of Heroic Times Remember] (Budapest: Kossuth, 1959), pp. 127-128.

31. Juhász Nagy, *op.cit.*, pp. 470-471; Bohm, *op.cit.*, p. 183.

32. Számuely, *op.cit.*, p. 313.

33. L. Nagy, *op.cit.*, p. 70.

34. See Stovall's press reports in the Wilson Papers, Series 5B.

35. L. Nagy, *op.cit.*, p. 70.

36. Számuely, *op.cit.*, p. 310.

37. Miklós Kozma, *Az összeomlás 1918-19* [The Collapse 1918-19] (Budapest: Athenaeum, 1933), p. 102; Tőkés, *op.cit.*, p. 127.

38. Franchet d'Esperey to Clemenceau and Foch, February 13, 1919, *CAP*, Roumanie, Vol. 47.

39. Rumanian Commission to Allied Supreme Council (Council of Ten), February 15, 1919, *CAP*, Roumanie, Vol. 47.

40. Sherman David Spector, *Rumania at the Paris Peace Conference: A Study of the Diplomacy of I. C. Bratianu* (New York: Bookman Associates, 1962), p. 103; Nicholas Roosevelt, *A Front Row Seat* (Norman: Oklahoma University Press, 1953), p. 105.

41. "Note lue par le General Alby devant leCommission des Affaires Roumanes," February 19, 1919, *CAP*, Roumanie, Vol. 47.

42. Ray Stannard Baker, *Woodrow Wilson and World Settlement* (Garden City: Doubleday, 1922), III, 29; W. K. Hancock and Jean van der Poel, (eds.), *Selections from the Smuts Papers*, Vol. IV (November 1918-August 1919) (Cambridge: Cambridge University Press), p. 86.

43. David Hunter Miller, *My Diary at the Conference of Paris with Documents: Minutes of the Supreme Council* (New York: 1925), XV, 52-54; *FRUS-PPC*, IV, 122.

44. "Plan d'action en Russie," February 17, 1919, *Sonnino Papers*, Reel 50.

45. Hunter Miller, *op.cit.*, XIV, 174-175.

46. Spector, *op.cit.*, p. 106.

47. Report on General Badoglio, January 29, 1919, *Sonnino Papers*, Reel 26; Tellegrammi in partenza, February 12, 1919, Sonnino Papers, *Reel 42*.

48. "Rapport sur la creation d'une zone neutre entre Hongrois et Roumains en Transylvanie," February 26, 1919, *CCA*, 20 N 729, Carton 42; *FRUS-PPC*, IV, 157-158.

49. Clemenceau to Franchet d'Esperey, March 1, 1919, *CAP*, Roumanie, Vol. 47; Confidential Report of Lansing, March 26, 1919, *Papers on Internal Affairs of Austria-Hungary*, file 864/00/37.

50. Franchet d'Esperey to Berthelot, March 5, 1919, *CCA*, N 732; Goodwin to Coolidge, March 15, 1919, *Coolidge Papers*, 184.01102/232; Spector, *op.cit.*, pp. 109-111.

51. Silverlight, *op.cit.*, p. 101; Bradley, *op.cit.*, p. 137; Azan, *op.cit.*, p. 240; Charbonneau, *op.cit.*, p. 150.

52. Franchet d'Esperey to Berthelot, March 6, 1919, *CCA*, 20 N 732.

53. Juhász Nagy, *op.cit.*, p. 422.

54. Commission Ministeriel d'Armistice to Vix, March 17, 1919, *CCA*, carton 3830-696-70 E.

55. Juhász Nagy, *op.cit.*, p. 457; Számuely, *op.cit.*, p. 320.

56. C. A. Macartney, *Hungary and Her Successors*, pp. 210-212.

57. *Ibid.*, p. 214.

58. Andics, *A Magyar nacionalizmus*, p. 258.

59. *Népszava*, March 13, 1g1g

60. Károlyiné, *op.cit.*, p. 460.

61. *Vörös Ujság*, March 13, 1919; Eckelt, *op.cit.*, p. 156.

62. Jászi, *Revolution and Counter-Revolution*, p. 87.

63. H. Rumbold to Lord Curzon, April 3, 1919, *F.O.*, 371/3515.

64. Károlyiné, *op.cit.*, p. 456.

65. *Ibid.*, p. 456.

66. Ellis Ashmead-Bartlett, *The Tragedy of Central Europe* (London: Thornton-Butterworth, 1923), p. 59.

67. Cuninghame, *op.cit.*, p. 328.

68. Ashmead-Bartlett, *op.cit.*, p. 61; Juhasz Nagy, *op.cit.*, p. 176.

69. Juhász Nagy, *op.cit.*, p. 170.

70. Szviezsényi, *op.cit.*, p. 90.

71. Resumé hebdomadaire de la situation Hongrie, Semaine 23 fevrier au ler mars, 1919, *CCA*, carton 106, dossier 3.

72. De Lobit to Franchet d'Esperey, March 1, 1919, *CCA*, carton 106, dossier 2.

73. Garami, *op.cit.*, pp. 107-108.

74. Böhm, *op.cit.*, pp. 101-102.

75. De Lobit to Vix, March 12, 1919, *CCA*, carton 106, dossier 2.

76. Béla Kun, *A Magyar tandcsköztársasagról* [Of the Hungarian Soviet Republic] (Budapest: Kossuth, 1958), p. 145.

77. Kozma, *op.cit.*, p. 137.

78. Szélpál, *op.cit.*, p. 81. For the text of the memorandum see Deák, *op.cit.*, p. 407. The examined material of the Archives Militaire did not contain the text of the memorandum.

79. De Lobit to Franchet d'Esperey, March 15, 1919, *CCA*, carton 106, dossier 2; Franchet d'Esperey to de Lobit, March 17, 1919, *ibid.*, dossier 3.

80. Dénes Berinkey to Vix, March 17, 1919, *CCA*, carton 106, dossier 3.

81. Vix to de Lobit, March 16, 1919, *CCA*, carton 106, dossier 3.

82. Goodwin to Coolidge, March 15, 1919, *Coolidge Papers*, 184.01102/232.

83. Vix to de Lobit, March 16, 1919, *CCA*, carton 106, dossier 3.

84. *Ibid.*

85. Dénes Berinkey to Vix, March 17, 1919, *CCA*, carton 106, dossier 3.

86. Franchet d'Esperey to Clemenceau and Foch, March 1, 1919, *CAP*, Russie, Vol. 33.

87. Clemenceau to Berthelot, March 7, 1919, *CCA*, 20 N 732.

88. Franchet d'Esperey to Clemenceau and Foch, March 11, 1919, *CAP*, Russie, Vol. 227.

89. William Henry Chamberlin, *The Russian Revolution* (New York: Grosset and Dunlap, 1965), II, 166.

90. Franchet d'Esperey to Clemenceau and Foch, March 12, 1919, *CAP*, Russie, Vol. 227.

91. *Ibid.*

92. Clemenceau to Franchet d'Esperey and Berthelot, March 13, 1919, *CAP*, Russie, Vol. 227.

93. Clemenceau to Franchet d'Esperey and Berthelot, March 14, 1919, Russie, Vol. 227.

94. "Note ramenée par M. Antonescu à M. Clemenceau," March 14, 1919, *CAP*, Roumanie, Vol. 47; Clemenceau to Franchet d'Esperey, March 14, 1919, *CAP*, Roumanie, Vol. 47; for a discussion on Rumania's exploitation of the "Red Scare," see Spector, *op.cit.*, p. 107.

95. Gondrecourt to Ambassador G. Barrère, March 26, 1919, *CAP*, Hongrie, Vol. 27; Bernachot, *op.cit.*, I, 85.

96. Franchet d'Esperey to Berthelot, March 19, *CCA*, 20 N 731; Franchet d'Esperey to de Lobit, March 20, 1919, *CCA*, 27 N 89.

97. Franchet d'Esperey to Clemenceau and Foch, March 20, 1919, *CAP*, Roumanie, Vol. 47.

98. *Ibid.*

99. De Lobit to Franchet d'Esperey, March 19, 1919, *CCA*, carton 106, dossier 2.

100. De Lobit to Károlyi, March 19, 1919; *CCA*, 20 N 732; lacking the documents now available, the author previously assumed that Vix had an open choice when to hand the memorandum to the Hungarians. Pastor, *op.cit.*, p. 496; for a revised interpretation stressing the Bolshevik angle as a background to the Vix ultimatum, see, Peter Pastor, "Franco-Rumanian Intervention in Russia and the *Vix Ultimatum*: Background to Hungary's Loss of Transylvania," *The Canadian-American Review of Hungarian Studies*, Vol. I, 1974.

101. De Lobit to Gondrecourt, March 19, 1919, *CCA*, 26 N 89.

102. "Rectification a l'instruction 129 relative a l'organisation zone neutre en Hongrie, March 19, 1919, *CCA*, 20 N 732; for the original order no. 129 sent to Vix on March 15, see *CCA*, 26 N 89; Bernachot, *op.cit.*, I, 97.

103. Goodwin to Grew, March 22, 1919, *Coolidge Papers*, 184.01102/284.

104. Roosevelt, *op.cit.*, p. 109.

105. *FRUS-PPC*, XII, 415-416.

106. Károlyiné, *op.cit.*, p. 466.

107. On the above mentioned issues, there is a difference of opinion between Vadász and me. Vadász seems to disregard the reports of Vix and de Lobit on the Yates encounter and claims that Károlyi was not aware that the Allies had no military force available to fight against Hungary. Also, he claims that Vix always acted in accordance with his orders. See Vadász, *op.cit.*, pp. 260-262.

108. Böhm, *op.cit.*, p. 191.

109. Garami, *op.cit.*, p. 111.

110. Böhm, *op.cit.*, p. 192.

111. Béla Godanecz, *A forradalom vezérkarában: Landler Jenő életeről* [In the General Staff of the Revolution: The Life of Jenő Landler] (Budapest: Táncsics, 1959), p. 149.

112. Böhm, *op.cit.*, pp. 192-194; *MMTVD*, V, 679-681; Számuely, *op.cit.*, p. 338.

113. Juhász Nagy, *op.cit.*, p. 494.

114. Erik Molnár, (ed.), *Magyarország története* [History of Hungary] (Budapest: Gondolat, 1967), II, 317. A Marxist monograph explains that Kun's decision to unite was motivated by the fear that the governmental interregnum would cause Allied occupation leading to the destruction of the Communist Party. See Mrs. Sándor Gábor, *A két munkáspárt egyesülése 1919-ben* [The Union of the Two Workers' Parties in 1919] (Budapest: Kossuth, 1961), p. 21.

115. Kelen, *op.cit.*, p. 91 (photocopy of original).

116. Kunfi later attempted to clear himself and the other socialist ministers by explaining that they thought that the accord was known to all the cabinet members. See Harrer, *op.cit.*, p. 406; Kunfi's biographers claim that since the cabinet was to resign, Kunfi's loyalty was rightly with the fusion government whose interest demanded his silence. See Köves and Erényi, *op.cit.*, pp. 116-120; another Marxist historian, Tibor Hajdu claims that the socialist silence "was dictated by the power relations of the labour movement, by the course of the revolution, and not by the will of certain individuals," Tibur Hajdu, "A Contribution to the History of the Proclamation of the Hungarian Republic of Councils in 1919," *Acta Historica Academica Scienticum Hungaricae*, 19, 1973, p. 81.

117. Károlyi, *Memoirs*, p. 154.

118. As quoted in Szélpál, *op.cit.*, p. 92.

119. Mihály Bihari, *Egy gyorsiró feljegyzései* [The Notes of a Stenographer] (Budapest: Kossuth, 1969), p. 147.

120. As quoted in *ibid.*, p. 147.

121. During a personal interview with Simonyi, the former secretary claimed that it was Károlyi who drew up his resignation with Kéri. He claimed that his resignation was therefore not by a coup but by his own design. Henri Simonyi, personal interview with the author at 22 Rue Brey, Paris, June 26, 1969; Simonyi, "Vissazaemlékezések," [Memories], *Századok*, 1966, no. 1, pp. 109-110. Whether Károlyi willfully resigned or not is still a controversial point. See, Gyula Illyés, "Egy

tanuvallomás" [Confessions of a Witness], *Népszabadság*, September 21, 1969; György Litván, "Meg egyszer Károlyi Mihály lemondásáról" [Once More About the Resignation of Mihály Károlyi], *Népszabadság*, October 5, 1969; Tibor Hajdu, "Adatok a Tanácsköztársaság kikiáltásának történetéhez," [Contributions to the Proclamation of the Soviet Republic], *Párttörténeti Közlemények*, 3, 1972, 150-152.

122. The author's explanation was constructed from memoirs. Cf. Károlyi, *Memoirs*, pp. 154-155; Böhm, *op.cit.*, pp. 195-205; Vince Nagy, *op.cit.*, pp. 135-136; Harrer, *op.cit.*, pp. 405-407; Garami, *op.cit.*, pp. 111-120; Károlyiné, *op.cit.*, pp. 467-468. For a secondary but imprecise account, see Mayer, *Politics and Diplomacy*, pp. 153-154.

123. Molnár, *op.cit.*, pp. 318-319.

124. Kelen, *op.cit.*, p. 93.

125. Szélpál, *op.cit.*, p. 81.

126. *Vörös Újság*, March 22, 1919.

127. *Ibid.*, March 23, 1919.

128. *MMTVD*, VI/a, p. 9. It is noteworthy that in a cable from Constantinople, General Franchet d'Esperey advised Paris on March 22 that the bourgeois parties in Hungary had made an offer to Vix to fight against Russian Bolshevism in return for a promise of Hungary's territorial integrity and 15,000 troops to keep internal order. Apparently this message was interpreted by the Hungarians as a call for troops. Mayer, *Politics and Diplomacy*, p. 549, fn. 1; the Archives of the Department of State Relating to Internal Affairs of Austria-Hungary, file No. 164.00/37, National Archives.

129. Károlyiné, *op.cit.*, pp. 470-471.

130. Paul Mantoux, *Paris Peace Conference, 1919: Proceedings of the Council of Four, March 24-April 18*, tr. by John B. Whitton (Geneva, Droz, 1964), p. 7.

131. *Ibid.*, pp. 35-36.

132. *Ibid.*, p. 55.

133. *Ibid.*, pp. 70-72.

134. W. K. Hancock and Jean van de Pool, *op.cit.*, p. 86.

CONCLUSION

1. In their memoirs the socialist leaders Bohm and Garami claimed that among the ranks of the socialists there were tens of thousands who were communists in all but name. Ironically Béla Kun complained that a significant number of communists were influenced by socialist democratic ideology. See: Vilmos Böhm, *A Magyar Tanácsköztársaság keletkezése és összeomlása* [The Rise and Fall of the Hungarian Soviet Republic] (New York: Hungarian Socialist Labor Federation, 1920), p. 25; Kun, *op.cit.*, p. 565.

2. *FRUS-PPC*, V, 61-62.

3. Károlyi, *Memoirs*, p. 159; Károlyi to Jászi, December 17, 1919, Oscar Jászi Papers.

4. R.W. Seton-Watson, ed., *Slovakia Then and Now* (London: Allen and Unwin, 1931), p. 83.

5. Franz Borkenau, *World Communism, A History of the Communist International* (Ann Arbor: University of Michigan Press, 1962), p. 123.

6. Meijer, Jan M., ed., *The Trotsky Papers 1917-1922* (The Hague: Mouton, 1964), I, 365-366, 431.

7. Hugh Seton-Watson,, *Eastern Europe between the Wars 1918-1941* (Cambridge University Press, 1946), p. 189.

BIBLIOGRAPHY

Manuscript Collections

The Archives of the American Commission to Negotiate Peace. Record Group 256. Volumes 177-185. (Coolidge Mission). National Archives.

The Archives of the Department of State Relating to Internal Affairs of Austria-Hungary and Hungary. File No. 864.00/0-169 National Archives.

The Ray Stannard Baker Papers. Box 8. Princeton University Library, Princeton, New Jersey.

Lord William H. Beveridge Papers. Box JI lg, JI lc. London School of Economics.

Great Britain, Foreign Office. Volumes 371/3134, 371/3136, 371/3139, 371/3141, 371/3443, 371/3514, 371/3515, 800/155, 800/161, 800/200. Public Record Office, London.

Great Britain, War Cabinet. Minutes. CAB 23-B. Public Record Office, London.

Great Britain, War Office. Volumes 106/683, 106/684, 144/8. Public Record Office, London.

David Lloyd George Papers. Series F, Box 197. Beaverbrook Library, London.

George David Herron Papers. Hungary, Czecho-Slovakia. Hoover Institute Archives.

Edward M. House Papers. Drawers 28-30, and 35. Yale University Library.

Hungary. Fegyverszüneti Bizottság [Armistice Commission] Hoover Institute Archives.

Oscar Jászi Papers. Columbia University Library.

Sidney E. Mezes Papers. Columbia University Library.

Ministère des Affaires Etrangères. Correspondance des Affaires Politiques. Hongrie, Volumes 27 and 44. Roumanie,Volumes 19, 32, 42, and 47. Russie, Volumes 33, 49 and 227. Serbie, Volume 25. Tchecoslovaquie, Volume 44. Archives des Affaires Etrangères, Paris.

Ministère de la Guerre. Etat-Major de l'Armée. Campagne contre Allemagne (1914-1918). Cartons 106, 3830-696-70 E, 10 N 731, 20 N 732. Archives historiques, Vincennes, Paris.

Rosika Schwimmer Papers. Box 1. Hoover Institution Archives.

Róza Bédy-Schwimmer Papers. Box A 125, A 127, A 129, A 133. The New York Public Library, Manuscript Division.

The Sonnino Papers. Reels 20, 22, 26, 42, 50. University Microfilms, Ann Arbor, Michigan.

Woodrow Wilson Papers. Series 5B. Library of Congress.

Personal Interviews

Interview with Ferenc Harrer, Garas utca 12, Budapest, July 10, 1969.

Interview with Mrs. Mihály Károlyi, Károlyi Muzeum, Budapest, July 8, 1969.

Interview with George Páll, former chief of Budapest Police, at Columbia University, 635 West 115 Street, New York, September 16, 1968.

Interview with Henri Simonyi, 22 Rue Brey, Paris, June 26, 1969.

Printed and Published Government Documents

Magyar Képviselőház, *Képviselőházi Napló* [Diary of the House of Representatives].
Vol. XLI (1918).

Ministerio degli affari esteri. *I Documenti diplomatici italiani.* Roma: Instituto
poligrafico dello stato, 1956. Vol. 1. 6. ser.

United States Department of State. *Papers Relating to the Foreign Relations of the
United States, the Lansing Papers 1914-1920.* Vol. II. Washington: 1939.

―――. *Papers Relating to the Foreign Affairs of the United States, 1917.
Supplement 1, The World War.* Washington: 1931.

―――. *Papers Relating to the Foreign Relations of the United States, 1917.
Supplement 2, The World War.* Washington: 1932. Vol. 1.

―――. *Papers Relating to the Foreign Relations of the United States, 1918,
Supplement 1, The World War.* Washington: 1933. Vol.1.

―――. *Papers Relating to the Foreign Relations of the United States, Paris
Peace Conference, 1919.* Washington: 1942-1947. Vols. I, II, IV, VII, IX,
XI, XII.

―――. *Papers Relating to the Foreign Relations of the United States, 1918,
Russia.* Washington: 1931.

Edited Collections of Documents and Papers

Baker, Ray Stannard. *Woodrow Wilson, Life and Letters.* Garden City: Doubleday,
Page and Co., 1939. Vol. VIII.

―――. *Woodrow Wilson and World Settlement.* New York: Doubleday, 1922.
Vols. II and III.

―――, and Dodd, William. *The Public Papers of Woodrow Wilson.* New York:
Harper and Brothers, 1927. Vol. I.

Bane, Suda Lorena and Lutz, Ralph H. *The Blockade of Germany after the
Armistice, 1918-1919.* Stanford: Stanford University Press, 1942.

Cumming, C. K. and Pettit, Walter W. *Russian American Relations, March 1917-
March 1920: Documents and Papers.* New York: Harcourt, Brace and Howe,
1920.

Gellért, Oszkár. *A diadalmas forradalom könyve* [The Book the Glorious
Revolution]. Budapest: 1919.

Hajdu, Tibor. "A KMP vezetőinek 1919 Februar 21-i letartoztatása a Minisztertanács
ellött" [The February 21 Arrest of the Leaders of the Hungarian Communist
Party before the Council of Ministers], *Párttörténeti Kozlemenyek* II. (1965).

Hancock, W. K. and Poel, Jean Van Der. *Selections from the Smuts Papers.*
Cambridge: Cambridge University Press, 1966. Vol. IV.

Iványi, Emma. *Magyar minisztertanácsi jegyzőkönyvek az Első Vildghdború korából*
[Minutes of the Hungarian Council of Ministers from the Era of World War One].
Budapest: Akademiai Kiado, 1960.

Kelen, Jolán. *Dicső Napok 1919* [Glorious Days 1919]. Budapest: Kossuth, 1960.

Lajos, Kossuth. *Válogatott Munkái* [Selected Works] Budapest: Lampel Robert,190?

Lenin, Vladimir Ilyich. *Lenin Magyarországról* [Lenin about Hungary]. Budapest: Kossuth, 1974.

Magyar Szocialista Munkaspárt Kozponti Bizottságának Pártörténeti Intézete. *A Magyar munkásmozgalom történetének válogatott dokumentumai* [Selected Documents to the History of the Hungarian Labor Movement]. Budapest: Kossuth, 1956. Vol. V.

——. *A Magyar munkásmozgalom történetének válogatott dokumentumai* [Selected Documents to the History of the Hungarian Labor Movement]. Budapest: Kossuth, 1959. Vol. VI/a.

Mantoux, Paul Joseph. *Paris Peace Conference, 1919: Proceedings of the Council of Four, March 24-April 18* (translated by John Boardman Whitton). Geneva: Droz, 1964.

Medvecky, K. A. *Slovensky Prevrat* [Slovak Revolution]. Bratislava: 1931.

Meijer, Jean M. *The Trotsky Papers, 1917-1922.* The Hague: Mouton, 1964. Vol. 1.

Miller, David Hunter. *My Diary at the Conference at Paris with Documents. Minutes of the Supreme Council.* New York: 1925. Vol. XIV.

Seymour, Charles. *Letters from the Paris Peace Conference.* New Haven: Yale University Press, 1965.

——. *The Intimate Papers of Colonel House.* Boston: Houghton Mifflin Co., 1928. Vols. II and IV.

Newspapers

Le Figaro.
Journal des Débats.
Népszava [People's Voice].
The New York Times.
Pravda.
Le Temps.
The Times (London).
Vörös Újság [The Red News].

Periodicals

The New Europe (London).
Sarlo és Kalapacs [Sickle and Hammer] (Moscow).

Autobiographies, Diaries, Memoirs and Other Miscellaneous Primary Sources

Ashmead-Bartlett, Ellis. *The Tragedy of Central Europe* London: Thorton-Butterworth, 1923.

Batthyány, Tivadar. *Beszámolóm* [My Account]. Budapest: Athenaeum, 1931. Vols. I and II.

Bauer, Otto. *The Austrian Revolution.* London: Leonard Parsons, 1925.

Beneš, Eduard. *My War Memoirs.* Boston: Houghton, Mifflin, 1928.

————. *Nemzetek Forradalma* [Revolt of Nations]. Bratislava: Eugene Prager, 1936. Vols. II and III.

Beveridge, Lord William H. *Power and Influence.* New York: The Beechhurst Press, 1955.

Bihari, Mihály. *Egy gyorsíró feljegyzései* [The Notes of a Stenographer]. Budapest: Kossuth, 1969.

Böhm, Vilmos. *Két forradalom tüzében* [In the Fire of Two Revolutions]. Budapest: Népszava, 1946.

————. *A Magyar Tanácsköztársaság keletkezése és összeomlása* [The Rise and Fall of the Hungarian Soviet Republic]. New York: Hungarian Socialist Labor Federation, 1920.

Buchinger, Manó. *Tanuvallomás: Az Oktoberi Forradalom tragédiája* [Testimony of a Witness: The Tragedy of the October Revolution]. Budapest: Népszava, 1936.

Charbonneau, Jean (ed.). *Franchet d'Esperey marechal de France.* Paris: Cahiers Charles de Foucauld, 1956.

Comte de Saint-Aulaire. *Confession d'un vieux diplomate.* Paris: Flamarion, 1953.

Coolidge, Harold J. and Lord, Robert H. *Archibald Cary Coolidge–Life and Letters.* Boston: Houghton Mifflin Co., 1932.

Creel, George. *How We Advertised America.* New York: Harper and Brothers, 1920.

Cuninghame, Thomas. "Between the War and Peace Treaties. A Contemporary Narrative," *Hungarian Quarterly,* V, No. 3 (1939).

————. *Dusty Measure.* London: John Murray, 1939.

Garami, Ernő. *Forrongó Magyarország* [Seditious Hungary]. Leipzig: Pegazus, 1922.

Goga, Octavian. "The Achievement of Rumanian Unity," *The New Europe,* IX, No. 116 (January 2, 1919).

Gondor, Ferenc. *Vallomások Könyve* [Book of Confessions] Vienna: 1922.

Harrer, Ferenc. *Egy magyar polgár élete* [The Life of a Hungarian Bourgeois]. Budapest: Gondolat, 1968.

Hatvany, Lajos. *Urak, polgárok, parasztok* [Lords, Citizens, Peasants]. Budapest: Revay, 1947.

Hevesi, Gyula. *Egy mérnök a forradalomban* [An Engineer in the Revolution]. Budapest: Europa, 1969.

Hoover, Herbert. *The Ordeals of Woodrow Wilson.* New York: McGraw-Hill, 1958.

Houston, David F. *Eight Years with Wilson's Cabinet.* Garden City: Doubleday, 1926.

International Committee for World Peace Prize to Rosika Schwimmer. *Rosika Schwimmer World Patriot.* New York: 1938.

Jászi, Oscár. *Revolution and Counter-Revolution in Hungary.* London: King and Son, 1924.

Juhász Nagy, Sándor. *A Magyar Oktoberi Forradalom története* [The History of the Hungarian October Revolution]. Budapest: Cserepfalvi, 1945.

Károlyi, Mihály. *Az uj Magyarországért* [For the New Hungary]. Budapest: Magvető Könyvkiadó, 1968.

————. *Egy egész világ ellen* [Against the Entire World]. Budapest: Gondolat, 1965.

————. Válogatott irásai [Selected Works]. Budapest: Gondolat, 1964.

Károlyi, Michael. *Memoirs of Michael Károlyi, Faith Without Illusion.* New York: Dutton and Co., 1957.

Károlyi, Mihályné (Mrs.). *Együtt a forradalomban, Emlékezések* [Together in the Revolution, Memoirs]. Budapest: Europa, 1967.

Kozma, Miklós. *Összeomlás 1918-19* [The Collapse 1918-19]. Budapest: Athenaeum, 1933.

Kristoffy, József. *A királyságtól a kommunizmusig* [From Monarchy to Communism]. Budapest: Kultura, 1920.

Kun, Béla. *A Magyar Tanácsköztársaságrol* [Of the Hungarian Soviet Republic]. Budapest: Kossuth, 1958.

Kun, Béláne (Mrs.). *Kun Béla (Emlékezések)* [Béla Kun (Memoirs)]. Budapest: Magvető, 1966.

Lansing, Robert L. *War Memoirs of Robert Lansing.* Indianapolis: Bobbs-Merill Co., 1935.

Laroche, Jules. *Au Quai d'Orsay avec Briand et Poincaré.* Paris: Hachette, 1957.

Lengyel, József. *Visegrádi utca. Lengyal József összegyüjtött munkái* [Visegrádi Street. The Collected Works of Jozsef Lengyel]. Budapest: Szépirodalmi, 1966.

Lloyd George, David. *The Truth About the Peace Treaties.* London: Victor Gollancz, 1938. Vol. II.

————. *War Memoirs.* Boston: Houghton Mifflin Co., 1933. Vol. I.

Masaryk, Thomas Garrigue. *Making of a State.* New York: F. A. Stokes Co., 1927.

Nagy, Vince. *Októbertől Oktoberig* [From October to October]. New York: Pro Arte Publishing Co., 1962.

Nicolson, Harold. *Peacemaking 1919.* London: Constable 1944.

Paléologue, Maurice. *An Ambassador's Memoirs.* New York: George H. Doran, 1925. Vol. I.

Poincaré, Raymond. *Aux service de la France.* Vol. X. *Victoire et Armistice 1918.* Paris: Plon, 1933.

Pound, Ezra. *Cantos.* New York: A New Directions Book, 1965.

Reed, John. *The War in Eastern Europe.* New York: Charles Scribner's Sons, 1919.

Roosevelt, Nicholas. *A Front Row Seat.* Norman: Oklahoma University Press, 1953.

Shotwell, James T. *At the Paris Peace Conference.* New York: Macmillan, 1937.

Simonyi, Henri. "Visszaemlékezések" [Memoirs], *Századok,* 1966, no. 1.

Szerémi, Borbála (ed.). *Nagy idők tanui emlékeznek* [Witnesses of Heroic Times Remember]. Budapest: Kossuth, 1959.

Szviezsenyi, Zoltán. *Hogyan veszett el a Felvidék* [How Ruthenia Was Lost]. Budapest: Franklin Tarsulat, 1921.

Tisza, István. *Lettres de Guerre, 1914-1916.* Paris: Les Oeuvres Representatives, 1931.

————. *Összes Munkái* [Collected Works]. Budapest: Franklin Tarsulat, 1926, Vol. III.

Varjassy, Louis. *Revolution, bolchevisme, reaction: L'Histoire de l'occupation française en Hongrie (1918-1919)*. Paris: 1934.

Weltner, Jakab. *Forradalom, Bolsevizmus, Emigráció* [Revolution, Bolshevism, Emigration]. Budapest: Weltner, 1929.

Whitehouse, Vira B. *A Year as a Government Agent*. New York: Harper and Brothers, 1920.

Wilson, Hugh R. *Diplomat Between Wars*. New York: Longmans, Green and Co., 1941.

Windischgraetz, Ludwig. *My Memoirs*. Boston: Houghton Mifflin Co., 1921.

Secondary Sources: Histories
Special Studies and Biographies

Albertini, Luigi. *The Origins of the War of 1914*. Oxford: Oxford University Press, 1957. Vol. II.

Andics, Erzsébet. *Munkásosztály és nemzet* [Working Class and Nation]. Budapest: Szikra, 1949.

————, (ed.). *A magyar nacionalizmus kialakulása és története* [The History and Development of Hungarian Nationalism]. Budapest: Kossuth, 1964.

Arday, Lajos. "Angol-Magyar viszony a polgári demokratikus forradalom idején az angol levéltari források tükrében" [English-Hungarian Relations during the Bourgeois Democratic Revolution as Reflected in English Archival Sources], *Történelmi Szemle* (1975), No. 2-3.

Azan, Paul. *Franchet d'Esperey*. Paris: Flamarion, 1949.

Bernachot, Jean. *Les Armées françaises après l'Armistice de 1918*. Paris: Imprimerie National, 1970. Vols. I and II.

Bolgár, Elek. *Válogatott tanulmányok* [Selected Essays] Budapest: Kossuth, 1958.

Bonsal, Stephen. *Suitors and Suppliants, The Little Nations at Versailles*. New York: Prentice-Hall, 1946.

Borkenau, Franz. *World Communism: A History of the Communist International*. Ann Arbor, University of Michigan Press, 1962.

Boros, Ferenc. *Magyar-Csehoslovak kapcsolatok 1918-1921-ben* [Hungarian-Czechoslovak Relations in 1918-1921]. Budapest: Adadémiai Kiadó, 1970.

Borsody, István. *Magyar-Szlovák kiegyezés* [Hungarian-Slovak Understanding]. Budapest: Officiana, 1946.

Bradley, John. *Allied Intervention in Russia*. New York: Basic Books, 1968.

Breit, Doberdoi József. *A magyarországi 1918-1919 évi forradalmak és a vörös háboru története* [The History of the Revolutionary Movements of 1918-1919 and the Red War]. Budapest: Magyar Királyi Levéltár, 1925.

Brook-Shepherd, Gordon. *The Last Habsburg*. New York: Weybright and Talley, 1968.

Carroll, E. Malcolm. *Soviet Communism and Western Opinion 1919-1921*. Chapel Hill: University of North Carolina Press, 1965.

Congdon, Lee, "History and Politics in Hungary: The Rehabilitation of Oszkár Jászi," *East European Quarterly*, IX, No. 3.

Connel, John. *The Office*. New York: St. Martin's Press, 1958.

Constantinescu, Miron and Pascu, Ştefan (eds.) *Unification of the Romanian State, The Union of Transylvania with Old Romania*. Bucharest: Academy of Romania, 1971.

Dallin, Alexander (ed.). *Russian Diplomacy and Eastern Europe 1914-1917*. New York: King's Crown, 1963.

Deak, Francis. *Hungary at the Paris Peace Conference*. New York: Columbia University Press, 1942.

Deák, István. "Budapest and the Hungarian Revolutions of 1918-1919," *Slavonic and East European Review*, Vol. XLVI (January, 1968).

Donáth, Regina. *A Tisza István elleni 1912-i merénylet a hirlapirodalom tükrében* [The Attempt Against the Life of István Tisza as Seen through the Journals]. Budapest: 1935.

Farkas, Márton. *Katonai összeomlás és forradalom 1918-ban* [Military Collapse and Revolution in 1918].Budapest: Akadémiai Kiadó, 1969.

Gábor, Sándorné (Mrs.). *A két munkáspárt egyesülése* [The Union of the Two Workmens' Parties]. Budapest: 1961.

Gelfand, Lawrence E. *The Inquiry, American Preparations for Peace, 1917-1919*. New Haven: Yale University Press, 1963.

Godanecz, Béla. *A forradalom vezérkarában. Landler Jenő életéről*. [In the General Staff of the Revolution. The Life of Jenő Landler]. Budapest: Tancsics, 1959.

Grátz, Gusztáv. *A dualizmus kora* [The Age of Dualism]. Budapest: Magyar Szemle, 1934. Vol. I.

————. *A forradalmak kora* [The Age of Revolutions] Budapest: Magyar Szemle, 1935.

Hajdu, Tibor. "A Contribution to the History of the Proclamation of the Hungarian Republic of Councils in 1919," *Acta Historica Academiae Scientiarum Hungaricae* (1973), No. 19.

————. "Adatok a Tanácsköztársaság kikiáltásának történetéhez,"[Contributions to the Proclamation of the Soviet Republic], *Párttörténeti Közlemények*, (1972), No. 3.

————. *Az 1918-as magyarországi polgári demokratikus forradalom* [The Bourgeois-Democratic Revolution of 1918]. Budapest: Kossuth, 1968.

————. *Az Őszirózsás Forradalom* [The Frostflower Revolution]. Budapest: Kossuth, 1963.

————. *Tanácsok Magyarországon 1918-1919-ben* [Councils in Hungary in 1918-1919]. Budapest: Kossuth, 1958.

Halecki, Oscar. *Borderlands of Western Europe: History of Eastern Europe*. New York: Ronald Press, 1952.

Hanak, Harry. *Great Britain and Austria-Hungary during the First World War*. (London: Oxford University Press, 1962).

Hershey, Burnet. *The Odyssey of Henry Ford and the Great Peace Ship*. New York: Taplinger Publishing Co., 1967.

Hodza, Michael. *Federalism in Central Europe.* London: 1942.

————. *Középeurópa országutján* [On the Highway of Central Europe] Bratislava: Eugen Prager, 1938.

Horváth, Jenő. *Magyarország és a nemzetiségi kérdés. 1815-1920* [Hungary and the Nationality Question. 1815-1920]. Budapest: Pfeifer, 1920.

————, (Eugene). *Transylvania and the Rumanians: A Reply to Professor R. W. Seton-Watson.* Budapest: Sárkány, 1935.

————. *A trianoni békeszerződés megalkotása és a revizió utja* [The Construction of the Trianon Peace Treaty and the Course of Revision]. Budapest: Magyar Tudomanyos Akademia, 1937.

Howard, John E. *Parliament and Foreign Policy in France.* London: Gasset Press, 1948.

Illyés, Gyula. "Egy tanuvallomás" [Confession of a Witness]. *Népszabadság,* September 21, 1969.

Jaksch, Wenzel. *Europe's Road to Potsdam.* New York: Frederick A. Praeger, 1963.

Jászi, Oscár. *The Dissolution of the Habsburg Monarchy.* Chicago: University of Chicago Press, 1961.

————. (Oszkár). *A nemzeti államok kialakulása és a nemzeti kérdés* [The Evolution of Nation States and the Nationality Question]. Budapest: 1912.

Kellen, Jolán and Barabás, Gyula. *A néptribün. Fejezetek Bokányi Dezső életéből* [The People's Tribunal. Chapters from the Life of Dezső Bokányi]. Budapest: Kossuth, 1964.

Király, Béla K. "The Danubian Problem in Oscar Jászi's Political Thought," *The Hungarian Quarterly,* V (April-June, 1965).

Kohn, Hans. *The Hapsburg Empire, 1804-1918.* New York: Van Nostrand, 1959.

Kosáry, Dominic. *A History of Hungary.* Cleveland: Benjamin Franklin Bibliophile Society, 1941.

Kővágó, László. *A magyarországi délszlávok 1918-1919-ben.* [The South Slavs of Hungary in 1918-1919]. Budapest: Akadémiai Könyvkiadó, 1964.

Köves, Rózsa and Erényi, Tibor. *Kunfi Zsigmond életutja* [The Life of Zsigmond Kunfi]. Budapest: Kossuth, 1974.

Krizman, Bogdan. "The Belgrade Armistice of November 1918," *Slavonic and Eastern European Review,* XLVIII (1970), No. 110.

L. Nagy, Zsuzsa. *A párizsi békekonferencia és Magyarország* [The Paris Peace Conference and Hungary]. Budapest: Kossuth, 1965.

————, es Zsilák, András (eds.). *Ötven év, A nagy Oktober és a magyarországi forradalmak. Tanulmányok* [Fifty Years, The Great October Revolution and the Revolutions in Hungary. Essays]. Budapest: Akadémiai Kiadó, 1967.

Lederer, Ivo J. *Yugoslavia at the Paris Peace Conference.* New Haven: Yale University Press, 1963.

Levin, Gordon N. *Woodrow Wilson and World Politics: America's Response to War and Revolution.* New York: Oxford University Press, 1968.

Liptai, Ervin. *A Magyar Tanácsköztársaság* [The Hungarian Soviet Republic]. Budapest: Kossuth, 1965.

Litván, György. "Az első vilagháboru és az 1918-19-es forradalmak magyar vonatkozású anyagai a francia levéltárakban" [French Archival Materials Relating to Hungary during World War I and during the Revolutions of 1918-19], *Történelmi Szemle* (1973), No. 1-2.

————. "Meg egyszer Károlyi Mihály lemondásáról" [Once More about the Resignation of Mihály Károlyi], *Népszabadság*, October 5, 1969.

Low, Alfred D. *The Soviet Hungarian Republic and the Paris Peace Conference.* Philadelphia: The American Philosophical Society, 1963.

Macartney, C. A. *Hungary and Her Successors: The Treaty and Its Consequences 1917-1919.* London: Oxford University Press, 1937.

————, and Palmer, A. W. *Independent Eastern Europe. A History.* New York: St. Martin's Press, 1966.

Mamatey, Victor S. *The United States and East Central Europe, 1914-1918.* Princeton: Princeton University Press, 1957.

May, Arthur J. "R. W. Seton-Watson and British Anti-Habsburg Sentiments," *The American Slavic and European Review* (February, 1961).

————. *The Passing of the Hapsburg Monarchy 1914-1918.* Philadelphia: University of Pennsylvania Press, 1964. Vol. II

Mayer, Arno. *Politics and Diplomacy of Peacemaking.* New York: Alfred A. Knopf, 1967.

Mérei, Gyula. *A magyar oktoberi forradalom és a polgári pártok* [The Hungarian Revolution of October and the Bourgeois Parties]. Budapest: Akadémiai Kiadó, 1969.

Mészáros, Károly. *Az őszirózsás forradalom és a Tanácsköztársasdg parasztpolitikája-1918-1919* [The Agricultural Policy of the October Revolution and of the Soviet Republic]. Budapest: Akadémiai Könyvkiadó, 1966.

Mock, James R., and Larson, Cedric. *Words that Won the War.* Princeton: Princeton University Press, 1938.

Mód, Aladár. *400 év küzdelem az önálló Magyarországért* [Four Hundred Years of Struggle for Independent Hungary]. Budapest: Szikra, 1951.

————. *Válaszutak 1918-1919* [Alternatives, 1918-1919]. Budapest: Magvető, 1970.

Molnár, Erik (ed.). *Magyarország története* [The History of Hungary]. Budapest: Gondolat, 1967. Vol. II.

Murray, Robert K. *Red Scare: A Study of National Hysteria, 1919-1920.* New York: McGraw-Hill, 1964.

Noble, George Bernard. *Policies and Opinions at Paris, 1919* New York: The Macmillan Co., 1935.

O'Grady, Joseph (ed.). *The Immigrants' Influence on Wilson's Peace Policies.* Lexington, Ky.: University of Kentucky Press, 1967.

Osusky, Stefan. "The Secret Negotiations between Vienna and Washington," *Slavonic Review,* IV (1926).

Pastor, Peter. "Franco-Rumanian Intervention in Russia and the *Vix Ultimatum:* Background to Hungary's Loss of Transylvania," *The Canadian-American Review of Hungarian Studies,* I (1974).

————. "The Vix Mission in Hungary, 1918-1919: A Re-examination," *Slavic Review*, XXIX (1970), No. 3.

Remak, Joachim. *Sarajevo*. New York: Criterion Books, 1959.

Remete, László. *Barikádok Budapest utcáin 1912*. [Barricades on the Streets of Budapest]. Budapest: Kossuth, 1972.

————. *Rengj csak, Föld* [Let's have Earthquake!]. Budapest: Kossuth, 1968.

Réti, László. *Lenin és a Magyar munkásmozgalom* [Lenin and the Hungarian Labor Movement]. Budapest: Kossuth, 1970.

Schönwald, Pál. *A magyarországi 1918-1919-es polgári demokratikus forradalom állam és jogtörténeti kérdései* [The Constitutional and Legal Questions of the Bourgeois-Democratic Revolution of 1918-1919]. Budapest: Akadémiai Könyvkiadó, 1969.

Seton-Watson, Hugh. *Eastern Europe Between Two Wars*. Cambridge: Cambridge University Press, 1946.

Seton-Watson, Robert William. *A History of the Czechs and Slovaks*. New York: Hutchinson, 1943.

————. *A History of the Roumanians*. Cambridge: Cambridge University Press, 1934.

Silverlight, John. *The Victors' Dilemma: Allied Intervention in the Russian Civil War*. New York: Weybright and Talley, 1970.

Society for the Dissemination of Scientific Information. *Hungarian-American Relations, 1918-1960*. Budapest: Pannonia Press, 1960.

Spector, Sherman David. *Rumania at the Paris Peace Conference: A Study of the Diplomacy of Ioan I. C. Bratinau*. New York: Bookman, 1962.

Stone, Norman. "Hungary and the Crisis of July 1914," *Journal of Contemporary History*, III (1967).

Sullivan, Mark. *Our Times: The United States*. New York: Charles Scribner's Sons, 1933. Vol. V.

Számuely, Tibor. *A Kommunisták Magyarországi Pártjának megalakulása és harca a proletárdiktaturáért* [The Organization and Fight of the Hungarian Party of the Communists for the Dictatorship of the Proletariat]. Budapest: Kossuth, 1964.

Szász, Zoltán. "Az erdélyi román polgárság szereplése 1918 öszén" / The Role of the Transylvanian Rumanian Bourgeoisie during the Fall of 1918/, Századok (1972), No. 2.

Szélpál, Árpád. *Les 133 jours de Béla Kun*. Paris: Artheme Fayard, 1959.

Szemere, Vera, *Az agrárkérdés 1918-1919-ben* [The Agrarian Question in 1918-1919]. Budapest: Kossuth, 1963.

Szende, Zoltán. "Count Michael Károlyi at Belgrade," *Hungarian Quarterly*, V. No. 3 (1939).

Tharaud, Jerome et Jean. *Quand Israël est roi*. Paris: Plon, 1921.

Thompson, John M. *Russia, Bolshevism and the Versailles Peace*. Princeton: Princeton University Press, 1966.

Thomson, Harrison. *Czechoslovakia in European History*. Hamden: Archon Books, 1965.

Tillman, Seth P. *Anglo-American Relations at the Paris Peace Conference of 1919.* Princeton: Princeton University Press, 1961.

Tőkés, Rudolf R. *Béla Kun and the Hungarian Soviet Republic.* New York: Praeger, 1967.

Unger, Mátyás as Szabolcs, Otto. *Magyarország története* [The History of Hungary]. Budapest: Gondolat, 1965.

Vadász, Sándor. "Vix és Károlyi," *Hadtörténelmi Közlemények,* XVI (1969), No. 2.

Valiani, Leo. "Italian-Austro-Hungarian Negotiations in 1914-1915," *Journal of Contemporary History,* III (1967).

Vermes, Gábor. "The Agony of Federalism in Hungary under the Károlyi Regime, 1918/1919," *East European Quarterly,* VI, No. 4.

────."The October Revolution in Hungary: from Károlyi to Kun," *Hungary in Revolution,* Iván Völgyes, (ed.), Lincoln: University of Nebraska Press, 1971.

Wandycz, Piotr S. *France and Her Eastern Allies 1919-1925: French-Czechoslovak-Polish Relations from the Paris Peace Conference to Locarno.* Minneapolis: University of Minnesota Press, 1962.

Dissertations

Eckelt, Frank. "The Rise and Fall of the Béla Kun Regime in 1919." Unpublished. New York University, 1965.

Fuchs, Mary B. "The Problem of the Hungarian-Czechoslovak Frontier, November 3rd 1918 to November 15, 1920." Unpublished. St. John's University, 1942.

E3